AT THE PLEASURE

OF THE MAYOR

AT THE

OF

Patronage and

PLEASURE

THE MAYOR

Power in New York City, 1898-1958

THEODORE J. LOWI

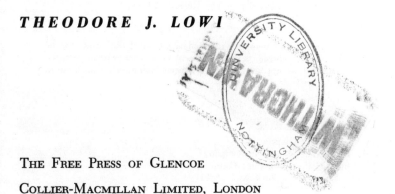

THE FREE PRESS OF GLENCOE
COLLIER-MACMILLAN LIMITED, LONDON

Copyright © 1964 by The Free Press of Glencoe

A Division of The Macmillan Company

Printed in the United States of America

FOR INFORMATION, ADDRESS:
The Free Press of Glencoe
A Division of The Macmillan Company
The Crowell-Collier Publishing Company
60 Fifth Avenue, New York, N. Y., 10011

Library of Congress Catalog Card Number: 64-11216

Collier-Macmillan Canada, Ltd., Toronto, Ontario

FOR
Angele
MY WIFE

PREFACE

THIS BOOK IS AN EXPLORATION into the politics of the world's largest city. I describe it as an exploration because there were so few specific expectations, hypotheses, and methodological guidelines in the theories of sociology and political systems with which to begin the task. For the most part it was necessary to depend upon discoveries and surprises. Consequently, if I offered it as a single study with a single thesis and a single observational standpoint, the book would be misrepresented. It is, rather, three books in one; or if you like, three separate approaches to a body of data.

First, it is an historical-descriptive study. In many respects I consider *At the Pleasure of the Mayor* a monographic extension of Sayre and Kaufman's masterful *Governing New York City*, as one of many studies anticipated by their work. The ideas for my project grew out of my association with Professors Sayre and Kaufman; and, while my interest in urban politics antedates that association, my experience and exposure during the months of 1956 and 1957 served to make urban politics and New York City almost indistinguishable. The top patronage and their major attributes constitute but a single strand of the political history of a single city. But the quantitative nature of the data has special utility for my own as well as future attempts at "middle-level" theory.

Second, the book is a recruitment study, comparable in many respects to the Hoover Institute Elite Studies, Janowitz' *The Pro-*

fessional Soldier, Warner and Abegglen's *Occupational Mobility,* and the papers in Dwaine Marvick's *Political Decision-Makers: Recruitment and Performance.* The data have an institutional as well as an historical context. Thus, for example, it was possible and desirable to assess not only the socioeconomic changes in the backgrounds of these political decision-makers[1] but also the significance of careers, nongovernmental groups, and parties for social and economic mobility in politics. It is particularly clear in urban political systems that corporations, interest groups, and many other organized social units perform the dual functions of defining problems that public policy must deal with *and* recruiting and grooming political personnel. The question is, then, how do these groups perform the latter function, and what difference does it make to the functioning of City government?

Third, the book is a case study in community power relations. In this respect the nature of the inquiry is not unlike Hunter's,[2] Dahl's,[3] Meyerson and Banfield's,[4] and other recent studies of urban politics, although the data herein offer an alternative approach, particularly with regard to the very largest cities. Questions of access, power, and influence have been dealt with largely as problems of the Mayoralty, but this was not felt to be a severe limitation because the Mayor of New York, if not of all cities, is so vital a source of initiative. Whether the undeniably pluralist social organization of the City results in a dynamic pluralist democracy or a static system of corporative privilege rests very heavily upon the strength or weakness of the Mayoralty and its relations, in unity or disunity, to the surrounding group struggle. These relationships are normatively as well as empirically significant, and I have not hesitated to offer generalizations of both types wherever I have felt them to be appropriate.

---

1. See, for example, Donald R. Matthews, *The Social Background of Political Decision-Makers.*

2. Floyd Hunter, *Community Power Structure.*

3. Robert A. Dahl, *Who Governs?* and companion volumes by Nelson W. Polsby, *Community Power and Political Theory* and Raymond E. Wolfinger, *The Politics of Progress.*

4. Martin Meyerson and Edward Banfield, *Politics, Planning and the Public Interest.*

Problems of community power and of good and bad community power are not and should not be separable.

Hopefully, the reader will find with the author that these three approaches are easily identifiable, related, and mutually reinforcing. I have set them forth in this Preface, however, so that the reader may be able to identify and integrate them if the author has failed to do so.

THEODORE J. LOWI

ACKNOWLEDGMENTS

Not all of a scholar's indebtedness can be found in his footnotes. Those who dismiss acknowledgments as mere ceremony are missing the rich network of mutual dependencies that constitute the scholarly way of life. I am happy to reveal these dependencies because they identify me with people, institutions, and traditions that can only lend some distinction to me and to my book.

Above all, I am indebted to Wallace S. Sayre and Herbert Kaufman for the experience and ideas I gained as their research associate for *Governing New York City*. While my reliance upon "Sayre and Kaufman" is apparent throughout the book, I am not able to acknowledge the full extent of their encouragement and guidance and the degree to which they allowed my work to intrude upon their time long after my formal association with the project ended. Thereafter, the enormous job of data collection, assimilation, and analysis was supported by a fellowship from the Metropolitan Region Program of Columbia University. Beyond the generous financial assistance of the Program, its directors, Wallace S. Sayre, David B. Truman, and Richard E. Neustadt, provided me with invaluable intellectual support.

Robert A. Dahl, Herbert Kaufman, James W. Fesler, Robert E. Lane, and Harold Lasswell, teachers and friends at Yale, spent countless hours going over early drafts of outline and manuscript.

Of equal importance were my graduate colleagues at Yale, whose fierce criticisms in the early planning stages and friendship since then deeply influenced my views of politics in general and communities in particular. Among these were Fred Greenstein, Herbert Jacob, Nelson Polsby, Morton Tenzer, Raymond Wolfinger, and Aaron Wildavsky.

I am the more indebted to the Metropolitan Region Program for the services of Mrs. Florence Perry Kaplan and Mr. Theodore Diamond. Mrs. Kaplan was editor and research associate rather than mere secretary. Theodore Diamond, while a candidate for the LL.B. and M.A., gave unselfishly of his time to the laborious task of collecting data. His enthusiasm for my work was a perpetual morale-booster, and his unflagging curiosity and uncanny political acumen continually forced me to sharpen my ideas. To the Hull Memorial Publication Fund of Cornell University, I wish to express my gratitude for its timely support in helping to keep in the book many of the expensive presentations of data. Finally, for permission to use part of a previously published paper, I wish to thank the American Political Science Review.*

Such an impressive list of support, superb advice, and guidance cannot help but magnify all flaws and errors in the final product. I gratefully acknowledge the assistance; the weaknesses I insist upon keeping as my very own.

---

* "Toward Functionalism in Political Science: The Case of Innovation in Party Systems." *American Political Science Review*, September, 1963.

CONTENTS

CONTENTS

PART ONE

Introduction

CHAPTER 1

APPOINTMENTS AND

COMMUNITY POWER

To ALL WHO HAVE EVER SERVED in urban government or who have watched its politics with more than casual interest, the title of this book is bitter irony. "At the pleasure of the Mayor" is a clause found in many city charters; it grants to the Mayor full discretion over certain appointments and removals. But if the top political appointments in New York City were truly chosen at the Mayor's pleasure I would be relating an entirely different story. The Mayor's pleasure becomes enmeshed with the demands of his constituency; as an elected and very much exposed chief executive, he lives in an environment that he disregards only at his peril. The Mayor is not a mute pawn, but neither is he a free agent. Every decision he makes, or attempts to make, involves the highly prized values of some organized elements in the community. The top political appointments are simply one type of policy decision—an indulgence of some participants, a deprivation of others. Not only must a Mayor see in these appointments a means for running an efficient operation, he must also view them as a means for effecting adjustments among the competing demands and expectations around him.

This, then, is a study of the top patronage in a large city—but not a study of patronage for its own sake. I use the characteristics of the appointees as indexes, or "tracer elements," for the purpose of discovering salient features of power structure

3

and dynamics in communities too large and complex for the generally accepted approaches. These officials, the subjects of the inquiry, head the large bureaucracies in the City and make, or share in the making of, the most important public policies; thus they are the focus for most of the City's prevailing demands and expectations. Quantitatively, the distribution of types of appointees (or their major attributes) can only be explained in terms of the larger, less quantifiable forces.

Most of the questions in this study—such as the class and group structure, party and other political institutions, the educational system, the economic system, and important changes among these elements in the past century—are questions political scientists have been pondering for a long time. Who makes the decisions in the political system that are binding upon us all? And why? What are the conditions for rule? Marx had a facile answer; the Italian school had more sophisticated, but still inadequate, answers. Contemporary behavioral scientists are again starting the inquiry, with much less certainty and therefore with a much more elaborate apparatus of inquiry.

The novelty of my own approach is that it combines the historical methods of earlier scholars with the quantitative, empirical methods of today. The sixty years incorporated in my study comprise the entire history of Greater New York. Most of the analysis is from *time series*, and the basic elements and conditions of power structure emerge from the secular trends and departures from those trends. Now that the study is completed, I am all the more convinced that quantitative analysis is more meaningful and powerful for the political historian than for the political chronicler.

APPOINTMENTS AND THE POLITICAL PROCESS

New York City operates under a "strong mayor" charter. The Mayor is the "chief executive officer of the city"; he appoints "the heads of departments and all other officers not elected by the people, except as otherwise provided by law"; and he may remove any public officer holding office by his appointment unless removal is otherwise provided for by law. The Mayor with his Budget Bureau has the primary authority over the expense budget, although it must be approved by the Board of Estimate.[1] The City Council may reduce or omit items, but it "may not add or increase any item or vary the titles, descriptions, terms or conditions of administration."

The New York City Mayoralty is not an unimpressive office, but it is weakened to a large extent by the powers and functions it shares with the Board of Estimate, the Comptroller, and certain State agencies. Of all the Mayor's powers, those of appointment and removal appear to be the most important. None of his appointments or removals are encumbered by the confirmation of the Council or the Board of Estimate, and legal restrictions of any sort are scant indeed.[2] However, "Mayors have found few opportunities to draw power from these provisions; they are instead mainly the source of expectations and demands from others."[3]

This is the factor that makes the study of top appointments significant. When an appointment decision is to be made the Mayor is the focal point, be he weak or strong; for he alone signs the commission, and he alone formally initiates the removal. There can be little pleasure for a Mayor who can reward some only at the sacrifice of others.

Just as much as decisions regarding substantive issues are policy decisions, so are the Mayor's appointments to strategic governmental posts. The holders of these positions are important wielders of power, at least during their periods of incumbency. The top political executives constitute an important segment of that construct called the "community power structure"; they are part of the theoretical class called the "ruling elite."

The Mayor's top administrative personnel set the tone of his administration. Although the overwhelming proportion of any large-scale agency activity is routine, increments of innovation at the center give each administration its own peculiar character. A Police Commissioner who would attempt a policy of saturating high-crime neighborhoods with policemen must take certain calculated risks in other areas, thereby deeply affecting the pattern of property protection. A Health Commissioner's crackdown on sanitary conditions of food-processing or eating establishments must consider the consequences on the profits of one group of citizens and on the health of another. A single ruling by the Welfare Commissioner tightening or loosening the categories of public assistance may change the very well-being of the down-and-out classes. Reformers in control of the Civil Service Commission will inevitably alter the position of political parties and may affect their own Mayor's chances for survival. To belabor

the obvious: The administration of the City's mayoral departments and agencies has a direct impact on practically every
citizen in the community. The differential impact of every agency
decision means differences in symbolic and tangible profits
throughout the community.

Because of the high stakes involved, community leaders of all
sorts seek to share in the shaping of these decisions. Every decision is in effect a political transaction, or part of a series of
political transactions, between the Mayor and others inside and
outside government.

THE VALUES INVOLVED

There is no cabinet at City Hall. Every department of government is headed by a commissioner or a board of several
commissioners. "Cabinet" is merely a convenient designation for
a particular level of government. The men who have held these
commissionerships—the cabinet-level appointees—are the subjects
of this book. Although they do not form a cabinet in the British
sense of the word, the Commissioners in New York City form,
like the President's Secretaries, a cabinet in every sense save
the most important: there is no collective responsibility. But
these appointees serve the same functions for the Mayor that
the President's Cabinet serves for him.

To see in these top appointments merely payoffs to those
responsible for the nomination and election of the Mayor is to
take an oversimplified as well as an old-fashioned view of urban
politics. Moreover, reformers who urge "the best man for the
job" cast the issue in the wrong terms. In the vast City of
New York, there are usually several candidates who can fill a job
more than adequately. All these candidates will be weighed for
those marginal qualities that convert able men into the most
appropriate appointee. A chief executive does not ask, "What
can I do for you," but, "What can you do for me?" A candidate
brings to the Mayor his skills and, hopefully, his knowledge of
the affairs of the department. But he must also bring the Mayor
some kind of a following. This is especially true in the line
departments. In some cases a candidate's following must be composed of members of the departmental bureaucracy itself; in
other cases it must be a segment of the Party hierarchy; and in
still others, composed of the more important clientele groups.[4]
All too often the need to galvanize support is so great that the
marginal factor of following becomes the central consideration.

Also for the candidates for office and their supporting groups, an appointment serves more than one purpose. The candidate receives the perquisites and honors of office. But the appointment also means a promotion either in his career or his Party hierarchy—a means for using either his skills or his political access in a more important context. For a surprising number of candidates, even if one only considers the nonsalaried commissionerships, an appointment is also an important exercise of civic virtue.

In addition, top appointments have special meanings for organized groups. Organized bureaucracies and other groups of government officials seek to influence the character of a new Commissioner as a means of self-defense and/or pursuit of policies more in keeping with some professional norm. Nongovernmental groups—groups aligned with or hostile to the party, "money-providing" and "service-demanding" groups, ethnic and religious groups, and, not least, the parties as interest groups—all see in the top appointments a recognition of their worth and a means of making increases in real power. Each group has its own conception of the "best man" for the job.

Appointment of a group representative is also a reaffirmation of group identity. This has been of particular importance to new ethnic and religious groups. Ethnic and religious stereotypes are part of the currency of political transactions; in political hands they function as symbols of status and influence, characteristics that are used by the ethnic components of the community to judge their treatment by the powerful. Recognition of a group representative serves to make the group more cohesive. The precise degree to which groups actually use these symbols as measurements of influence and accept them as inducements for support will never be known, because it is unlikely that politicians will ever put the myth to the test. The use of ethnic and religious stereotypes in politics is to a great extent self-perpetuating and, to varying degrees, effective.

It would be impossible to trace the influence of all possible values involved in political transactions. Even though I have dealt with types or categories of values, I could not exhaust the possibilities. Those included in the study are types that have appeared to be the most prominently involved at one time or another in the past six decades.

Some attributes, like ethnicity, religion, party membership, Borough of residence, and socioeconomic status, are traditional ones. They have been, and continue to be, important characteristics in balancing elective and appointive slates. Each follows it own peculiar historical pattern, and the secular shifts and sudden variations are most revealing (see Part Two, especially Chapter 8).

Traditional political values were of greatest importance in the days when politics was dominated by the politically-professional, administratively-amateur leaders. In large part, ethnic and religious balancing and party and residential considerations, though still important, are holdovers from the nineteenth century. Traditionally, the "capable" appointee was, in modern parlance, a generalist, not a specialist. For most positions, lawyers were ideal. But new needs arising out of more complicated social relations and elaborate technology have demanded new values that have partially displaced the older ones. These values have to do with efficient administration and specialized knowledge of the area to be administered. In this study these values are referred to as *job-oriented skills*, the appointment of men who are equipped specifically for office by their training and career.[5] Closely related to this equipment is affiliation with the new professional and skill groups and an array of civic and economic "interest groups."

The Channels of Recruitment

Values, traditional and new, are the currency of political transactions. The bid for party or group influence on the Mayor's decisions is made in terms of these and related attributes. But values are inseparable from the personnel who bear them. In the process of claiming representation for their values, groups must offer persons or types as candidates for appointment. Membership and, especially, leadership in parties and various types of groups are characteristics to be treated as values in and of themselves. But, in addition to this, these organizations are social structures through which every kind of characteristic may flow. Groups in the community, including political parties, serve as channels for the recruitment of political personnel.

The most important channel of recruitment in New York City is the party organization or, synonymously, the political club. Influencing the choices of appointing officers is one of the party organization's historic functions.[6] Although its role has been steadily narrowed since 1898, the party-organization channel continues to supply a larger proportion of cabinet personnel than any other single channel. The interest of party leaders in appointments is systematic and general, reaching into every area of governmental activity.[7] And the orientation of the party channel is personal; its bias favors party loyalty and service over any other values.[8]

Whereas the party orientation is general and personal, interest groups as channels of recruitment tend to be specialized and impersonal. To a great extent, their interests are specialized along subject-matter lines; seldom does one find a group involved in the activities of more than a few agencies. Providing personnel for public office is not an overriding purpose of interest-group action. Unlike political parties, these groups are not constantly attempting to name specific appointees. Instead, they try to establish the criteria of appointment for the Mayor, to narrow the range of eligibility. Sometimes this range becomes so narrow that only a group-recruited person is satisfactory;[9] nevertheless, the orientation tends to be impersonal or objective. If not held too rigidly, the conventional distinction between parties and interest groups—personnel versus policy—is accurate. Applied to the appointment process, the distinction in orientation is "personal" versus "type of person."

If the recruitment role of interest groups has grown it is because these organizations appear to have more of the appropriate talent than parties. But the real influence of interest groups comes more from their role as departmental guardians, seeing to it that appointments are made according to pre-established standards. Each satisfactory appointment by the Mayor becomes in varying degrees a commitment that affects his successor. The "capturing" of posts occurs when the expectations as to the type of commissioner are fulfilled with a high degree of regularity (see Chapter 7, "Attribute Continuity").

THE POLITICAL POSITION OF THE MAYOR

PARTIES AND THE MAYORALTY

The Mayor faces a dazzling array of forces and competing claims. But he is not without his own resources and prior commitments. New York is a city of strong party organizations that monopolize the nomination and electoral processes. The mayoralty is tied so closely to these party processes that it is quite remarkable that nonparty forces have been able to gain any

Table 1.1 The Mayors of New York, 1898–1957*

Mayor	Incumbency	Number of Cabinet Appointments	Religion	National Origin	Preceding Office
Robert A. Van Wyck	1898–1901	62	Protestant	Native	Judge, City Court, 1889–1897
Seth Low	1902–1903	93	"	"	Mayor of old Brooklyn, 1882–1886; President, Columbia University, 1889–1901
George B. McClellan	1904–1909	161	"	"	Congressman, 1894–1903
William Jay Gaynor	1910–1913	95	"	Irish	Justice, Supreme Court, 1893–1909
John Purroy Mitchel	1914–1917	94	Catholic	"	Pres., Board of Aldermen, 1910–1913; Collector of Port of New York, 1913
John F. Hylan	1918–1925	119	"	"	Judge, Kings County Court, 1914–1917
James J. Walker	1926–1932	90	"	"	State Senator, 1914–1925
John P. O'Brien	1933	50	"	"	Surrogate, New York County, 1923–1932
Fiorello H. La Guardia	1934–1945	170	Protestant	Italian	Congressman, 1917 and 1923–1933; President, Board of Aldermen, 1920–1922
William O'Dwyer	1946–1950	108	Catholic	Irish	District Attorney, Kings County, 1940–1945
Vincent R. Impellitteri	1951–1953	63	"	Italian	Pres., City Council, 1946–1950
Robert F. Wagner	1954–1957	86	"	German-Irish	Pres., Borough of Manhattan, 1950–1953
Total appointments		1,191			

* Acting Mayors: Ardolph Kline, September–December, 1913; Joseph V. McKee, September–December, 1932; Vincent R. Impellitteri, September–December, 1950.

direct access at all. The party machinery is a vital part of
the context of appointment politics, for it explains much about
the nature of the mayoralty and the Mayor's problems in dealing
with all who claim a share of his pleasure.

The Mayor of New York is one of the highest paid and most
powerful public officials in the United States. Yet no centralized
party machinery exists for his nomination and election. And there
is no central pool from which he can select capable *and* party-
loyal candidates for appointive office. The Greater City of
New York was created in 1897, consolidating Manhattan with
the Bronx and three other surrounding Counties;[10] but *political*
consolidation was never accomplished.

Very much like the organization that provides us with our
presidential candidates, the citywide organizations of the two
major parties in New York City are periodic alliances of local
chieftains. The "real" organization in the City is the County
organization, and the key figure is the County Leader. In both
parties and in all five Counties, he is elected by the Executive
Committee of the County Committee. The Executive Committee
is composed of all Assembly District ("AD," "ward") Leaders
and their female Co-Leaders. According to the rules of each
of the County organizations, the Executive Committee is the
interim committee of the full County Committee—a very large
body of members biennially elected by precinct in the primary—
which usually convenes only once in its two-year life to adopt
the rules. The Executive Committee is the effective policy-making
and conflict-resolving body of the County organization.

The County Leader is a powerful figure only to the extent
that he holds a stable majority on the Executive Committee.
Almost always the County Leader is also leader of a District.[11]
Inside the County, the County Leader's role is primarily one of
resolving disputes that involve more than one District. Any
elective office whose constituency is fully within a District is
almost exclusively the concern of that Assembly District Leader.
Except for the Assemblymen, however, all constituencies do in
fact cut across District lines.[12] If the party is to work at all
efficiently and therefore reduce the number of primary fights
and electoral defeats, it must have a means of anticipating and
settling conflicting claims that arise out of the District clubhouses.

Often two or more District Leaders will have no problem
settling on a proper candidate. The County Leader enters the

scene to help settle the "hard cases" and to achieve a total
County slate "balancing" the outstanding ethnic, religious, and
other elements of the County. A strong County Leader has probably seldom dictated the choice of designee to his Assembly
District Leaders, but very often he will specify beforehand some
of the qualifications the candidate ought to possess. The County
Leader is strongest with respect to filling County-Borough offices,
such as that of District Attorney and Borough President. One
might say that his role grows larger as the number of participating
Assembly District Leaders increases.

The Democrats Nominate a Mayor: Making arrangements
for the three *citywide* elective offices[13] is a unique political
problem in the City, for there is no City committee in either
party. The five Democratic County Leaders must settle this
ticket *ad hoc,* among themselves. Little is publicly known about
the types of bargains that are struck or how these decisions are
finally made. But it is probably not unlike an ordinary executive
session of the Board of Estimate—a bargaining among men who
have independent sources of power. The County Leaders cannot, as the Board so often does, avoid a decision. To allow
bargaining to break down would almost inevitably mean a citywide primary fight. Nothing in New York politics can be so
bitter or revealing as a closely contested primary, even though,
on the average, less than 25 per cent of the enrolled Democrats
bother to vote. Seldom do all five Leaders survive a primary
fight. The strongest and probably "presiding" Leader is the one
from whose County the incumbent Mayor has been recruited,
or the Leader who is also the Democratic National Committeeman. Carmine DeSapio enjoyed both distinctions until the 1961
primary; Ed Flynn was for many years the National Committeeman.[14]

The Republicans: Citywide Democratic politics moves along,
then, on the basis of tenuous, shifting coalitions of the five
County Leaders in the two parties. The Republican pattern is
complicated by the fact that that party so seldom wins, in fact
has never won except in coalition with dissident Democrats and
reform groups. There are several consequences.

First, the Republican County Leaders are more prone to accept
the initiative of the Republican State Chairman. Influence tends
in the other direction for the Democrats. The Republican State
Chairman, in recent years at least, has convened the meetings
of the five Republican County Leaders and has often provided

the thrust necessary to get these Leaders, some quite passive, to the brink of decision.

Second, the Republican scheme is permeated more readily by interest groups,[15] especially the "money-providing" groups that seek reductions in City expenditures by increasing the efficiency and more sharply limiting the growth of governmental functions. On several occasions during the history of the Greater City, these groups have been brought together in an ephemeral, but highly energetic, party or movement, the Fusion ticket. The Republican-Fusion coalition has elected a Mayor three times (see Chapter 8). But during the reform ferment, the Republican organizations are fully permeated, sometimes overwhelmed, by the Fusion groups and their leaders. Seth Low had been a distinguished Mayor of the now defunct City of Brooklyn and President of Columbia University. He had run in 1897 on a Citizens' Union nomination against Van Wyck and as the regular Republican nominee as well. In 1902 Low, elected Mayor on the first Republican-Fusion ticket, was the price State Leader Platt and the regular City Republicans had to pay for victory. In 1913, the Republican-Fusion nominee was John Purroy Mitchel, again the choice of the Fusionists. Mitchel was known as an Independent Democrat and had no organization affiliation at all. He had been a Commissioner of Accounts under Mayor McClellan after McClellan's break with the regular Democrats and had been groomed for the Mayoralty by three years as a Fusion Aldermanic President and one year as a Wilsonian Collector of the Port of New York. Fiorello LaGuardia was a renegade Republican all of his political life, and his nomination for Mayor in 1933 was very much against the wishes of the regular Republicans. One reason there was no Fusion movement in 1961 was that the regular Republicans designated Lefkowitz before Fusion was organized. No wonder one old-line politician once said that rather than do what is necessary to win— nominate and share power with an "independent"—"It is better to preside over the wreckage."

A third consequence of the continuing voter preference for Democrats is that Democratic leaders are also able to influence Republican decisions. The Bronx GOP has been most strongly affected by interparty collusion. For many years prior to his death in the mid-1950s, the Bronx Republican Leader held a sinecure in the offices of a Democratic judge. Many local Republican Leaders find that in the long run they can extract from the majority-Democrats almost as much by cooperation (or collusion) as by an occasional victory. And the risks are so much less. This is another reason Republican leaders resist Fusion. Their leverage with the Republican-dominated State Legislature, and often in the Governorship, gives them not a little bargaining power with the Democrats.

The Democrats usually win City and County elections, but most often with a plurality, indicating a fragmented but widespread opposition. When the opposition begins to solidify behind an issue or a candidate, the Republicans become the keystone of the alliance and share in the victory. But they also face the risk of being forced into a secondary role by their allies.

THE PATTERN OF DISTRIBUTION

Parties: In the distribution of appointive offices, similar relationships among party levels exist. Legislators, judges, District Attorneys, and Borough Presidents can deal directly with the Leaders in their jurisdictions. Often the County Leader steps in with a candidate, but, more often probably, his role below the County level is one of clarifying the *type* of appointee required for the political balance. At all levels the County Leaders are arbitrators, and the successful Leader keeps accurate records of the types and proportion of offices each of his Districts has to its credit. The County Leaders, in turn, become claimants for the patronage of the three citywide officials, the most important being the Mayor. It is a rare occasion when an Assembly District Leader deals directly with City Hall, either at his own or the Mayor's initiative.[16] Such occasions usually indicate that the Mayor is attempting to remove a County Leader, and the risks are great.

Groups: Campaigns by interest groups for influence vary greatly; yet all groups enjoy a considerable amount of direct access to the Mayor.[17] Support of prominent groups is often solicited by candidates for the Mayor's pleasure; by far the largest single category of business in the papers of the Mayors held by the City Archives is that regarding letters of recommendation for appointment. The press is also a readily available channel for groups, but in the appointment process this medium is more often used to oppose an appointment already made. When the Mayor anticipates the opposition of a group, he will

probably not consult with them; so they turn to the press when
direct bargaining has broken down.

Often the Mayor takes the initiative for consultation with
groups, especially with professional associations whose membership is regional or national. It is not unusual for a Mayor to
initiate a nationwide search for the most outstanding member
of a profession. Two Health Commissioners, for example, had
received coveted professional awards.

An appointment is one of the Mayor's handiest mechanisms
for coopting support, but it involves a complicated calculus. A
story by Mayor McClellan (1904–1910) illustrates one of the
problems of cooption—and also one serious limitation on the
data of this study:

I called on [Archbishop] Farley and consulted him in reference to
the three departments in which he would presumably have been
most interested, Charities, Correction and Tenement Houses. I
asked him if he had any candidates to propose or any suggestions
to make. He replied, "I have no candidate for any of these offices
and only one suggestion to offer: That is, that in making these
appointments you do not name Catholics. I should much prefer that
you appoint fair-minded Protestants. All that the Church wants is a
square deal from these three commissioners, that we shall always
receive from fair-minded Protestants; on the other hand, Catholics
of the kind you should appoint will lean over backwards in their
effort to avoid appearance of favoring their own church, and the
church will suffer as a consequence.[18]

Beyond cooption, however, lies the Mayor's great need for advice
about appropriate candidates. Many groups provide this service
unselfishly. But, paradoxical as it may seem, they are not always
happy for the opportunity, for from it follows considerable
responsibility for the performances of the men so recruited. This
is why many groups prefer to set standards and act as departmental watchdogs. Again, Mayor McClellan:

Dr. Charles Parkhurst [a minister who became famous for his reform
crusades] . . . came to see me with a delegation of his admirers.
He said to me, "We are not satisfied with the way McAdoo [not the
former national figure] is running the Police Department, and
demand that you do not retain him." I replied much to the good
doctor's surprise, "I quite agree with you. McAdoo has been a failure,
and I shall not retain him. If you gentlemen will submit the name of

a candidate for the office who is qualified for the job I shall be very happy to appoint him." Thereupon Parkhurst replied, "It is not our duty to find you officials. Our duty is to see that they do their work after you have found them." [19]

APPOINTMENTS AS HISTORY

During the twentieth century New York City has been the vanguard of change in the United States. The City was the first to see the market of small, independent enterprises subordinated to a system of centralized capital. Dispersed land-use was swept away by concentrated land-use, only to return again on rubber tires. Transportation system on top of transportation system, communication system within communication system have woven the new society together and in turn have created new opportunities for change. Successive waves of international and domestic immigration have contributed ever-new elements of color, ardor, and taste. The circle of scientific-to-technological-to-societal development completes 360 degrees in months rather than years or generations.

The City's institutional and class context has changed to an extent that we cannot yet fully comprehend. The sons of the independent farmer, small proprietor, and sturdy yeoman no longer toil; they pursue a career. Their world is a simple *blue-and-white*, according to the collars they are wont to wear. The salaried members of the new industrial and business bureaucracies constitute a large and ever-growing propertyless middle class that lives by a set of values considerably different from those of the older classes. To this new middle class, the accumulation of skill is more relevant than the accumulation of property, and its orientation is less toward business and product and more toward the job.

Politics and government are organic parts of this society. The leadership of the community is rooted in and sustained by the society. There is necessarily an intimate relation between social and political change. In response to social change the range and scope of governmental activities have expanded at an almost geometric rate since the 1890s. In 1902 the City employed 33,017; by 1957, 246,316. So, while the City's population more than doubled in those years, the size of its government expanded over seven times.[20] Service and welfare activities, either unknown or unacceptable then, now take an enormously large proportion of

the City's budget. And whereas the City's population has increased by some four million, City government services have
increased from around $8.30 per capita in 1899 to $126.40 per
capita in 1958.[21] In addition, the City government has, in its
autonomous authorities, become a vast empire of public enterprise, these activities not being reflected in the annual expense
budget. Except for public health and police regulation, most of
the regulatory activity came after the turn of the century. Some
examples are traffic control,[22] tenement regulation (1902), comprehensive zoning and zoning appeals (1916), strict markets
supervision (1917), city planning (1938), air pollution control
(1952), and labor regulation (1954). Two other important
changes in government operation were the establishment of centralized purchasing (1923) and budgeting (1924). Many, many
other examples of governmental adaptation could be cited.

However, many of the profound changes in government and,
especially, politics are not reflected in structure and activities.
Social change has affected the *leadership* of the community.
Those who rule the City are not insulated from changes in the
class and occupational structure of the community, changes in
the things people are concerned about, and changes in governmental responsibilities. In the long run, the community leadership group is "representative" in some form or fashion:

As a political term, representation has some connections with the
legal idea of agency, but it is much more than this. Sociologically,
political representation may be viewed as the *process* whereby the
structure of society is reflected in the policy-and-decision-making
machinery of government. In political terms, problems of representation concern (1) the composition and organization of the governmental agencies of political decision . . . [to the end that they reflect
adequately the diverse interest of the population] and (2) the direction and coordination of the deliberative processes of government . . .
[with maximum effectiveness and popular satisfaction].[23]

Like substantive policy, strategic appointment decisions tend to
reflect the prevailing values and influences in the community.[24]

That there is a relation between strategic decisions and prevailing values is an assumption vital to later interpretations.
Like most assumptions, it is tautological. But it is a powerful
tautology because it forms the beginning, not the end, of the
inquiry. The precise nature of these values and influences has

yet to be determined. The data, not the assumptions, will tell
the story: Who are these top appointees? How did they attain
their positions? What factors have attracted the Mayor's attention? In what respects and to what extent do they reflect the
values of the population over which they exercise their authority? What changes in their distribution have occurred since the
beginning of the Greater City in 1898? What are the conditions
underlying these changes?

In brief—Who rules and why? This is an issue at the very core
of the political scientist's discipline. The problem has been approached in many ways, the one currently fashionable being to
identify and analyze all types of Leaders in a single cross-
section of time—the so-called studies of "community power
structure." In contrast, I have isolated a single type of political
decision—appointments—and have attempted to discover patterns
in depth. The top appointees do not constitute a random sample
of community leadership; rather, they comprise a special population chosen in an institutionally meaningful way. Since my statistical population is only a segment of the whole, generalizations
about power and its conditions are limited to this arena and can
only be suggestive of the whole. However, the offices included in
this study deal with practically the total array of governmental
activities, and, in the long run, most types of interests and leaders
will involve themselves in getting the "right man" at the top.

Moreover, the study reaches back into history in order to
overcome one of the fundamental problems of the community-
power-structure approach: These studies are *"time-bound."*
Structures are the *"continuing arrangement* . . . by which power
is shaped and shared within the community. . . ." [25] A simple
cross-section of time is inadequate because the pattern of leadership at any given moment may be a peculiar departure from the
typical. Trend analysis is an important tool in the study of
political dynamics as well as statics, for the identification of
norms and departures from norms leads to the discovery of conditions, of independent variables, new correlates of political
change.

When one deals with history, his starting point will always
be arbitrary. To move also into the contemporary means a second arbitrary decision. Where does one stop? The year 1898
was chosen as a starting point because it was the first year
under the new charter of consolidation. The end of Mayor
Wagner's first term, December 1957, is the cutting-off point,

rounding out the first sixty years of Greater New York's history. A few of the more recent events are recorded in the footnotes and in the final chapters. But data on the appointees do not extend beyond 1957.

TYPES OF DECISIONS NOT REPRESENTED IN THE STUDY OF CABINETS

The reader should be warned that political leaders and interest groups deal in all types of decisions and that a single political parlay might involve several types of each. For example, if an Italian bloc is frustrated by the absence of an Italian on the citywide elective slate or the weakness of Italians on the full slate, the group might be propitiated with additional appointive offices. Or, several deputy commissionerships and lesser posts might serve as the equivalent to a single department commissionership for a County Leader's share of patronage. More important, perhaps, is the fact that one bloc of support may consistently prefer representation of another type altogether, and thus would be willing to settle over a long period for less representation in the cabinet. Jewish groups allegedly prefer judicial posts to any others; and many economic and occupational groups tend to prefer a new law or interpretation to an office. To repeat a point made earlier, the population of this study was not selected for its "representativeness" of the "ruling class" of the City. The appointing process involves decisions quite distinct from others in the political process. A full profile of power in the City would require systematic inventories of decisions and decision-makers in all of the following areas:[26]

Filling Elective Offices: The nominating process is comprised of strategies and decisions regarding selection of candidates for elective office. Political parties continue to monopolize the recruitment of candidates, and the party's richest resource is the consequent hope for designation which springs eternal in the breasts of the loyal. A primary fight indicates the breakdown of bargaining techniques inside the party. For a party organization, the primary is a last resort. But it has also been a means by which the entrenched party oligarchies can more easily be attacked by outsiders. To say that nomination is strictly party business is only to say that in New York, in order to participate one must have been an enrolled member of the party for several months prior to the primary.

Party Hierarchies: The selection of individuals to fill party posts is another decision process dominated by the top party cadres. However, like the nominating process, monopoly by party leaders is far from complete, for there are often bitter fights for these posts by leaders of ethnic blocs or neighborhood economic interests. This is an important means through which new ethnic groups have achieved their first representation in other processes as well (see Chapter 2, "Social Lag"). Party office often precedes public office for new groups.

Other Appointing Authorities: All elective offices possess some appointing authority, the Mayor being most important. Appointed officials may in turn control a number of jobs. All judges, the Comptroller, and the department heads, among others, are important dispensers of patronage. Often these individuals clear appointments with the Leader, or Leaders, most responsible for their own nomination and election or appointment. Often the Mayor commits his top excutives to certain deputies prior to filling any posts. Still other deputies and bureau chiefs must be appointed in strict accordance with statutory standards. And the Commissioner has problems with his own departmental constituency.

The types of decisions so far discussed all involve personnel, and it may well be that the characteristics of the office holders in each are distributed in patterns entirely different from the ones discussed in the following chapters. However, this involves questions that only comparative analysis will settle.

Substantive Policy: Party leaders as entrepreneurs become interested in policy as this policy affects their positions or the position of the party. Policy in such areas as housing, redevelopment, zoning, and assessments often evokes intense interest. In general, however, the party leaders are far more interested in manipulating existing policies such as exceptions to zoning or parking regulations, tax relief, and so on for electoral gain. Most often, policy expressions and aspirations issuing from the party come from adjuncts to the party; the "upper-class" functionaries or "councillors"; intellectuals who have access to the Leaders or to the various campaign organizations; and the compaign organizations themselves, members of which are seldom members of the inner cores of the machine. The major participants in the policy-formulation area are, however, the responsible officials, the departmental bureaucracies, and an array of organized

interest groups. And the access that the nongovernmental groups
have to the process is direct, no longer through party leaders or
any other intermediaries.[27]

The Implementation of Policy: Seldom does interest stop
with the successful filling of offices or signing of laws. However,
with the bureaucratization and professionalization of the civil
service, access to the implementation of policies has become as
formal as it is difficult. No longer can the parties depend upon
the petty official. Bribery, no longer systematic, has probably
been reduced as far as possible, unless there are improvements
in the general social milieu. And as much by way of defense as
for more positive reasons, the civil service cultivates the ethic of
neutrality.

In all of these, party control has declined, but the nature of
this decline requires considerable elaboration. Party control has
been replaced by what de Grazia has termed "essential pluralism":[28] Many groups with independent sources of power are
competing for a share in shaping decisions that have significance
for the whole community. Of all nongovernmental groups, party
is probably the only type whose interest is both continuing and—
in the terms set forth above—universal. But the interests of most
other participants and the influence of *all* participants including party are probably segmented along subject-matter lines.[29]
In the large urban center there is specialization of function to
such a high degree that it is most unlikely that political structures and functions remain simple and undifferentiated. But let
us hold off on this issue until we see what patterns emerge from
the data. My immediate purpose is simply to introduce the question, not to argue it.

THE PLAN OF THE BOOK

In this chapter my intention has been to set the ground rules,
the boundaries, and the issues of the study. The next two chapters deal with the sociology of officialdom. Chapter 2 is devoted
to ethnic, religious, and social class factors. It shows fairly
conclusively that the political tone of the large urban center is
set more by ethno-religious forces than by class factors in the
Marxian sense. I also go to some lengths to show the process by
which the newer immigrant groups were absorbed into the political system. Chapter 3 deals with the specialization and professionalization of urban government, and also shows the concomi-

tant changes in occupational recruitment. As far as possible I also show how shifts in occupational sources account for the secular decline of mobility in politics (as described but not explained in Chapter 2).

Chapters 4 and 5 are devoted to the major channels of political recruitment—the urban machines and the nongovernmental interest groups. Chapter 4 plots out rather vividly the breakup of the virtual monopoly of access held by the parties at the turn of the century. It shows with quantitative and illustrative data the transformation of the political structure from a single, party-centered elite to a multicentered, pluralist system. Chapter 5 assesses the political role of interest groups and also compares groups with parties as channels for a variety of social and occupational types. For example, it clarifies not only the nature of group leaders' displacement of party functionaries in the command posts of government but also demonstrates that groups have become a more significant channel of social mobility than the parties.

Chapters 6 and 7 attempt to make greater theoretical sense out of the superficially confusing pluralist configuration suggested in the earlier chapters of this work and in most of the recent analyses of local as well as national politics; in other words, if there are many sources of power and no single elite in the system, is it possible nonetheless to find any established patterns (structures)? My answer is a very elaborate *yes*. With indexes of tenure, personal continuity (see Chapter 6), and attribute continuity (see Chapter 7), controlling statistically for areas of governmental activity, quantitative differences emerge that can only be explained by essential and lasting *structural* differences in the politics of public policy. Power tends to develop along subject-matter or functional lines. Each area of governmental activity or policy tends to develop its own distinct political process or power structure: To control for areas of policy is to expose arenas of power. For example, the politics of welfare and service agencies together is quite different from the politics of regulatory activities. Decisions in the former are *redistributive* and thus develop essentially a class-based politics. It is a politics of the big "peak associations," where the money-providing groups are highly coalesced against the service-demanding groups. Owing to the strength and stability of both sides, most of the decisions are submerged in the bureaucracies; since neither side can allow clear victory to the other nor get victory for itself, both tend to fall back on professionalism and elaborately objective legal formulas. In contrast, the regulatory arena is highly pluralistic; combat may follow economic lines, but never class lines. A regulatory decision is quite specialized and individualized, and this specificity of impact tends to create a highly dispersed and fluctuating set of power relations. It is every man for himself; the laws allow and the clientele groups demand discretion in regulatory decisions; peace pacts between official and clientele do not last. In both arenas, party recruitment has declined drastically (but has been displaced by entirely different channels in each arena); but in a third arena, taxes and assessments, the party monopoly still holds fast. And so on.

Chapter 8, the final empirical chapter, returns to time-series methods to get at the question: What are the sources of innovation in a big city that tends toward *stasis?* Time series is ideal for the purpose. I focus on the "reform cycle," assessing the consequences of the three periods in which the minority party held power. My major conclusions revolve around the thesis that it is the minority, or majority-in-the-making, party that is the source of innovation. It absorbs the new, no-access interests; its electoral weakness makes it permeable, whereas the electoral strength of the majority party (regardless of whether it is called Democratic or Republican) makes it a consolidative, essentially conservative force. For example, almost all the gains made by the new minority groups (Jews, Italians, Negroes) were through the Republican-Fusion coalition, not through the Democratic party. And most of the structural innovations were also Republican efforts.

The final chapter reviews both the moral and methodological significance of the findings. First I focus on what is lost and gained by the weakening of the machines and the rise of direct access to government by interest groups. The destruction of the boss-system, or party-centered power, has not been all to the good because it has left the chief executive naked to accommodate himself to and effect adjustments among competing claims in an *ad hoc* manner. Eventually I propose some suggestions toward restoration of the machine. In the methodological section I attempt to raise doubts about the recent studies of community power structure on the grounds that they have abandoned the worthy crafts of history and public administration, which approaches should set the theoretical framework for the empirical study.

I have tried to place the appointing process in the larger context of the total political process. The data of the analysis are quantitative; however, my speculations about cause and effect have often led me far, perhaps too far, beyond the data. Frequently the propositions generated to explain the distributions seem to explain phenomena outside the appointment process or beyond the City itself. I have not hesitated to offer these, unsatisfactory as they may be, as general propositions—with the ever-present proviso that they are to be treated as hypotheses for further inquiry. Just as frequently, the variations and discontinuities in the time series can only be explained by such nonquantifiable "critical events" as a Party changeover, a primary fight, or a first appointment representing a new ethnic group. These qualitative variables are, it seems to me, of critical importance although many may wish to invoke the old Scottish doctrine, "Not Proved."

Because of the vast areas of the political system *not* covered here, this study is essentially exploratory. But that fact serves well to emphasize a point that I hope to make time and again in the pages to come: It is a great mistake to treat a political system from the beginning as though there were only a single power structure or a single influence process; it is extremely misleading to refer glibly to "*the* power structure" and "*the* political process" as though we knew exactly what we are talking about. I hope this study will be a small contribution to a more sophisticated approach to politics, in which students will be searching for *conditions* under rigorous controls rather than for universal, timeless, invariant, and authoritative generalizations.

NOTES*

* For full publication information, see Bibliography.

1. The Board of Estimate is composed of the Mayor, Comptroller, and the President of the Council (four votes apiece), and the five Borough Presidents (two votes apiece). This is the Board of Directors of the City. The Board shares the legislative powers with the Council and exercises "all the powers vested in the city except as otherwise provided by law" (Charter, Section 70).

2. See Appendix (page 237) for a full classification of the offices and appointments of "cabinet" status.

3. Wallace S. Sayre and Herbert Kaufman, *Governing New York City,* Russell Sage, New York, 1960, p. 670.

4. In some instances the appointees may not need a "following" in the strict sense of the word. These "political eunuchs" are to be found almost exclusively in overhead agencies (e.g., the Budget Bureau), where loyalty to the chief and/or professional competence alone might suffice.

5. "Merit" might have been used instead, except for the moral connotations associated with the term.

6. Sayre and Kaufman, *op. cit.,* pp. 218-220.

7. However, the Party hold varies extremely from one area to another. See Chapter 7, "Attribute Continuity," especially the section on "Governmental Inputs."

8. Of course, other values, especially the "traditional" ones, can be, and are, taken into account, for no values are incompatible with political parties.

9. This is particularly true of professional associations (see Chapter 5) and organized bureaucracies (see Sayre and Kaufman, *op. cit.,* p. 222).

10. The Bronx did not become a separate County until 1914.

11. Ed Flynn was a significant exception to this rule.

12. Particularly in Manhattan, many Assembly Districts are subdivided into Parts, each Part with a Leader and Co-Leader, so that *no* elective office is fully contained.

13. Mayor, Comptroller, and President of the City Council.

14. The 1961 primary appears to be no exception in this regard. In spite of Bronx Leader Buckley's special access to the national Party Leaders, the initiative remained in DeSapio's hands, perhaps for the last time. However, 1961 is exceptional in that the five County Leaders had never before unanimously opposed an incumbent Democratic Mayor. Part of the reason for this can be seen in Wagner's use of his top patronage (see Chapter 4).

After his remarkable victory in 1961, Wagner attempted to become the real City Leader, the earliest move being to appoint his own Party coordinator, J. Raymond Jones. Only time will tell whether this move was simply a means of preventing a Negro from becoming County Leader or part of a concerted effort to unify the five County organizations.

15. For the special significance of minority-party status, see Chapter 8.

16. Every Party functionary who consented to an interview has confirmed this assertion.

17. As we shall see, this has not always been the case. The pattern is covered in detail in Chapter 4, the "Monopoly of Access."

18. Harold C. Syrett (ed.), *The Gentleman and the Tiger,* The Autobiography of George B. McClellan, Jr., Lippincott, Philadelphia, 1956, pp. 237-238.

19. *Ibid.,* p. 235.

20. *Annual Reports* of Municipal Civil Service Commission and Mayor's *Annual Reports.*

21. These are expenditures for Education and Welfare, Health, Hospitals and Sanitation, and Recreation. Even in constant value dollars there has been nearly an eightfold per capita increase.

22. Mayor George B. McClellan relates the difficulty he had in getting even the concept of traffic regulation accepted in 1905: "In Brooklyn that strange and eccentric person Justice Gaynor of the Supreme Court, who succeeded me as mayor, did all in his power to prevent my putting the traffic regulations

into force. He enjoined me permanently on the ground that any regulation of traffic was a curtailment of the constitutional liberty of the individual. It required nearly a year to win a victory over Gaynor in the Courts of Appeals. . . ." (Syrett, *op. cit.*, pp. 201-202).

23. Avery Leiserson, *Parties and Politics*, Knopf, New York, 1958, pp. 315-316.

24. Cf. Harold D. Lasswell *et al.*, *Comparative Study of Elites*, Stanford University Press, Stanford, Calif., 1952, p. 1: "The 'leadership' of a society is a criterion of the values by which the society lives. The manner in which the 'leadership' is chosen; the breadth of the social base from which it is recruited; the way in which it exercises the decision-making power; the extent and nature of its accountability—these and other attributes are indicators of the degree of shared power, shared respect, shared well-being and shared safety in a given society at a given time. By learning the nature of the elite, we learn much about the nature of the society."

25. Harold D. Lasswell and Abraham Kaplan, *Power and Society*, Yale University Press, New Haven, 1950, p. 200. Emphasis added.

26. My remarks here are intended only to suggest the key participants in each area in comparison and contrast to what will be presented in succeeding chapters. Admittedly, many of these observations remain controversial.

27. We shall see, however, that there are many significant variations in the actual pattern (see Chapters 6 and 7).

28. Alfred de Grazia, *Public and Republic*, Knopf, New York, 1951, p. 210.

29. Cf. George Belknap, "The Socio-Political Dynamics of Metropolitan Areas," a plan for research presented to the Social Science Research Council seminar, New York, 1957 (mimeo).

PART TWO

Representation

CHAPTER 2

THE SOCIAL ORIGINS OF

POLITICAL EXECUTIVES

THE BOARD OF EDUCATION: A CASE REPORT

THE DEPARTMENT OF EDUCATION forms the largest single activity in the government of New York City. The annual budgets of the Department exceed $600 million, and its personnel exceeds 50 thousand. A million students of every race, nationality, creed, and linguistic background depend on its services. Formally, the Board of Education is responsible for this vast establishment; in reality, the Board shares power with the Superintendent of Schools and the Board of Superintendents—all of whom are appointed by the Board of Education. But the Board, with its various standing committees, exercises a very real influence on the City's education policies. In fact, the Board has been a buffer between the school system and those who seek to influence what is taught, where the schools are located, what supplies and materials are bought, what architects and designs and construction companies are to be employed, and so on. Many government agencies, party organizations, professional associations, civic groups, and, not least, nationality and religious groups are vitally interested in the Department and Board of Education, and all seek representation of their interests in departmental policy.

Given the gigantic constituency of the Board of Education, no participant in education policy-making has a guarantee of

perpetual access. One of the most important strategies used to
gain a favorable position is to influence the composition of the
Board and other important departmental agencies. The scramble
for positions has been so intense that special arrangements have
long been made for the competing groups.

Representation of the five Boroughs on the Board of Education
was fixed by the first Charter of the Greater City. But representation of the ethnic and religious components of the City has
been a perennial problem for the Mayor. Between 1902—when
appointment of Board members became a mayoral power—and
1917 these problems could be solved, for two good reasons.
First, the Board was very large—forty-six members distributed
by law among the five Boroughs—and various subdivisions were
possible. Second, by virtue of its cumbersomeness and weak
statutory powers, the Board was not the object of extremely
strong desire.

Between 1902 and 1917, the Board of Education was almost
strictly an "honorific" body. Membership could be considered a
more or less symbolic recognition of local groups or of conspicuous civic virtue; but Board members seldom had a share
in framing important policies by virtue of that membership.
The old Board was one of the last enclaves of the "Gentleman
in public office." One third of the first forty-six members—
appointed by Republican Seth Low (1902-1903)—were listed in
the Social Register. During the ten Democratic years following
Low, 15 per cent of the members were in the Social Register, as
were 31 per cent of Fusionist Mitchel's appointees during the
four final years of the old Board. Alongside the seventeen Social
Register appointments, Mayor Low made fifteen that were
clearly affiliated with an ethnic group; forty-nine representatives
of ethnic minorities served with the eighteen Social Register
Board members during the McClellan and Gaynor administrations; and alongside the twelve Social Register appointees of
Mayor Mitchel served ten hyphenated Americans.

In 1917, the Board of Education was reorganized. The forty-
six-member "advisory" Board was replaced by a seven-member
Board with enlarged powers. The new Board was set up to take
an effective part in policy-making; the reduced size of the Board
put the stamp of genuineness firmly upon that fact. Further confirmation of the Board's new governmental role was seen in the
behavior of the seven initial members. Two were women who
had already devoted a lifetime to civic work; the five men who

served with them retired thenceforth from all business and professional commitments and joined the women in an almost full-time commitment to this nonsalaried government service.

Its new governmental role pushed the Board of Education irrevocably into the vortex of politics. The chips were down once it became clear that important public stakes were involved in the Board's proceedings. The pulling and hauling of groups for representation intensified, and the Mayor's appointment problem increased accordingly. No division of the number seven was ideal, for, unless a man could be found with no reliigous affiliation whatsoever, one of the big three religions would always feel deprived. Not a month passed without complaints from representatives of nationality groups; and the law granting two members for Manhattan and Brooklyn discriminated mightily against the three other Boroughs, which each had one man—one vote respectively on such matters as the building and location of the new schools.

The first consequence of the Board's new position was the disappearance of the enclave of Gentlemen. It was not a gradual disappearance, but immediate and absolute. Since 1917, not a single member of Society has served on the Board of Education. No law was passed, no accord was reached; but no Mayor

Table 2.1   Members of Society on the Board of Education, 1902–1957

Mayor	SOCIAL REGISTER		Total	Per Cent Social Register
	Yes	No		
Van Wyck	*	*	*	*
Low	17	36	53	32
McClellan	12	53	65	18
Gaynor	6	38	44	14
Mitchel	12	27	39	31
Hylan	—	17	17	—
Walker	—	8	8	—
O'Brien	—	3	3	—
La Guardia	—	14	14	—
O'Dwyer	—	10	10	—
Impellitteri	—	4	4	—
Wagner	—	9	9	—

* Board of Education made up of delegates from Borough Boards, approved but not appointed by the Mayor.

since 1917 has seen fit to appoint anyone to the Board whose credentials included a niche in the Social Register.

Since 1918, membership on the Board has followed the shifting currents of religion and nationality. However, given only seven members with seven-year staggered terms, Mayors had to make accommodations over several years. The pattern set by one Mayor was more or less a commitment for his successor. The first appointments to the new Board included three Catholics, three Protestants, and one Jew. In the first two vacancies (1920) the replacements were of the same religion as their predecessors—Protestant replaced Protestant and Jew replaced Jew. In 1921, a "Protestant vacancy" was filled by a Protestant, but in 1923 the successor was a Catholic. In 1922, another Protestant vacancy was filled by a Catholic, in 1924 returning again to a Protestant. Thus, during the first ten years, the new Board's membership shifted from three Protestants, three Catholics, and one Jew to 2:4:1, 3:3:1, and 1:4:2, respectively.

Table 2.2   Board of Education: Characteristics of Members Serving in Selected Years, 1917–1957

	1917	1918	1927	1937	1947	1948	1957
Religion							
Protestant	23	3	1	3	3	3	3
Catholic	7	3	4	3	2	3	3
Jew	5	1	2	1	2	3	3
N.A.*	11	—	—	—	—	—	—
Total	46	7	7	7	7	9	9
Ethnicity							
Am.-Eng.	19	2	2	2	2	2	2
Irish	6	2	3	2	—	—	2
Italian	1	—	—	1	2	3	1
Jewish	5	—	1	1	2	3	3
Other	2	—	—	1	—	—	—
Negro	1	—	—	—	—	1	1
N.A.*	12	3	1	—	1	—	—
Total	46	7	7	7	7	9	9

* Not Ascertained

In the 1930s the pattern continued to shift in about the same manner, except that the Jews were able to make a claim for a second member. The 1930s was also a period when two new ethnic groups rose to complicate matters. No longer could the Mayor mix religion and national origin on the Board by having only Irish-Catholics, native-American Protestants, and Jews. *Jewish* is both a religious and an ethnic category; and although national distinctions may be an issue of some importance in some contexts, it seems to matter little in political parlance whether an individual is German-Jewish or Russian-Jewish. But both the Italians and Negroes had to be accommodated, and this meant the sacrifice of at least one Catholic spot by the Irish and one Protestant spot by the native Americans.[1]

Thus, by 1948 a final solution was required. On January 13, Senator Paul Fino and Assemblywoman Elizabeth Hanniford, both Bronx Republicans, introduced a bill in the State Legislature, increasing the size of the New York City Board of Education to nine members. Ostensibly, this increase was proposed to give the Bronx and Queens equal representation with Manhattan and Brooklyn. But it also made possible a much more acceptable social distribution. Mayor O'Dwyer's two additional appointments established the 3:3:3 pattern that has remained inviolable since 1948.[2] The Catholic bloc shifts from time to time between one and two Italians; and the Protestant group includes one Negro. The two Negroes who have served since 1948 have been prominent Protestant ministers.

The Board of Education is a dramatic example of the development of ethno-religious politics in the City. Like geography, ethnic and religious characteristics are primary variables in the political calculus. The "balanced ticket" is clearly an integral part of *nominating* politics. One of the most important functions of the County Leader has been to exert pressure on AD Leaders to designate candidates for election in such a manner that the entire County electoral slate resembles the social composition of the county. Of appointments, at least this much can be said: Representation of one group in high office must be accompanied by at least a token effort on behalf of other groups. And, as for geographic balancing, the Mayor must never forget, even when the Charter and laws allow, that the Counties are independent entities in the City's party structure. County representation on the City electoral ticket and in patronage from City Hall is a rough measure of the relative power of the County Leaders. AD Leaders jealously study the pattern to test the efficacy of their Boss; they may act to deprive the Leader of

his majority in the County executive committee if he is shown
to have no leverage with City Hall (see Chapter 4).

There is a fourth social characteristic of importance to the
sociology of community power: social mobility. The members
of the cabinet are successful by the standards of relative income
and prominence, and I shall attempt to assess roughly the relative social distance traveled to reach this level. This will add
an important dimension to our picture of "circulation of elites"
in the City. However, as far as can be determined from histories, biographies, and other sources, the factor of mobility
or class position seldom enters into the arena as another requirement for calculating the balance of elective or appointive slates.
As a matter of human interest, the press often notes the fact
that a man is "self-made"; but, except with regard to the extremely rich—in which case class position is likely to be a liability—there is no evidence to indicate that this factor is considered in the distribution of offices. It is the large *social*, not
economic, substrata, the numerous ethno-religious subcultures,
in the vast City that give its politics its flavor. In New York,
"class consciousness" never appears so strongly as ethnic awareness.

MELTING POT OR TOSSED SALAD?

Decisions on nominations and appointments in New York City
have always been weighted heavily with ethnic and religious
considerations. Although the balancing of political stakes has
never been made according to any arithmetic formula, "Dealings
of this kind are neither clandestine nor unconscious." [3] All that
has changed in sixty years have been the number and types of
characteristics that Leaders feel they must accommodate.

At the turn of the century, political power in the City was
being shared almost exclusively by the Irish and the native
Americans. The Irish base was the party organization; for over
twenty years they had held a large and growing proportion of
the Democratic County and AD Leaderships and a fair proportion of Republican Party posts as well. Irishmen had perceived in politics a rare opportunity for legitimate or pseudo-
legitimate social self-promotion; urban politics was well suited
to the Irish temperament and style. The very term "Boss" was
made a political designation after Hughey McLaughlin of the
Brooklyn Democracy. McLaughlin's extension of power from

the Brooklyn Navy Yard throughout the County was as typically Irish as it was successful for him: "Big and strong, handy with his fists in a fight, he commanded the respect of the lads who hung around the firehouse."[4] Or, Boss Murphy of Tammany Hall, whose vocational life also began in a shipyard: "Having to fight among rough youths, he developed both physical prowess and a sort of domineering ascendancy which gave him marked leadership qualities among the virile youths. . . ."[5] These are superb portraits of the Irish political leader of the *fin-de-siècle*. Men like McLaughlin and Murphy had created and now controlled the political machine of the day.

The native-American-Protestant claim to power was as traditional as it was anything else. Despite Irish control of the nominating machinery, the first four Mayors of the Greater City were Yankees. But many old-stock Americans were still party leaders or functionaries, and a large part of the treasuries of both parties came from the old fortunes and established businesses.

In terms of ethnic distribution in appointment politics, the old regime lasted through the 1920s. Clearly identified native-American, English, and Irish stock comprised between 60 and 70 per cent of all Cabinet appointments, and at no time did the Mayors of that period yield over 15 to 20 per cent of top patronage to all other groups combined, although the share of the latter was slowly increasing (Figure 2.1).[6] Except for Van Wyck and Walker, at the beginning of the century and the end of the 1920s, native-Americans received much the larger share of the top posts, regardless of the party in power. Nonetheless, relative proportions varied according to party, the Irish faring best during Democratic rule. There were similar variations in the religious complex of the cabinet, which, of course, resulted by and large from one maneuver involving Irish Catholics and native-American Protestants (see Figures 2.1 and 2.2).

Given the grip of these two groups on both the politics and the economics of the City, it is surprising that this internal distribution of the stakes did not maintain itself. But the competition of the two parties for new voters was irresistible; a policy of excluding new ethnic minorities would have been most unprofitable in the long run. For the same reasons, the Irish had made their way into the higher political councils earlier in the nineteenth century. Tammany Hall had bitterly opposed recognition of naturalized citizens for at least the first forty years of its existence:

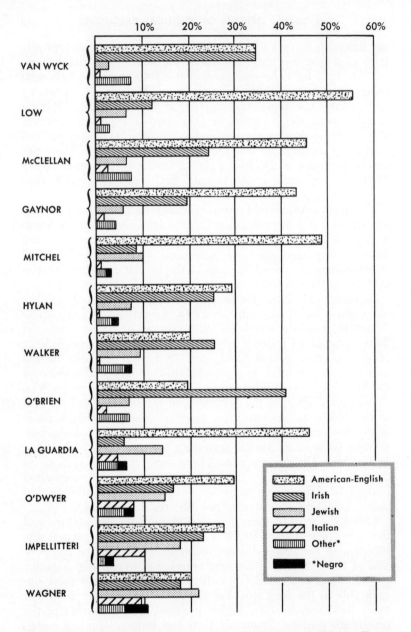

Figure 2.1   Ethnic Distribution: The Balancing of Ethnic Types by Mayor

The prejudice against allowing "adopted citizens" to mingle in politics was deep; and Tammany claimed to be a thoroughly native body. As early as May 12, 1791, at Campbell's Tavern, Greenwich, the Tammany Society had announced that being a national body, it consisted of Americans born, who would fill all offices; though adopted Americans were eligible to honorary posts, such as warriors and hunters. An "adopted citizen" was looked upon as an "exotic." [7]

In its fight against the Whigs for control of the old City, Tammany Hall finally voted itself a naturalization bureau to help recruit the expanding population. This step was taken on the eve of the great Irish immigrations: 1840. Within twenty years, naturalized Tammany affiliates outnumbered the native-born as a result of a willingness to set prejudice aside.

And so it was with the new immigrant groups of the late nineteenth century. Not only did they have to be served by the naturalization bureaus of both parties; a place had to be made for them in the distribution of the spoils. Between 1898 and 1958, the representation of all national groups other than native-born and Irish rose from 12 per cent to 43 per cent. The native-American and Irish share of cabinet appointments taken together declined from 70 per cent to 39 per cent.

The distribution of appointments did not respond steadily to the movement of new minorities into politics. The rate of entry into the cabinet of the three most significant new groups was governed largely by the minority party—Republican-Fusion Mayors Low, Mitchel, and La Guardia. Each of these Mayors appointed substantially larger numbers of Jewish, Italian, and Negro representatives than had their Democratic predecessors. If the Democratic successors reduced the number of these appointments it was never to earlier levels.

It has been the role of the minority party in New York to provide a channel of mobility for new ethnic groups (see Chapter 7 and Figure 8.2). The "club core" of the dominant party, while an important assimilating channel in the City, seems to have had a retarding effect on new elements. The grooming of party members for higher and higher party and governmental office is methodical, almost hierarchal, in the dominant party; seniority and length of service are important considerations as long as the party can afford them. The entrenched Democratic leadership has resisted the intrusion of types of people who might have spoiled the *camaraderie* of the Irish-Catholic in-

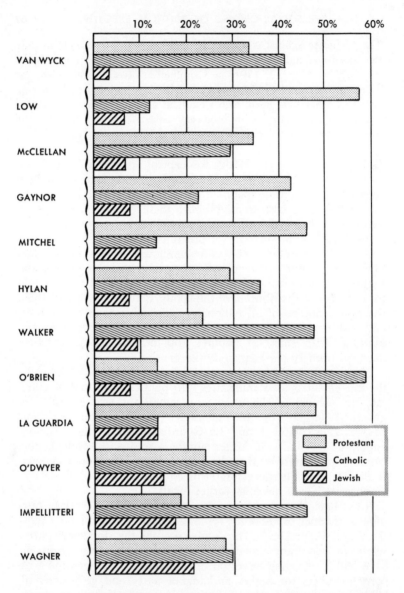

Figure 2.2 Distribution of Religions: The Balance of Major Religious Groups by Mayor

group. This *camaraderie* has always been a strong cohesive factor in the New York City Democracy.

The City's Republican organizations are also built around the local clubhouses. Further, they have typically been composed of the "better classes." But the coalition necessary to capture City Hall has made the mayoral cadre much more permeable to all sorts of nonorganization forces. The role of the minority party in the twentieth century is not so clear as in the nineteenth. Tammany Hall had had an open field in 1840 and 1850 because the Whigs had been incapable of competing with them. "The Whigs were bewildered at this systematic gathering in of the naturalized citizens," [8] and all they could do was to issue statements of condemnation:

After the election of April, 1840, when Tammany re-elected Varian Mayor and carried the Common Council, the Committee of Whig Young Men issued a long address on the subject. After specifically charging that prisoners had been marched from their cells in the City Prison by their jailers to the polls to vote the Tammany ticket, the address declared that . . . naturalization papers had been granted at the Marine Court on tickets from Tammany Hall, under circumstances of great abuse.[9]

The dominant Democratic organizations of the twentieth century have made efforts to attract the immigrants, but the minority Republicans made greater use of top patronage for these purposes.

THE SOCIAL LAG

The representation of a new minority in places of power occurs long after it has reached considerable size in the population and electorate. No political system or segment thereof has ever attempted to give proportional representation to every element, even a major one, in the society. Elites everywhere must pay close attention, however, to any group—whether its base be economic, geographic, or social—that accepts the community and tries to orient its behavior into channels that are functional for it. As these groups assimilate the prevailing myths and practices of their adopted land, they start the process of "coming of age" politically. Italian and Jewish greenhorns started the process by reading the local newspaper printed in their native tongue; slowly they learned English and began reading English-language dailies. The economically blessed joined local civic ac-

tivities, especially nationality and religious clubs. Then, with
the aid of the District political clubs, they became citizens and
voters. It was inevitable that many would become loyal club
members in return. From this moment they became part of the
political process, not merely its subjects.[10] But they did not become politically potent until long after they were many in
number.[11]

Each new nationality group went through a waiting period of
practically a generation before gaining a voice in party councils.
Perhaps the Irish grip on New York politics was most tenacious
because they had suffered the longest wait. The 1830s and
1840s swelled the entire Eastern seaboard with sons of Erin; by
1890 their control on three of the New York Counties—Manhattan, Queens, and Kings—was secure, thereby rooting out most
of the remaining Dutch, Germans, and Anglo-Saxons. According
to Peel, however, even as late as Tweed's reign in the 1860s,
political power was still firmly in the hands of the Scotch and
Scotch-Irish.[12]

The tidal waves of Jewish immigration occurred at just about
the point when the Irish were beginning to take the political
reins.[13] The Jews were absorbed politically by whatever party
controlled their new neighborhoods. As a group their strength
was dissipated. Many drifted to the Republican party and later
to the Socialist and Communist parties. Those who chose the
New York Democratic party were not cordially invited to share
leadership with the Irish. When, upon occasion, a Jew succeeded
to AD leadership or some other spot of political importance, he
was generally content with Irish leadership and an office for
himself.

Italian immigration began to stabilize a decade or two after
the Jews had arrived. For a generation, according to Peel, the
Italians were content to serve the causes of the "Irish-Jewish
Democrats and the Jewish-Irish-'native American' Republicans
without protest."[14] Like the Jews, they were at first dissipated by
district lines; but after 1925 La Guardia became the rallying cry
for Italians of all parties. Literally hundreds of Italian clubs
sprang up all over the City and its environs.[15] Perhaps even more
than Protestant La Guardia, Carmine De Sapio symbolizes the
coming of age of the Italians. In the late 1930s he destroyed the
seventy-five-year old Battery Dan Finn dynasty in Greenwich
Village and permanently altered the nature of Tammany leadership.

As early as 1902–1904, Jews were receiving 5 to 8 per cent of the Mayor's top appointments—closer to 10 per cent under Mayor Mitchel. La Guardia was the watershed for Jewish and Italian patronage, almost doubling the representation of both groups between 1933 and 1945. Largely due to La Guardia's appointment pattern, ethnic and religious representation entered a new and perhaps stable phase: the balancing of appointments, in a manner resembling the balancing of electoral tickets, in rough proportion to group electoral strength. Mayor O'Dwyer appears to be the first to make such an attempt, and his two successors worked out an even more careful balancing.

THE FIRST APPOINTMENTS

The vanguard of an ethnic minority is of fundamental importance to the campaign of the group for representation. The manner in which precedents are broken largely determines whether new precedents are established; a poor first representative can easily set back the cause of a new minority by many years. In the twentieth century, three of the important ethnic blocs in New York passed through political infancy, political grooming, and political maturity. Like the Irish before them, all three depended largely, although not exclusively, on the minority party, but all three blocs long ago began to enjoy the recognition of both parties. And although their coming of age was separated by a decade or more, the first representatives of each group bear a surprising number of common attributes.

The Jews were, to a certain extent, already established politically by 1898 and were receiving a few crumbs of top patronage. However, although "first appointments" of Jews cannot be identified within the time limits of this study, it is still possible to observe some significant common characteristics among the earliest Jews after 1898. Eight Jews received cabinet posts in the first decade after Consolidation. Without exception they served on boards; no Jewish appointee headed a department alone. Six of the eight served on *nonsalaried* boards (Board of Education and Board of Health), a fact that suggests that their economic positions were far above the average for their ethnic group and for the total New York City population. The other two served on the Board of Taxes and Assessments. Seven[16] were very prominently associated with Jewish philanthropic and fraternal societies, and all ranked high in their respective political parties, despite the fact that the Boards of Education and Health have never been Party enclaves. Three were Democrats. Of the five about whom relevant information could be found, two were foreign-born; and these two—Nathan Straus and Felix Warburg—were probably the most prominent Jews ever to serve the City.

Only three Italians served as Commissioners in the first decade following Consolidation. All three were members of boards, two on the Board of Education and one as President of the Board of Assessors. All three were outstanding members of Italian welfare and fraternal groups. The two foreign-born members were sons of well-established Italian merchant families; both were from northern Italy, and one was Protestant. The third Italian was somewhat closer to the ethnic stereotype. However, although born in lower Manhattan of an immigrant shoemaker, he became a doctor at 23 years of age. He achieved ethnic, civic, and professional prominence not long afterward, and was appointed to the Board of Education at the age of 36. The two Board of Education members were not politically prominent; the Board of Assessors member was a Sachem of Tammany Hall and a founder and President of the Italo-Democratic Union, a Tammany affiliate.

The first and only Negro to serve prior to 1920 was Dr. Eugene P. Roberts. A son of freed slaves, he was graduated from Lincoln University, studied medicine in New York City, and practiced for a short while before being appointed a medical examiner by the New York City Board of Health in 1897. His service with the Health Department and practice in Harlem led to his appointment to the Board of Education in 1917. A founder of the National Urban League, he was prominent in all phases of Negro community life. His biography reveals no political activity, although it is possible that his brother's activities leading to election as the first Negro Alderman in 1918 added to his credentials.

Since 1917, only eight other Negroes have received cabinet appointments. The second was Ferdinand Q. Morton's appointment to the Civil Service Commission in 1922. Morton served on the Commission until 1946, and his three successors on the Commission were also Negroes. The third Negro cabinet appointment was to the Tax Commission in 1934; Hubert T. Delany served as Tax Commissioner through 1942 and went from there into elective judicial office. Two other Negroes, the Reverends John M. Coleman and Gardner C. Taylor, were appointed to the Board of Education. The eighth, Arthur C. Ford, was ap-

pointed Commissioner of Water Supply, Gas, and Electricity by
Mayor Wagner in 1954. Ford was the first Negro Commissioner
of a single-headed department, serving for over three years in
that capacity.[17]

Morton and Delany, the second and third Negro appointees,
were party functionaries; Morton was an organizer for Democrats in Harlem, and Delany figured prominently in La Guardia's
1933 campaign. However, the other five, including Commissioner
Ford, were Democrats with no background of party service at
all. Four of the eight had been officers in large civic and philanthropic organizations, and seven were prominent in the affairs
of the Negro community. In contrast to the first Jewish and
Italian appointments, seven of the nine (including Eugene Roberts) had used governmental bureaucracies to rise to the top.
Two made a career in the civil service, four spent most of their
occupational lives in exempt City and State jobs, and one was
a practicing lawyer who had held other public offices prior to
his Cabinet appointment. The only two without considerable
government service prior to appointment were the two clergy-
man Board of Education appointees.

All of the earliest appointments from new ethnic groups were
members of Boards. Appointment to the commissionership of a
single-headed department did not come their way until long
after their respective groups were firmly established politically.
Group representation has been the "latent function" of the
Boards and Commissions that head up so many of the departments. The Board of Education was the most important point
of entry for the first Italian and Jewish representatives, but the
Civil Service Commission served most frequently for the
Negroes. This in itself is a significant difference reflecting the
perspectives of the groups toward the stakes of government.
Jewish and Italian leaders sought the high status of public office
for themselves and as symbols for their own kind; but they had
specific religious ties to their communities that could be fur-
thered in public education policies. In contrast, Negroes have
so far seen in government opportunities for the nondiscriminatory
employment that is closed to them in so many private economic sectors. The first Negro Civil Service Commissioner,
Morton, chose his position from several offered him in return for
Party services rendered.

Most of the Jewish and Italian appointees had been active
in party organizations prior to appointment, and two of the

first three Negro appointees had also been functionaries. The fact that the later six Negroes were not active at all does not necessarily suggest differences either in opportunities or perspectives of Negroes regarding political organizations. These appointments were made in the 1940s and 1950s; as we shall see in later chapters, the position of the political party had by then been drastically altered.

POLITICAL ASSIMILATION

Melting pot or tossed salad? The social process metaphor in America has been the crucible; those who approve of our style call the process "Americanization," and those who disapprove call it "assimilation." The extraordinary degree to which immigrants have adopted the norms of the majority is undeniable. But what of the maintenance of old-country identifications? Dual loyalties are nothing new to the United States. Irish-American funds helped finance the independence of Ireland. So with German- and Polish-Americans long before Zionism. Assimilation was seldom ultimate.

The political process, too, is often thought to be an assimilating force.[18] Political activity works toward the maximum of consensus in the community. The need for majorities, around which political organizations were formed, makes necessary the forging together of many elements into a stable coalition. Differences of group aims and interests must be put aside for the good of the party. But political strategies have a strong *conservative* impact on the society: *the pulling and hauling of party activity tend to maintain the awareness of differences among minorities.* Between campaigns, the community moves toward majority norms, toward uniformity and lack of class, ethnic, or religious consciousness. As party political activity mounts, so are the various social differences reaffirmed.[19] Political leaders, in attempting to forge together a winning coalition by "representing" the important minorities on elective and appointive slates, help perpetuate traditional ethnic and religious groupings. In New York City, these ethnic and religious groupings are real, perhaps to a greater extent and variety than in any other city in America. *And in behaving as though they are in fact true units of political force, the political leaders help to maintain them.*

The balancing of social characteristics in the appointment process is not the result of a precise policy of apportionment. It is not a balancing of electorates but a balancing of claims. A calculus is involved, but the calculations are made according to the Mayor's crude perceptions of power. Great effort is exerted by political leaders to apportion electoral candidacies in terms of voting strength. A ticket must, after all, be presented all at once and at a time when political leaders are most vulnerable, so that the every existence of a large ethnic group in the electorate has particular efficacy.

By contrast, the Mayor's appointments are made at various times during his incumbency. Yet, with regularity, each appointment is considered in terms of all that were made before. Balancing maneuvers are fully apparent in the appointment process, but being a step removed from the election, mayoral appointments are less responsive to electoral strength. Many different resources—electoral, social, personal, economic—or simply the mythology of group power can make a claim effective; but without *access*, none of these valuable resources will require the Mayor's attention. And access takes time; it lags well behind the emergence of a significant number of votes.

Given access to the Mayor, the actual size of a group in the electorate plays essentially a negative role. *Electoral size tends to establish an upper limit on the amount of recognition a group can expect.* Otherwise, during most of the Democratic Mayoralties before the 1930s the Irish-Catholic in-group might well have had the power to take all of the choice posts for their own. During the late 1930s, Mayor La Guardia is alleged to have expressed concern that there were "too many Jews" in office. In recent years, the pattern of cabinet appointments has come to resemble ticket balancing in its approach to electoral apportionment. However, this is for the most part due to the gradual equalization of political power among ethnic groups, and this pattern of apportionment is likely to continue as it, like the balanced ticket, becomes embedded in the political folklore.

When the Mayor recognizes a group demand he does not necessarily gain the support of the group for himself; but if he too often goes counter to expectations he can expect to lose support as a bigot. Very few of the Mayor's appointments of ethnic representatives, especially the earliest of a· group just risen to power, have closely fit the stereotype. While they have been, in most cases, closely identified with their respective groups, they were *from,* but not *of,* the group. Most of them— including the Negro appointees—have been at least a generation removed from the lower economic brackets. But all have symbolized the American ideal of success; each appointment made on ethnic or religious grounds has reaffirmed faith in that ideal and has also reaffirmed the identification of the members of the group with each other.

The social balancing of appointments is thus part of a general process of assimilation. But political assimilation, unlike assimilation through occupation, education, sports, entertainment, organized crime, and other economic endeavors, has a dual impact. Political decision-makers, being no more liberal than the average citizen, have been pushed through competition for support to offer special inducements to marginal groups. In so doing, their actions have had consequences far beyond the intended. Success in economic fields is highly individualized; notwithstanding the occasional Jackie Robinson, there is relatively little group symbolization of success. In contrast, political success, particularly in the big cities, is symbolized very strongly in group terms. Economic mobility is more truly assimilative because economic success homogenizes values and tends to erase social differences. If the melting pot is insisted upon as the proper metaphor for the American social process, then it should be added that the political process reduces the flame.

SOCIAL CLASS MOBILITY: A PROFILE OF THE SOCIETY

The rise of new ethnic groups in the cabinet does not necessarily imply an increase of class mobility in politics. Most representatives of the new minorities in the cabinet have been a generation or more removed from the lowest economic brackets; they or their parents used the educational system, technical training, or small business as the channel of initial mobility (see Chapter 3). Those who found their way into the political elite were the blessed compared to the group of their origin. Thus, the entry of representatives of new ethnic groups has in fact tended to *reduce* the degree of class mobility in politics.

Cabinet members have always been a heterogeneous lot in terms of class as well as ethnic origin. In the period prior to the 1930s only once did more than 30 per cent of the cabinet come from a single stratum of the community. During the two-year incumbency of aristocratic Mayor Seth Low, almost 40 per cent of the top appointments originated in the upper class; the Social Register was his eligible list (Figure 2.3).[20] But this was an

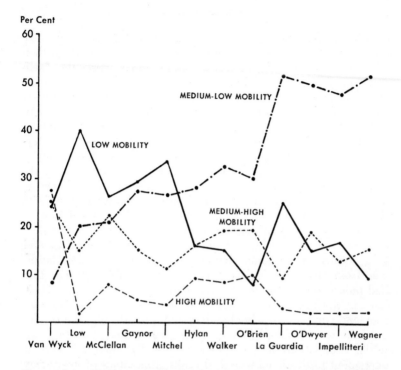

Per Cent

Figure 2.3 **Mobility in the Cabinet: Per Cent of Appointments by Degree of Mobility for Each Mayor, 1898–1957**

exception to a rather continuous decline of upper class origins in the appointive elite, a decline retarded only by the interjections of the three Republican-Fusion Mayors. Otherwise, cabinets of the period before 1933 were drawn from all class strata. Clearly the largest proportion in this period were drawn from the middle strata, both medium-high- and medium-low-mobility personnel. Those of highest mobility, from lower-class origins, made up almost 30 per cent of Mayor Van Wyck's cabinet, which perhaps reflects the pattern of the late nineteenth century; but after 1902 they never again comprised more than 10 per cent of the cabinet.

The most marked change to be noted in the sixty years of Greater New York's history is the rise of the medium-low mobiles, those who had acquired college education and training before entering the work force. For all the class strata, La Guardia and the 1930s were the break with the past, but the 1930s

merely accelerated trends already apparent for the middle- to
upper-middle-class strata. Cabinet members who had begun their
adult lives with little education and menial work—the "self-
made men"—became highly exceptional cases. The upper class
also continued to diminish as a source of political executives.
And even the high school graduate with a clerical and semi-
technical background—the medium-high mobile—could no longer
look to City Hall for an expanding opportunity to reach the top.

So appointive politics declined as an avenue of class mobility.
It was replaced primarily by the educational system and the
modern business establishments. In the late nineteenth century
the ambitious sons of the poor had entered the work force with
the barest exposure to formal education. Their livelihoods, if
any, were taken from manual labor and clerical jobs, but their
true vocation was politics. Politics was an end in itself as well
as a means of economic betterment. Their promotion ladder
was from "ward heeler" to functionary to public official; they
had moved out of the lower class with political leverage. Those
born in the lower strata after 1900, however, had an elaborate,
free, and compulsory school system and, periodically, the staying
hand of mass unemployment. Owing to higher education and
initial occupations in the upper white-collar, salaried, and independent professional-technical ranks, appointees of lower-class
parentage traveled a shorter social distance to reach the political
elite. The extension of free public education and inexpensive
higher education, coupled with the phenomenal growth of higher
white-collar tasks in industry, expanded the *availability* of
middle- versus high-mobility personnel.

The extent to which politics in the City of New York has
declined as a channel of mobility can best be shown by comparing proportions of each class category in the cabinet with their
proportions in the community at large. Otherwise the changes of
representation in any given social stratum might seem merely
reflections of similar changes in the community. Such would tend
to be the case only if high political position were completely un-
influenced by class origins.[21] That is to say, if the opportunity
for entry into the political elite were the same for persons of
all class origins—if opportunity were distributed randomly—the
ratio for any comparison between class representation in the
cabinet and the social structure of the community could approach unity. Any ratio over 1:0 indicates "over-representation"
of a class; the farther below 1:0 for the lower strata, the lower

the *degree of mobility* in the cabinet. (For further discussion of these comparisons, see the Appendix.)

Between 1870 and 1900, wage laborers in New York City's work force declined from 72.5 per cent to 61.8 per cent; by 1930 the proportion of wage laborers in the work force had dropped still further to 53.8 per cent. During the same sixty-year period, the percentage of lower white-collar clerical personnel grew as a proportion of the City's work force from 9.6 to 10.7 to 21.2 per cent. From the manual laboring class of around 1870, Mayor Van Wyck drew 29 per cent of his cabinet; Mayor Wagner appointed only 2 per cent of his 1954–1957 cabinet from

Table 2.3   Degree of Mobility: Ratios of Per Cent of Each Class Stratum in New York City Population to Per Cent of Each Original Class Stratum in the Cabinet, 1898–1957

Categories of Original Class Position	Per Cent 1898–1901 Cabinet/ Per Cent 1870 Census*	Per Cent 1925–1932 Cabinet/ Per Cent 1900 Census	Per Cent 1954–1957 Cabinet/ Per Cent 1930 Census
Low (high mobility)	.40	.15	.04
Middle (medium-high mobility	2.71	1.87	.75
Upper (medium-low and low mobility)	1.79	1.78	2.48

* Since this was prior to Consolidation, the best available census figures for 1870 were for Brooklyn and old New York City taken together. See 1870 *Census of Population*, Vol. I. The figures for 1900 and 1930 were derived from the Census of Occupations for the entire City. See 1900 Census, *Special Reports: Occupations*, pp. 634-641, and 1930 Census, *Population*, Vol. IV, pp. 1130-1134.

men who had started as manual laborers in the 1920s. The ratio of manual labor origins in the cabinet to manual laborers in the work force dropped, therefore, from .40 in 1898–1902 to .04 in 1954–1957, a tenfold decline in relative mobility. This was accompanied by a reduction from 2.71 to .75 in the relative mobility of clerical-worker origins. When we add to this the average age at the time of appointment to a cabinet post of those of humble origins, we can see that the attrition rate has become not only higher but the process of rise is more arduous: In Van Wyck's day the average age for the larger proportion of high mobiles to receive appointments was 47.1 years, whereas for Walker's and Wagner's appointees it had risen to 53.6 and 53.4, respectively. How does this compare with the business elites?

Mobility in politics, as reflected in the top appointments, is apparently responsive to factors other than those affecting mobility rates in the business elite. For while the Mayor's cabinet has come to be dominated by recruitment from a single stratum— over 50 per cent from a professional or technically educated class (and still increasing)—the American business elite has become more heterogeneous. New forms of organization have emerged from the growth and centralization of contemporary production. A trained white-collar, educated class has all but displaced the ordinary laborer.[22] Yet as many as 14 per cent of the American business leaders in 1952 started out as laborers. Comparing this proportion with the proportion of laborers in the total work force of 1920, Warner and Abegglen found the "ratio of under-representation" to be .30; that ratio in the Wagner cabinet was .04.[23]

The change from family to corporate control of business has very likely loosened many class barriers to business leadership. According to Warner, the " . . . stronghold of inherited position in America today is in the smaller enterprises; the freest and most open positions are in the largest enterprises." [24] The proportion of laborer origins among business leaders was relatively high in 1952 and may well have increased compared to earlier times; and perhaps of even greater significance is the fact that the number of members of the business elite who were *sons* of business leaders has dropped since 1928.[25]

Meanwhile, political structure and party organization have undergone no such drastic transformation. What has changed is the economic world around the clubhouse. In our day there are more and more opportunities in industry for those of humble backgrounds, whereas once politics appeared to many to be the only channel of mobility (see Chapter 5). Thus, the very economic changes that increase class circulation in industry have provided many of the conditions for reduction of circulation in the political order. Industry needs new skills in ever-expanding supply, and industry has provided for this supply with on-the-job training, subsidized college training, and secure and clear promotion ladders based on merit. The industrial system is attractive to those who do not have the means to educate themselves. The fact that these new skills are needed by government gives the skilled person access to many types of public office which he enters, if at all, after his initial rise in industry.

SUMMARY

The claims made upon the Mayor on behalf of social groupings in the community are ethnic and religious claims. Aid to the economically underprivileged is extended by many private and public institutions; in our time welfare has become a profession. But no groups exist for the promotion of the self-made or the conscientious underprivileged for office. Ordinarily the wooing of lower-class support is done through policies, not offices. This is true, for example, even of the trade unions. Although they attempt to exercise a veto over many prospective appointments, they seldom promote one of their own leaders for a commissionership. A few bona fide trade unionists have served in the cabinet, but they were old union managers who were, almost without exception, prominent in political parties or campaigns. Economic class origin is not taken into account by appointing authorities unless that origin is extreme wealth or high status, in which case it tends to work negatively.

Direct comparisons of ethnic and religious distributions in the cabinet with those in the population are illegitimate because the intervening effects of access and political power must be accounted for. But direct comparisons of this sort can be made for economic factors since they are not involved in political transactions. Such comparisons are crude at best, but they give some indication of long-run changes in mobility patterns and rough, yet clear, differences between the political and business elites.

Much of the change in the mobility of the cabinet is to be explained by changes in the educational system and occupational structure of the community. However one might measure social class or social mobility, he would find secular changes in the stratification of the community reflected eventually in the political structure. But when some political trends go contrary to or far in excess of community trends, relationships between the political and the social cannot be interpreted innocently. One must look for changes of the perspectives of political leaders, changes, more specifically, in the use of the Commissionerships by the Mayor, and changes in the values of Mayors toward skills and the use of them.

Throughout the sixty years of Greater New York's history, the rise of an educated class to politics has been apparent. However, the variations within the trend must be explained by differences in the character and outlook of the types of administrations that have ruled the City. At first, the increase of formally educated personnel in the cabinet was attributable to reform Mayors.[26] Following World War II, the pattern became typical rather than exceptional. This does not signify a return of the older, liberally educated class. Middle-class "generalists-with-experience" remain a small proportion of cabinet appointments. A newer middle class is displacing the highest and lowest classes as well as a large segment of the older middle class. Because of their formal education, members of this growing segment of the cabinet are to be classified as having medium-low mobility, or middle class in origin. But they are *trained* as well as educated; they possess specialized knowledge—not general ability or administrative skills, but *job-oriented skills*. It will be the main burden of Chapter 3 to examine the developing pattern of occupations and skills within the class context developed in this chapter.

NOTES

1. This category does not include Negroes.

2. The highly publicized reorganization and reform of the Board in 1961 apparently did not change this.

3. Sayre and Kaufman, *op. cit.*, p. 539.

4. Oscar Handlin, *The Uprooted*, Grosset and Dunlap, New York, 1951, p. 209. See also James McGuire (ed.), *Democratic Party of the State of New York*, United States History Co., New York, 1905, Vol. II, pp. 236-260.

5. Gustavus Myers, *The History of Tammany Hall*, Boni and Liveright, New York, 1917, p. 299.

6. Summary of Figure 2.1:
Percentage of Cabinet Appointments of native-Americans—Irish and the other minority groups:

Mayor	Native Americans-Irish	Other Groups	Origin Not Asct.
Van Wyck	70	12	18
Low	69	11	20
McClellan	72	18	10
Gaynor	64	15	22
Mitchel	68	15	17

Mayor	Native Americans-Irish	Other Groups	Origin Not Asct.
Hylan	56	12	32
Walker	59	20	21
O'Brien	61	18	21
La Guardia	53	25	22
O'Dwyer	47	31	22
Impellitteri	49	32	19
Wagner	39	43	18

7. Myers, *op. cit.*, p. 30.

8. *Ibid.*, p. 129.

9. *Ibid.*

10. For a poignant description of the changes in orientation and activity of immigrants, see Oscar Handlin, *op. cit.*, especially Chapter VIII.

11. The Chinese community of New York is an excellent case in relief. Of substantial size, this group has firmly remained a subcommunity of the City, taking little part in activities outside those of the nationality. During the entire sixty-year period covered by this study there were no Chinese appointments, although one commissioner had a Chinese mother.

12. Roy V. Peel, *The Political Clubs of New York City*, Putnam's, New York, 1935, p. 252. For a full treatment of this subject covering arenas outside the scope of this study, see pp. 251 ff.

13. According to the *Jewish Communal Survey of Greater New York* (1928), the great Jewish immigration started in 1882, almost entirely to the lower East Side:

Year	Jews in New York City	Per Cent
1890	300,306	11.98
1900	597,674	17.39
1910	1,252,135	26.28
1920	1,643,012	29.23

The crest of the wave was in 1916, or thereabouts (Regional Plan Association, *Regional Survey*, The Association, New York, 1928, Vol. II, pp. 63-64, 105-106).

14. *Ibid.*, p. 254.

15. *Ibid.*, p. 256.

16. No detailed biographical information could be found on the eighth.

17. The second full-fledged Negro commissioner, James R. Dumpson, was appointed Commissioner of Welfare in August, 1959.

18. See, for example, Elmer E. Cornwell, "Party Absorption of Ethnic Groups: The Case of Providence, Rhode Island," *Social Forces*, 28 (March, 1950), pp. 205-210, and studies cited there.

19. Cf. Bernard Berelson, *et al.*, *Voting*, University of Chicago Press, 1954, pp. 142-143.

20. Definitions of the four class strata are given in the Appendix.

21. See W. Lloyd Warner and James C. Abegglen, *Occupational Mobility*, University of Minnesota Press, Minneapolis, 1955, pp. 39-44.

22. The impact of new industry on the work force has been carefully studied by Lewis Corey, "The Middle Class," in Reinhard Bendix and S. M.

Lipset (eds.), *Class, Status and Power,* Free Press, New York, 1953, pp. 371-380.

23. This is admittedly a crude comparison, but, given the available figures, it is the best possible one. One objection to the comparison might be that Warner used Census data for the total population whereas we used it for New York City only; another objection follows from the use of 1920 figures for the business elite ratio and 1930 figures for the political ratio. However, convert the Warner ratio by using the 1930 New York City Census and you get a ratio of .26 as compared to our ratio of .04—still a great difference.

Most unfortunately, there are no figures by which to compare differences in trends between the business and political ratios. That is, we have no data on lower-class origins of earlier business elites. The 1928 study of business leaders (F. W. Taussig and C. S. Joslyn, *American Business Leaders*) that Warner used for many comparisons did not collect any data on initial occupations. It would, however, be remarkable if the ratio of per cent laborer origins in business leadership to per cent laborers in the Census was much higher than .30 or .26 in 1928 *or* 1900, so that it is most unlikely that mobility in the business elite has declined.

24. *Ibid.,* pp. 168-169.

25. *Ibid.,* p. 164.

26. Low, Gaynor, Mitchel, and La Guardia. Analysis of this phenomenon, as well as Democrat Gaynor's place, is one of the purposes of Chapter 8 (see "The Reform Cycle").

CABINET SPECIALIZATION AND

ITS CONSEQUENCES

NEW ROLE FOR THE HIGH PRIESTS:
A CASE REPORT

THE LAWYER has more or less justifiably been called the "high priest of American politics." Throughout American history the largest occupational source for public officials of all types and at every level of government has been the law. Although comprising less than one half of one per cent of our labor force, the legal profession supplied the Presidency and his Cabinet with 70 per cent of the occupants of those offices between 1877 and 1934.[1] Over 55 per cent of the Eighty-First Congress, and during the 1930s over 50 per cent of all State Governors, were from the legal profession. In the Mayor's cabinet of New York the law has also been an important occupational source. Thirty per cent of all cabinet appointees in the Greater City's history were trained as lawyers, over one half of whom had pursued a career in legal practice prior to appointment. Ours has indeed been "a government of lawyers and not of men."

There are many reasons for the dominance of the lawyer in public office despite the small size of his profession in the work force. The lawyer has the "skill" in interpersonal relations and the "skill" in the use of words so vital in the political trade. He can easily master the mysteries of the legal framework within which all governmental activity takes place. What is more, politics is one of the few ethical means for client promotion and advertisement open to the lawyer; politics and his professional calling are symbiotically related.

The lawyer and the image of the generalist administrator have been an almost perfect fit in every field:

. . . the lawyer is today . . . the one indispensable adviser of every responsible policy-maker of our society—whether we speak of the head of a government department or agency, of the executive of a corporation or a labor union, of the secretary of a trade or other private association, or even of the humble independent enterpriser or professional man. . . . For better or worse our decision-makers and our lawyers are bound together in a relation of dependence or of identity.[2]

Yet looking beyond the simple classification "the law," and beyond a simple counting of occupational heads, one finds that the function of the lawyer in government has changed. Despite the continuing prevalence of his profession in public office, the lawyer's role as political executive is becoming less and less distinguishable.[3]

The image of the good administrator has changed, and with it the role of the lawyer, because the position and responsibility of Chief Executives have changed. Such changes in the New York mayoralty have been dramatic. Early in the century a lawyer might be found in practically any position in the cabinet. Only in such departments as Law and Investigations (Accounts) could it be said that the lawyer was a specialist; for it is only in essentially legal activities that the lawyer-as-Commissioner uses job-oriented skills.[4] Yet lawyers were serving as Welfare, Housing, Sanitation, Tax, or other Commissioners. Under Mayor Van Wyck and his immediate successors the large majority of lawyers were, in fact, Commissioners of departments in which their specific career skills were only tangentially related to the technology of the departments themselves. A legal background and "a way with people" made a man omnicompetent.

In those days the concept of management was unclear, and the demands upon the managers only rudimentary because mayors "for a good century of our national history were chiefly interested in policy and politics:"[5]

Table 3.1   Appointees with Legal Background in the Mayor's Cabinet

Mayor	Per Cent in Cabinet With LL.B. Degree	Per Cent in Cabinet With Career in Legal Practice
Van Wyck	21	16
Low	35	31
McClellan	30	23
Gaynor	34	22
Mitchel	28	21
Hylan	22	10
Walker	23	10
O'Brien	26	14
La Guardia	26	13
O'Dwyer	39	13
Impellitteri	44	25
Wagner	41	15
Total	30	18

The principal historical fact concerning American chief executives as administrators is that, until 1900, most of them had little to do with administration. In early years this situation arose in part from preference for the legislative branch, a reaction against unpopular colonial governors; in part from the highly decentralized character of administration in the states; and in large part from the mere absence of much administration at any level of government, anywhere.[6]

However, after Consolidation, if not before 1898, disregard of the administrative functions of the executive had become anachronistic. Since that time the Mayor has been general manager of the second largest principality in the United States. His administrative burden is probably greater than that of the large corporation manager because of the "irrationalities" of access in a democratic political system. The Mayor can no longer content himself with the political and ceremonial features of his office because he lives among the complicated community problems that require a vast array of laws, skills, and esoteric technology. However well or poorly the cabinet serves the traditional functions of representation and the adjustment of relations among potent interests in the community, the cabinet *members* now serve the Mayor only when they share some of the newer administrative burdens, or at least act as buffers between him and everyday departmental business. The new image of managership has not demoted lawyers to staff and advisory positions; the proportion of commissioners with legal backgrounds is higher than ever. But the place for the generalist has given way to the specialist in the modern administrative environment; the role of the lawyer in top policy positions has become more and more circumscribed.

During the four years under Mayor Van Wyck, over 90 per cent of the lawyers in the cabinet held commissionerships in

Table 3.2 Proportions of Job-Oriented and Non-Job-Oriented Skills for All Career Independent Professionals in the Cabinet

	A *Job-Oriented Skills*	B *Non-Job-Oriented Skills*	*Ratio A:B*
1898–1909 (N=100)			
Lawyers	13	63	.21
All other independent professionals	18	6	3.00
1910–1925 (N=86)			
Lawyers	11	43	.26
All other independent professionals	26	6	4.33
1926–1945 (N=93)			
Lawyers	8	31	.26
All other independent professionals	50	4	12.50
1946–1957 (N=72)			
Lawyers	15	27	.56
All other independent professionals	23	7	3.29

departments unrelated to their training. Therefore, in the entire first decade of the Greater City's history, only 20 per cent of the lawyers in the cabinet possessed job-oriented skills. The rest were generalists. Counting only those whose entire pre-cabinet careers were in legal practice, there were almost five times as many generalists as specialists (see Table 3.2).

The intervening years that saw a phenomenal growth in governmental tasks and complexities also saw equivalent increases in the use of lawyers for their special skills. Those trained in the law but who were generalists in Mayor Van Wyck's cabinet outnumbered the specialists by about three to two. Among career practicing lawyers in the cabinet, the ratio of specialists to generalists almost tripled between 1898–1909 and 1946–1957 (Table 3.2). At the present time, doctors, engineers, and other independent professionals overwhelmingly continue to hold commissionerships in career-related departments. The lawyer's role in the cabinet is slowly coming to resemble that of his fellow professionals. And as specialization of the cabinet has developed, the need for lawyers has declined relative to other professions. From 1898 to 1925, 70 per cent of all independent professionals in the cabinet were career lawyers; from 1926 to 1957, only 41 per cent were career lawyers.[7]

Many lawyers continue to serve as generalist commissioners; in fact, most of the appointees without job-oriented skills are lawyers. But there is an ever-smaller enclave of career lawyers in the cabinet performing more and more often in those areas for which they were specifically trained. Why has the place of the lawyer been narrowed? What does it mean for the functioning of the City government and its politics?

CABINET SPECIALIZATION

According to Max Weber, there is in the history of all "corporate groups" a transformation from amateurs or dilettantes to specialists:

Both immediate democracy [e.g., town meetings] and government by amateurs are technically inadequate, on the one hand in organization beyond a certain limit of size . . . or on the other hand, where functions are involved which require technical training or continuity of policy. [Specialists rise to power whenever there are] very urgent economic or administrative needs for precise action.[8]

As the Mayor has become the "single predominant center of administrative responsibility"[9] in the City, he has, regardless of party or group commitments, seen an increasing hiatus between administrative power and political controls. The successful organization of agencies for voluminous routine business, together

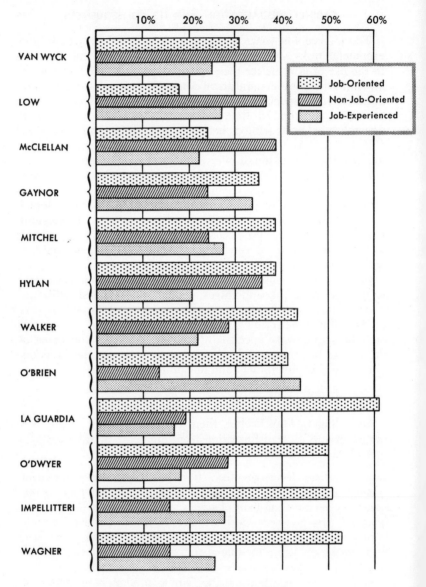

Figure 3.1   Orientation of Skills

with the development of career bureaucracies trained in and identified with the contrived functions of their departments, has created "islands of functional power" around the Mayor. The possibility of establishing coordinative control of these virtually antonomous agencies immediately upon gaining office is remote. Even to establish beachheads for making incremental changes in departmental policy requires four years of incessant toil. And yet, the Mayor is "held hostage . . . for the conduct of all officials and all employees of the city, for their personal integrity, their wisdom in policy, and their efficiency in performance." [10]

The adaptive reaction of New York mayors has increasingly been to appoint as political executives men who have made careers of departmental specialties. These can be seen as actions of personal survival or of a general reorientation of all who seek to be Mayor. Very likely the selection of job-oriented skills at the top of his establishment is a combination of both motives, since these appointments are occurring at the expense of the Mayor's immediate cadre and his party (see Chapter 5).

The appointment of men with job-oriented skills has greatly increased in sixty years (Figure 3.1). In Van Wyck's cabinet of 1898–1901, 32 per cent were using job-oriented skills. Almost half these appointments were required by the City Charter.[11] In Wagner's cabinet of 1954–1957, 52 per cent of all those who served possessed job-oriented skills, about one fourth of which were required by the Charter. And the proportion of job-oriented appointments has increased steadily with almost every mayor in between. The high point was reached with La Guardia's 63 per cent; the cabinets of the three succeeding Democratic mayors stabilized the proportion to around the 50 per cent mark. By far the smallest proportion of job-oriented skills occurred in the Low cabinet of 1902–1903. This was not because Low rejected the merit arguments of the reformers of his day. Rather, it was because so many of the Low appointees were prominent socially and economically, and would, as generalists, have been expected to satisfy his reformist supporters. Preference for job-oriented skills had not yet become a central tenet of reform.

Since the Charter limits the Mayor's choice in some offices, the figures on skills in each cabinet do not entirely reflect his values. However, the rise of job-oriented skills cannot be attributed to Charter changes. For, when these offices are eliminated, the *rate* of change appears to be even greater (see Table 3.3).

Strictly at the pleasure of the Mayor, Van Wyck staffed 23 per cent of his Cabinet with men having job-oriented skills; Wagner appointed 43 per cent of such men to his Cabinet—almost twice as many. Thus, it has become the Mayor's pleasure to fill over 40 per cent of his Cabinet with specialists; another 10 per cent is in accordance with the Charter.

Table 3.3   Proportions of Job-Oriented Skills in Each Cabinet Appointed at the Pleasure of the Mayor*

Mayor	Per Cent	Mayor	Per Cent
Van Wyck	23	Walker	28
Low	16	O'Brien	33
McClellan	18	La Guardia	50
Gaynor	29	O'Dwyer	39
Mitchel	33	Impellitteri	42
Hylan	24	Wagner	43

* Those with job-oriented skills who are appointed to offices where such backgrounds are not required by the Charter.

There has been a concomitant decline of non-job-oriented cabinet members. In spite of relatively wide fluctuations from cabinet to cabinet, amateurs, generalists, and utility men have dropped from first to last in importance. The proportion of job-experienced executives, second in importance for most of the period, has fluctuated around the 25–30 per cent mark except for a discontinuous spurt upward in Mayor O'Brien's cabinet (1932). This spurt was caused by O'Brien's reappointment of so many of Mayor Walker's commissioners. O'Brien had become Mayor in a special election following Walker's resignation, and he ran what was essentially a caretaker government. Non-job-oriented under Walker, these commissioners were (by definition) job-experienced under O'Brien.

The specialization of the work force has been reflected *in extremis* in the cabinet. Among cabinet members of recent years who were educated beyond the high school level, specialized education outnumbered general education by more than ten to one (Figure 3.2).[12] Coming out of a period when universal public education was beginning to take hold and liberal subjects were replacing classical ones, the pre-World-War-I Cabinet members with general educations approached almost 40 per cent

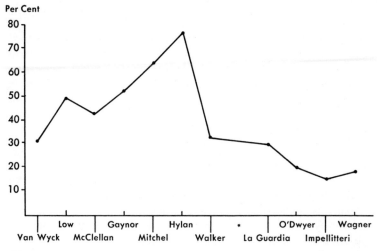

Per Cent

80
70
60
50
40
30
20
10

| Low | Gaynor | Hylan | * | O'Dwyer | Wagner |
Van Wyck McClellan Mitchel Walker La Guardia Impellitteri

*O'Brien omitted.

Figure 3.2   Ratio: Per Cent General to Per Cent Special Training

of all those trained in special fields. Following World War I, however, the ratio dropped steadily[13] until the specialist educations were in a ten-to-one majority.

The problem of chief executive has become essentially the same for every mayor of New York: Achieving efficiency of specialization while making policy implementation, if any, responsive to his own and his party's goals. The data of this study are not appropriate for evaluating the success of each mayor in balancing policy and administration, but they do reflect every Mayor's increasing efforts to do so. New skills and the new uses of old skills have become unquestionably necessary to control the large and complicated City bureaucracies. But the cry of the reformers to extend merit-system values "upward, outward, and downward" is deceptively simple. For although the gains of a specialized Cabinet may be immediate, the costs are conditional and more difficult to evaluate.

Cabinet specialization creates a dilemma for the Chief Executive. On the one hand, the Mayor and his political executives are likely to be considered birds of passage by the permanent civil servants. Lacking the resources and equipment for effective departmental control, the new political executive might well begin his descent almost immediately into the Weberian Hell:

the capturing of power by his specialist, career subordinates. If a commissioner is not already well-versed in departmental business before taking command, he will have to depend strongly upon his subordinates, most of whom militate against innovation. Most neophyte political executives find that their choices lie between fighting a losing battle against the bureaucracy and identifying fully with it; the latter is the more typical resolution.

They can easily create a general impression of vigor and drive by working assiduously to intensify prevailing activities . . . in short, to do more of what has traditionally been done, and to do it in the customary way. In such efforts they can normally count on the enthusiastic support of their career bureaucracies, partly because the bureaucrats, as specialists, believe ardently in the importance and desirability of the programs they administer, and partly because expansion of this kind opens additional opportunities for advancement without disturbing the settled arrangements. . . . [14]

On the other hand, the job-oriented, specialist political executive is no sure solution for the Mayor, for his identification with his specialty might simply reinforce his department's resistance to central political coordination. In government the specialist must obey two masters—his professional ethic or bureaucratic tradition (or a combination) and his political chieftain—and the imperatives of the two are often conflicting. A career fireman might, as Fire Commissioner, fight every effort to add more fire prevention activity rather than use the respect he enjoys in the Department to alter the perspectives of the force. An old-line health administrator can be expected, as Health Commissioner, to resist reorganization of his bureaus, say, along District rather than functional lines, in the face of successful experiments in other cities.

Each mayor must find his own way out of the dilemma. But there has been a pattern of attempted solutions. There has been a growing dependence upon the salaried expert, so that the "bureaucrats" and "new professionals" alike have shown an upward secular trend in the Cabinet (Figure 3.3).[15] Taken all together, careers in salaried occupations rose from 2 per cent of Van Wyck's cabinet to almost one quarter of Wagner's. But fluctuations within such trends have been completely "out of phase." Organization Mayors have selected job-oriented political executives primarily from the City bureaucracies and officialdom;

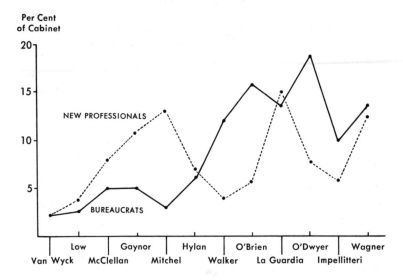

Per Cent
of Cabinet

20

15

NEW PROFESSIONALS

10

5

BUREAUCRATS

| Low | Gaynor | Hylan | O'Brien | O'Dwyer | Wagner |
| Van Wyck | McClellan | Mitchel | Walker | La Guardia | Impellitteri |

Figure 3.3 Salaried Technical, Managerial, and Professional Bureaucrats and New Professionals

and nonorganization Mayors from the professions outside the City and State governments. Mayor McClellan, following his break with Tammany Hall, sought his job-oriented skills outside the civil service because of organization loyalties suspected there. The pattern established by McClellan was repeated by the other insurgent and reform Mayors: Gaynor, Mitchel, and La Guardia.

The City's civil service prior to World War I had hardly been graduated from the spoils system. Each extension of the competitive service had meant for the most part a simple covering-in of patronage personnel. At the upper reaches of departmental bureaucracies, these men might well have been capable as well as skilled administrators; but sabotage could always be expected when an interloping nonorganization, or antiorganization, man became Mayor. Following many years of Democratic rule, Mitchel and La Guardia were especially wary of the civil service and officialdom. Also, many of the new professionals who were appointed had been members of local societies supporting the Fusion coalition (see Chapter 7).

The fact that both bureaucrats and new professionals were about equally present in Wagner's cabinet suggests that perhaps the civil service has finally come of age, that its political neutrality has now been accomplished. However, the "lateral-entry" pattern of the new professionals is essentially antibureaucratic; in an important sense the new professional and the bureaucrat are natural enemies. Bureaucrats are recruited organizationally, new professions by the labor market. The bureaucratic career follows a prearranged pattern, whereby credit is given for seniority as well as for experience and skill. The new professional, following a chance pattern among bureaucracies or small nonbureaucratic enterprises, must depend upon skill and regional or professional prominence—i.e., through publication and/or "contact" in professional societies. The professional is not merely an interloper, coming in at the top without proper grooming; he fully understands the business of his department without suffering classic bureaucratic myopia. But as a consequence he is likely to face a conspiracy of resistance. This is one particularly good reason why the tenure of professionals, as well as of the average Fusion cabinet member, is low (see Chapter 6).

CONSEQUENCES OF CABINET SPECIALIZATION

THE CAREER LADDERS

Cabinet specialization has brought about a transformation in the relationship of occupations to public office. Careers that had once been in a strategic position to provide the City with its top personnel have given way to the shifting demand for specific skills in public administration and the shifting values of the Mayor toward the use of his commissionerships. The transformation has been from occupations of the "old middle class" to those of a "new middle class." Although the shift has not been a total one, it has been clear and unmistakable—so pronounced that even the older careers still in the Cabinet are being put to new uses. The case of the lawyers, presented earlier in this chapter, offers ample dramatization of the fact.

The new middle class is composed of those whose careers have been in salaried occupations: Managers, technicians, and professionals who have developed their skills in, and sell them to, the large public and private bureaucracies and men who have spent the greater part of their adult lives in exempt appointive and elective office.[16] Careers of the old middle class are primarily in self-employed businesses and the independent professions, or as entrepreneurs of goods and services. In the work force at large the old-middle-class occupations have declined in proportion to other types;[17] this shift has been reflected in the cabinet.

Table 3.4   **Careers in the Cabinet: Distribution of Types of Primary Occupations of all Cabinet Appointees Prior to Appointment, 1898–1957**

I. Nonsalaried: The "Old Middle Class"		571
A. Business Enterprisers		
1. Business Leaders	107	
2. Trade (proprietors, major salesmen, agents, etc.)	124	
B. Independent Professionals	340	
II. Salaried: The "New Middle Class"		597
A. Salaried managerial, technical, professional	203	
B. Officialdom (all elective and exempt appointive)	178	
C. Wage-earners	13	
Total		1,168*

* Total population is 1,191. Not ascertained and "nonsalaried civic" omitted.

In the aggregate, the shift from dominance of old-middle- to new-middle-class careers in the Cabinet has been a steady one. Full-time administrative posts in the Cabinet, once about 60 per cent filled by the old middle class, are now over 70 per cent staffed by the new middle class. Of all the types of careers within these two broad classes only those of the new middle class have increased. Business leaders, highest in status of the old middle class, were never a very important segment of the cabinet; nevertheless their proportion has declined still further except for a temporary revival during the La Guardia administra-

Table 3.5   **Proportions of Old-Middle-Class and New-Middle-Class Careers in the Cabinet, 1898–1957 (In Per Cent)**

Career	1898–1909	1910–1925	1926–1945	1946–1957
Old Middle Class	57	50	36	29
New Middle Class	43	50	64	71

tion. Small business and sales careers have been declining at an even greater rate—from over one fifth of all full-time commissionerships in earlier cabinets to only 8 per cent of the most recent. And most of these were from real estate and stock brokerages. Thus, if a "major-salesman" category were created, the "small business proprietor" would appear to be practically vanishing from high public office. This is a far cry from the days when the saloon proprietor, construction man, and retail merchant were familiar figures around City Hall.

Table 3.6 Careers in the Cabinet: Appointees in Full-Time Salaried Positions from the Five Major Careers, 1898–1957 (In Per Cent)

Career	1898–1909	1910–1925	1926–1945	1946–1957
Old Middle Class				
Business leader	8	9	5	2
Sales and trade	22	22	11	8
Independent professional	28	19	19	19
New Middle Class				
Salaried professional-technical	16	20	32	30
Officialdom	27	30	32	41

The independent professions have also declined appreciably as a proportion of salaried cabinet personnel, largely due to the decline of the lawyer. He remains the most important type on nonsalaried and salaried policy-making boards, but has become less appropriate for the large single-headed departments.

The dominance of salaried careers in the cabinet is due only in small part to increasing availabilities in the work force, for the status of these careers in the community still rates a poor second to entrepreneurial careers. Many continue to move from salaried to entrepreneurial work when the opportunity arises. For example, only 5 per cent of the 1,191 cabinet appointees so far have chosen salaried careers after a period in a self-employed occupation. And over 35 per cent of those whose initial occupation was salaried have moved into entrepreneurial work for a career. The bureaucratic doctor continues to be thought of as one who "couldn't make the grade" as a practitioner.

The peculiar specialities of the salaried person are what have become so attractive to the Mayor, regardless of their availability or status in the community. Salaried careerists are not simply the bearers of conventional technical and professional skills attached to new institutions. Their education and training are similar in substance and degree to those of the old middle class, but their occupational style differs completely. Although they share many of the traditional middle-class values, they are essentially a propertyless class. No matter how prominent one of its members becomes he remains basically an economically dependent functionary in a large establishment. And success in the large establishments is, above all else, related to the steady accretion of skills, not the accumulation of property.[18]

Having been recruited and groomed by large, bureaucratic establishments in public and private sectors, salaried personnel are specialized to a degree unknown to their fellows in the independent professions. They have made a life's work of fields that are perhaps only tangential to the profession of which they are a part. When their peculiar skills are appropriate to the work of a department of City government they appear to be a far greater attraction to the Mayor than some other professional who would still have to learn the esoteric language and proprieties of the department.

The salaried person is also more accustomed to the collective environment of public administration. On his way to the top he has, regardless of specialty, become a manager of men. Further, a cabinet post is generally more attractive to the salaried person, for in return for substantial boosts in salary and status he can accept an appointment without feeling that has altered his career at all. For the entrepreneur and the independent professional, acceptance of a cabinet post involves a career transition which, even if temporary, can be quite poignant:

. . . the greater success is paid for by complete abandonment of the activities symbolically most closely associated with the occupation, a consequent loss of skill in those activities, and passage from identification with the basic colleagueship to some other. This is a career contingency of much importance to the individual's self-conception.[19]

Commissioners who have made a career in exempt appointive and elective office—"officialdom"—constitute the largest segment of the contemporary cabinet because of their strategic position in the appointing process. After virtually a lifetime in government, they are, very likely, known personally by the Mayor, and many have served in the department to which they were later appointed as Commissioner. Through experience, if not training, they command many of the political, administrative, and technical requirements of office. And as officials they are in a position to use the resources of their own offices to bargain with the Mayor for a cabinet post. The increasing use of officialdom in the cabinet is due primarily to the gradual displacement of the purely political payoff by trained personnel; hence the modern Mayor can find more cabinet talent in his departments.[20] Exempt appointments in the City government are still subject to a high degree of political manipulation; but more and more often, appointing authorities at every level use their most important exempt offices as opportunities for appointing people who can share the burden of administration. Today, those who rise through officialdom are vastly different from their earlier counterparts.

No doubt, many of the commissioners with backgrounds in salaried professional and technical careers are in effect agents of the big corporations. To whatever extent this may be the case, the point remains that the relation of big business to government is increasingly *indirect*. Business leaders appear to be less and less able to acquire power for themselves; as candidates for office, even in Fusion administrations, the holder of great business influence is likely to be a liability to the Mayor. One might argue that the decline of business leaders in the cabinet to a mere one or two appointments per Mayor indicates only their increasing lack of willingness to accept local public office. Perhaps this is true; but, given the constant improvement of public morality and the expanding role of executive vice-presidents and the like in civic affairs, an even stronger case could be made the other way around. Big businessmen could hardly be *less* willing now than in the days of Croker and Murphy.

There is no simple nexus between economic and political power. The degree of interchangeability is conditioned by many things and varies in every area of the community political system. The professionalization of government bureaucracies and specialization of the Cabinet have made the interchange between business and government considerably more difficult. Although true of all types of entrepreneurs, the conditions of interchange have proved especially difficult for the small proprietor "whose distinctive success trait is effective bargaining for private gains . . . , [who] . . . tends not to survive because this trait is not readily adaptable to the goal of maximizing gains for others through a central decision-making apparatus." [21] Economic leaders continue to wield political influence in the community, but the Cabinet is no longer a meeting-place for men who have accumulated influence through property and "contact." It has become a place for men who can accumulate influence through the vigorous use of skills and professional respect.

CAREERS AND THE "CIRCULATION OF ELITES"

Ethnicity and Career: During most of the twentieth century, officialdom has provided a larger number of cabinet members than any other single career. As reported earlier, this segment of the cabinet has expanded from one quarter to over 40 per cent of the fulltime salaried commissionerships, and the end is not yet in sight. Accompanying the increase of such appointments has been an ever-expanding use of officialdom as a channel of recruitment by ethnic Americans. Throughout the sixty years of Greater New York's history, the most marked contrast between "ethnic" and "native" Americans has been the extent to which they have made use of officialdom for entry into the political elite (Table 3.7). The proportion of clearly ethnic appointments out of officialdom, always important, grew from 22 per cent in the first quarter of the period to 45 per cent in the last. Native-Americans have almost ceased to enter the cabinet by way of officialdom.[22]

Table 3.7   **Ethnicity and Career: Distribution of Ethnic and Native-Americans According to Four Major Careers, 1898–1957 (In Per Cent)**

	1898–1909		1910–1925		1926–1945		1946–1957	
	Ethnic	*Native*	*Ethnic*	*Native*	*Ethnic*	*Native*	*Ethnic*	*Native*
Business	47	26	29	27	19	19	14	16
Independent professional	23	53	28	42	27	40	24	52
Salaried	8	14	16	22	20	29	17	31
Officialdom	22	7	27	9	34	12	45	1
N =	114	128	89	119	132	109	133	58

It is no wonder that Negroes sought to establish and maintain a Negro seat on the Civil Service Commission. Public service appears to be one of the few nondiscriminatory economic structures in the City, with the additional promise of a greater share of the best exempt, "political" positions. And, as increasing demands have been made on the Mayor both for more ethnic balancing *and* for more administrative experience, he has had to depend the more strongly upon officialdom to fill the top posts. For although either attribute can be found independently, they are to be found best *together* in officialdom. Commissionerships are visible appointments, and the Mayor can hurt himself with the ethnic group and with the entire community if, say, one of his "Italian" Commissioners turned out to be a poor political executive. In officialdom there appear to be more safe solutions.

As careers in business and trade declined in cabinet representation they also dropped from first to last in importance for ethnic recruitment (see Table 3.7). It is most unlikely that the newer minorities are abandoning business in the community at large, for the number of self-employed businessmen in the City has actually increased since 1870.[23] Nonetheless, the data here suggest either that small business has become practically a dead end for the politically ambitious ethnic American or that small businessmen no longer have political ambitions.

Differences between ethnic and native commissioners have been greatest in recruitment through careers in officialdom. But evidence of difference in recruitment between the two is only slightly weaker in the independent and salaried professional careers; and the passage of time has not brought any change in these differences. These contrasts between ethnic and native appointees in three of the four major career categories suggest a very considerable and continuing difference in style of life associated with the two social types. Such differences have been maintained in recent years despite the fact that the second and third generations of immigrant parentage have supposedly adopted the patterns of the native American. The data here again suggest that the old saw about politics being an assimilating force has at most a weak justification. Campaign appeals, as was earlier suggested, clearly function to reaffirm ethnic identifications; and special ethnic consideration in the making of appointments is a reward for ethnic solidarity, not dispersion. Now it can be seen that the pattern of appointments serves to maintain such distinctions in another way. Ethnic and native Americans may bear similar political values in general—i.e., assimilation of ideologies and proprieties may be taking place—but there are clearly some major differences in specific interests and organizational identifications that would result from the quite different occupational and career backgrounds shown in this chapter.

Mobility and Career: Study of the social stratification of the careers in the cabinet emphasizes once again that ethnicity and high social mobility are independent of one another. Although officialdom has become by far the most important career channel for minorities, it is far from being the most important channel of social mobility (Table 3.8). In the earlier period of the City's history, mobility was most strongly associated with small business; in later years, primarily with small business and salaried careers other than officialdom. The general decline of business careers in the cabinet has clearly been the most important factor in slowing down class circulation; as the Mayor has turned away

Table 3.8 **Mobility and Career: Distribution of High- and Low-Mobility Cabinet Members by Major Career, 1898–1957 (In Per Cent)**

	1898–1909 Mobility		1910–1925 Mobility		1926–1945 Mobility		1946–1957 Mobility	
	High	Low	High	Low	High	Low	High	Low
Business	50	23	46	21	31	16	34	7
Independent professional	8	59	9	49	6	45	9	40
Salaried	12	11	22	18	40	23	43	20
Officialdom	30	7	23	12	23	16	14	33
N =	99	150	65	159	62	192	47	163

from the small entrepreneur he has also apparently cut down on the number of lower-class origins in the elite. Particularly in the years since the 1930s, salaried careerists including officialdom have, like the independent professionals, come from more privileged backgrounds and have had on the average a higher education. Since 1946, for example, fifty-two of the fifty-nine appointees from careers in officialdom have had medium to low mobility, as have thirty-three of the fifty-three other salaried careerists. In contrast, twelve of the sixteen appointees from small business and trade have been from lower-class origins. The fact that so many of those of lower-class origins in the contemporary cabinet have risen through salaried careers indicates that even high mobility has become less a matter of accumulating goods and capital and more a matter of the most intensive use of education and skills.

SUMMARY

A career is more than a primary occupation; it has a social value as well as an economic function. A career consists " . . . of moving . . . within the institutional setting in which the occupation exists." [24] Thus, it is an identifiable channel on which those who become a part of it focus their expectations for recognition as well as livelihood. "An 'occupational group' is also a status group. For normally, it successfully claims social honor only by virtue of the special style of life which may be determined by it." [25] Each career has its own distinctive ethnic and class composition, which was determined by rates of expansion, shifts in the status of skills and occupations in the community, and shifts in the investment required for entry. For instance, college teaching has become a channel of ethnic and class mobility because of the enormous expansion of demand and of attractive scholarships and fellowships, whereas law and medicine remain career channels of much lower mobility.

Changes in the social composition of careers are probably the most important conditioners of mobility in politics.[26] However, changes in the career composition of the cabinet have been determined in large part by the skills associated with the careers and the changing values of the Mayor toward them.

The term *skill* is widely used in studies of leadership, yet it has been much abused. Every member of an elite possesses skills. This is particularly true if the term is broadened to include all such talents and special sensitivities as "skills" in human relations or in political dealing or in getting attention. Lasswell and his Hoover Institute associates, for example, traced the transformation of elites from the decline of the preindustrial aristocratic amateur to the rise of two new types, those "skilled" in coercion and those "skilled" in persuasion.[27] All of these are important considerations, but *skill* ought to be reserved for more precise uses. Skill is "behavior which is essentially technical. . . . Much of this behavior may be thought of as non-social." [28] One possesses skill to the degree that he commands the techniques and vocabulary of his job; skill refers to the *education, training, and experience called upon in pursuit of a career.*

In actuality, the categories employed by the Hoover Institute studies are not categories of skill. They are *functions of the state,* areas of governmental activity. An individual member of the executive may perform in one or any other of these areas irrespective of his skills; the executive's functional responsibility and his skills are independent factors.[29] *The role of the political executive is defined by his career skills and by his function in the cabinet, not by either of these factors alone.* What is the relation between a man's career and the task he is brought into the elite to perform? Is the political executive appointed to the commissionership that calls essentially for a continuation of the work for which his career has equipped him? Or is he appointed to a position wholly unrelated to his skills?[30] And what are the consequences in changing occupations and circulation in the cabinet as the standard of selection changes to a career-related or specialized function? These questions have been the main burden of this chapter.

Cabinet specialization has been the Mayor's response to administrative exigencies, and it continues even at the expense of the Mayor's party organization. But specialization has been no solution in itself because it does not solve the problem of central coordination. The appointment of a specialist commissioner with a mayor's promise of "no political interference" tends to compound political separatism with administrative particularism, giving departmental autonomy a special moral rationale. Cabinet specialization makes the Mayor all the more clearly responsible for integrating the separatist agencies at a time when the legitimacy of organized partisan support and of the party-loyal political executive, his key resources for integration, are declining.

Shall the Mayor be leader or clerk? Professor Neustadt's question is posed for all chief executives.[31] In making his appointments on the basis of job-oriented skills, the Mayor must take care that the answer is not made *for* him. Commissioners who "know their business" and identify with it tend to reduce the Mayor's role as chief executive to one of ratifying agreements already worked out between the Commissioner, his bureaucracy, and contending clientele groups.[32] Executive leadership is a political problem; POSDCORB[33] does not provide the Mayor with an adequate science of government. Administrative as well as legislative leadership requires organized partisan support.

This need not be *party* support, but it must be organized and continuing. The relationship of political organizations to the appointing process is, thus, the burden of the next two chapters.

NOTES

1. These and other figures on national and State governmental leaders are found in Donald Matthews, *The Social Background of Political Decision-Makers*, Doubleday, New York, 1954, p. 30. Cf. Joseph A. Schlesinger, "Lawyers and American Politics," *Midwest Journal of Political Science*, vol. 1, no. 1. pp. 26-29.

2. Harold D. Lasswell and Myers McDougal, "Legal Education and Public Policy," in Harold Lasswell (ed.), *The Analysis of Political Behavior*, Kegan Paul, London, 1947, p. 27.

3. Cf. Joseph A. Schlesinger, *op. cit.*, pp. 33 and *passim*, whose trend analyses of the careers of State governors shows clearly how the lawyer is becoming more and more the specialist in the law enforcement offices.

4. Members of the Cabinet whose functions require skills similar to those for which they were equipped by some formal training or that were developed and used in pursuit of a career. The category "non-job-oriented" refers to those who were not serving as commissioners of Departments that called for their career training or experience. These are the "generalists." See also the Appendix.

5. Leonard D. White, *Introduction to the Study of Public Administration*, Macmillan, New York, 1948, 3rd ed., pp. 40-41.

6. *Ibid.*, p. 40.

7. To guard against apparently inconsistent figures given earlier, let it be emphasized that the proportion of commissioners with legal training has actually increased but that the proportion of those who had careers in the practice of law has declined.

8. A. M. Henderson and Talcott Parsons, *Max Weber: The Theory of Social and Economic Organization*, Oxford, New York, 1947, p. 415.

9. Leonard White, *op. cit.*, p. 42.

10. Sayre and Kaufman, *op. cit.*, p. 659.

11. For example, the Charter required that the Corporation Counsel be a lawyer in good standing; one of the two Commissioners of Accounts (predecessors to the Commissioner of Investigation) had to be a certified accountant.

12. Taking all Cabinet members educated beyond high school, a ratio was computed between the proportion of those receiving general education (B.A. or general B.S. curricula) and those receiving training in special fields. Plotted on Figure 3.2, the higher the point the closer the proportion of general to special education.

13. Mayor O'Brien's Cabinet was omitted from Figure 3.2. He mudded up an otherwise clear pattern. O'Brien appointed very few college graduates during his one-year term, and from the small numerical differences resulted quite large percentage variations.

14. Sayre and Kaufman, *op. cit.*, pp. 303-304.

15. See the Appendix for a discussion of "bureaucrat" and "new professional." "Bureaucrat" is simply a convenient designation for salaried professional, managerial, technical careers pursued almost exclusively in a single, large establishment. In my population this means predominantly the City Departments. The "new professional" is also a salaried person but one whose career was either in a small establishment (e.g., an academic Department) or involved a movement among several larger bureaucracies.

16. This latter category is referred to as "officialdom." It is a *bona fide* salaried career, regardless of the political activities associated with it. In the context of this study, officialdom frequently requires separate treatment, but in comparison with the "old middle class" it is included with the other salaried careers. See the Appendix.

17. C. Wright Mills estimates that between 1870 and 1940 old-middle-class occupations declined from almost one-third to one-fifth of the work force (*White Collar*, pp. 63-65). In New York City the shift would be less extreme because there was not a concomitant decline of farm population.

18. Cf. Hans Speier, *Social Order and the Risks of War*, Stewart, New York, 1952, pp. 372, 376-379. Cf. also Lasswell, *Politics*, Meridian, New York, 1958, pp. 125 ff.; and Daniel Lerner, *The Nazi Elite*, Stanford University Press, 1951, pp. 5-8.

19. Everett C. Hughes, "The Study of Occupations," in Merton, *et al.* (eds.), *Sociology Today*, Basic Books, New York, 1959, p. 457.

20. Another factor is the concentration of ethnic Americans in officialdom. See *infra.*

21. Lerner, *op. cit.*, p. 6.

22. Slicing the distribution the other way, of thirty-five Cabinet appointments out of officialdom between 1898 and 1909, twenty-six or 74 per cent were ethnics. Between 1946 and 1957, sixty of the sixty-one appointments from officialdom were ethnics.

23. Between 1870 and 1900, self-employed businessmen rose from 12.9 to 19.6 per cent of all gainfully employed persons in New York; in 1930 the proportion was 14.4.

24. Everett C. Hughes, *op. cit.*, p. 457.

25. Hans Gerth and C. Wright Mills (eds.), *From Max Weber*, Oxford, New York, 1958, p. 193.

26. In Chapter 5 differences will be observed in the degree of mobility associated with parties and groups. However, those differences are hardly so extreme as the ones observed here, and were to a great extent determined by the occupations associated with each type of organization.

27. Lasswell, *Comparative Study of Elites, op. cit.*; Maxwell E. Knight, *The German Executive*, Stanford University Press, 1952; and Daniel Lerner, *op. cit.*

28. Miller and Form, *Industrial Sociology*, p. 278.

29. For example, a military man (a "coercer") might be recruited into the elite precisely for manipulative skills. General Eisenhower is perhaps an historic case in point.

30. As long as function and skill are kept separate, it is possible to control for one while assessing the other. Thus, in Chapters 6 and 7 specialization in

the Cabinet is analyzed in terms of the four key functions or areas of governmental activity in the City.

31. Richard E. Neustadt, *Presidential Power*, Wiley, New York, 1960, Chapter I, *passim*.

32. Cf. Sayre and Kaufman, *op. cit.*, p. 304.

33. This is an acronym coined by Luther Gulick from the initial letters of planning, organizing, staffing, directing, coordinating, reporting, and budgeting ("Notes on the Theory of Organization," in Gulick and Urwick (eds.), *Papers on the Science of Administration*, Institute of Public Administration, New York, 1937, p. 13).

CHAPTER 4

CHANNELS OF RECRUITMENT I:

POLITICAL PARTIES AND

THE TOP PATRONAGE

CROKER'S TAMMANY AND TAMMANY'S CROKER:
A CASE REPORT

J. SERGEANT CRAM served on the old Dock Board for four years in Mayor Van Wyck's cabinet. Cram was scion of an old New York family whose ancestors could be traced back to 1640. His grandfather was a wealthy New York merchant and his father had both a lucrative law practice and an almost distinguished career as Assemblyman, Speaker of the Assembly, U. S. Consul in Milan, and Democratic candidate for Lieutenant Governor.

The young Cram was prepared at St. Paul's School, Harvard College, and Harvard Law School to succeed to his father's law business, to a place in the Social Register, and to New York's most exclusive social clubs. In 1882 at the age of 29, Cram became affiliated with the Society of St. Tammany as Associate Leader of the 29th Assembly District, and in 1898 left his law practice to become Secretary to Democratic Mayor Green. Shortly thereafter, Mayor Grant appointed Cram to the Dock Board, to which he was reappointed by Van Wyck.

In the 1890s, the name of J. Sergeant Cram climbed high upon the rolls of the loyal. He was made a Sachem of Tammany Hall and served a term as Chairman of the Democratic Committee of New York, an honorific position. On the Dock Board, Cram became a close friend of Charles F. Murphy, soon to be Croker's successor to the Tammany Leadership. Cram became Murphy's social mentor, teaching Murphy to "eat peas with a fork," and they remained closely associated throughout the remainder of their lives.

Cram's association with Tammany and Murphy was not an untarnished asset. During the bitter leadership struggle following Croker's retirement, Cram became an issue in the hands of the colorful insurgent "Big Bill" Devery:

Since Charlie Murphy has got to running with J. Sergeant Cram, he's turned up his trousers at the bottom, and he's wearing glasses. One of these days . . . Charlie'll have only one pane of glass, like Cram, and then it'll be, "Ah, there, chappie," and when you go to ask him for a job it'll be "Ah really cawn't do it, old chappie, don't you know." [1]

However, both Cram and Murphy managed to survive Big Bill, and Cram remained one of Tammany's best "respectability" councilors until his death in 1935. Cram served as Grand Sachem of Tammany Hall for much of Murphy's long reign as Leader, held the posts of Deputy Attorney General and Public Service Commissioner, and was one of the more important brokers between Tammany and the large business donors.

Lazarus Straus was a Jewish Horatio Alger. An escapee from the 1848 German Revolution, Straus immigrated to Columbus, Ga., where he made and lost a fortune in cotton during the Civil War. After the war he moved with his family to New York and set up a china-importing business in the basement of R. H. Macy's. Within a decade the firm of L. Straus and Sons had become one of the largest of its kind in the country. One of the sons was Nathan Straus, born on the eve of the departure from Germany. Under Nathan Straus the family fortunes were further expanded; by 1888 they were extended to a controlling interest in Macy's, and in 1892 Abraham and Straus was formed in Brooklyn.

Nathan Straus was also interested in community affairs. He maintained extensive philanthropic commitments both to the Jewish community and beyond. He was particularly active on behalf of that new and still distrusted process called pasteurization, and such activities led to his appointment as member of the Board of Health in 1898. His activities also included politics. Straus was identified by the Mazet Committee as "prominent in the councils of the party." [2] He held public office as early as 1889, and in 1894 declined the Democratic nomination for Mayor. His affiliation with Tammany Hall began before and lasted beyond Boss Croker's rule.

Dr. Thomas Darlington was one of the foremost physicians of his day. His accomplishments as scholar, author, practitioner, and public health consultant were noted in *Who's Who in America*, the *National Cyclopedia of American Biography*, and in professional directories. He was a descendant of the Scottish Earls of Darlington and was listed in the earliest editions of the Social Register.

Mayor McClellan's appointment of Dr. Darlington as Health Commissioner in 1904 was hailed by professional groups, civic groups, and the press. But it was also seen by Tammany Hall as recognition for long service. For Darlington was a member of a Tammany club as well as his Social Register clubs. Darlington's Tammany affiliation was in fact stronger than his loyalty to his Mayor. Darlington did not join McClellan's 1906 revolt against Tammany Hall but instead went on to become Chairman of the New York Democratic County Committee (1910–1912), candidate for Manhattan Borough President in 1913, Grand Sachem of Tammany Hall from 1914 to 1925, Father of the Council of Sachems from 1925 to 1932, and again Grand Sachem from 1932 until his death in 1945.

These men were products of organization politics in the days of Croker's Tammany. If they were exceptional it is only because they were exceptional in background and personal attainments. Politically they were typical. Regardless of high status, great wealth, fame, competence, or all of these worthy attributes, if a man held high office in New York at the turn of the century he was above all else a Sachem[3] of Tammany Hall or held some other organization position gained by long and loyal service.

Croker's Tammany held a virtual monopoly of access to the government of New York City. The backgrounds of political dignitaries are mere reflections of the phenomenon. The power of the urban machine was based upon the control of a number of votes, arrangements with other district bosses, and the patronage, bribes, and tips that followed electoral victory. The bosses were, in the main, socially detested, but they handled contributions and claims with discretion and thus became indispensable to the merchants, industrialists, and aspirants to high office. The civil servant or professional could hardly be trusted by those who sought special treatment or privilege.[4] Following the Civil War, most of the members of the plutocracy of the City slowly isolated themselves from direct participation in City government.[5] Control of government fell upon the political entrepreneur, for he alone had the resources for filling the elective and appointive positions. His base of power was organization, not economics.

As V. O. Key has observed, it was "by the combination of the party machine, the utilities and the underworld that control of the city could be gained, and by that control each segment of the power combination could obtain what it wanted."[6] But the party machine at the turn of the century was not an agent of the "economic dominants" of the day. In the City, party leaders were on top of the political heap, and the business leaders had to deal with them. In traction and utility franchises, city contracts of every sort, and inside information, the politicos controlled the commodities for which the capitalists had to pay the price. Once established, the companies with franchises and other public privileges had to support the system to keep what they had and hope for more. Control was not simply "Tammany control"; Croker's Tammany was the keystone of an arch comprised of both parties and the business community. It was an alliance between the party *system* and certain elements in the economic sector:

During the period of the 1890's, when Richard Croker and Tammany Hall were demoralizing the City of New York more systematically and more efficiently than it had ever been done before or has ever been done since, another wider demoralizing force was at work even more efficiently, if not so systematically, in the form of that listless but energetic, polite but firm, cautious but essentially dishonest Republican politician [State "Boss"], Thomas C. Platt, who, more than any one man in the history of America, was responsible for the corrupt alliance between millionaires and their corporations and those whose business was supposed to be the government of the state.

Thomas C. Platt and Richard Croker, like Chinese bandits, worked together frequently in spite of the fact that they were the leaders of opposite parties, but since their interests were both essentially predatory, they sometimes found themselves in conflict.[7]

The alliance was a particularly intimate one because the welfare of every professional politician depended upon it. No arrangements were ever made for the personal income of a party leader out of the treasury. Every boss was expected to fend for himself, and most often he did very well. Many of the leaders took government sinecures for stable income. More often, however, they were involved in types of businesses that benefited from their position. Boss Croker was a partner in a very successful real estate auctioneering firm, although he must have had many dealings, both legitimate and illegitimate, in order to have built up an estate valued well into the millions. Charles Murphy was involved in several successful business enterprises, and, according to Werner, it was his "great and lasting contribution to the philosophy of Tammany Hall that he taught the organization that more money could be made by legal contract than by petty blackmail." [8] As a rule they followed the dictum of the notorious Plunkett: The politician lives by honest graft—what you get as a result of inside, advance information— "He seen his opportunities and he took 'em."

Elements of this alliance were building up from at least the 1850s with the rising star of William Marcy Tweed. The great contribution of the Scotch chairmaker was his extension of Tammany Hall's domain. A fraternal-convivial organization with roots extending back to the Columbian Society of 1789, Tammany Hall had been converted to the search for political influence as early as 1805. By mid-century Tammany had become perhaps the most important political organization in the City, but it was far from the only one, even in the Democratic Party. Its most important rival was Mozart Hall, led by Fernando Wood, a former Mayor. Consolidation of these two organizations required the efforts of a Tweed, who became chairman of the general committee of Tammany Hall and Grand Sachem of the Tammany Society in 1863. A few concessions to Mozart Hall and the two organizations were eventually combined under Tweed's leadership. By 1869, Samuel Tilden could say, "the Ring became completely organized and mature." [9]

Tweed's Tammany Hall was an ancient megatherium compared to Croker's Tammany. Croker took over a blindly selfish brotherhood and transformed it into a rationally self-seeking enterprise.[10] What Tweed did for the domain of Tammany's power, Croker did for its internal processes. Croker established an inviolable principle of loyalty to organization and proceeded to enforce it.[11] His first nominee for Mayor was Abraham S. Hewitt, a respectability candidate. Hewitt's independence of action as Mayor (1886–1888) led to his rejection for an insider, Hugh T. Grant. All elective and almost all appointive offices—except for an occasional "loss leader" at the top—were filled by clubhouse recruits, and the reins were held tight to insure continuing loyalty after taking office. Even officials as important as department heads were expected to appear at Party headquarters every evening to make themselves available to Leaders and functionaries:

Q.   . . . [I]t is a fact is it not, that practically all heads of departments in the city meet at the Democratic club every evening?
CROKER: Yes, sir.[12]

Croker also systematized Party finances. The Wiskinkie of the Tammany Society was his official agent or "bag man" for collecting 5 to 10 per cent of the salaries of every office holder Tammany recruited and the large but indeterminate contributions of organization candidates.[13] Croker was unashamed of his own selfish goals, but he enunciated the principle for the entire party, not only for himself:

Q.   . . . if you have a controlling voice in the affairs of your party, and secure the nomination of true man, you may be sure that at least in part the real estate exchange and in the firm of Meyer and Croker you will, as a true democrat, get some of that patronage?
A.   We at least expect he will be friendly to us.

Q.   Then you are working for your own pocket, are you not?
A.   All the time; the same as you.

Q.   It is not then a matter of wide statesmanship or patriotism altogether, but it is a wide statesmanship's patriotism and personal gain mixed up, is it not?
A.   It is "to the *party* belongs the spoils. . . . " We win and we expect everyone to stand by us.[14]

Croker's most important and lasting contribution to party organization in New York was his recognition of the Assembly District Leaders as the chief patronage dispensers. From a central pool—the desk of Richard Croker at New York County Democratic headquarters—all spoils from City Hall were apportioned to the AD Leaders on the basis of size of District, degree of support, and related factors.[15] In nominations and in patronage management Croker followed a principle of public administration enunciated long after his death: Centralize the organization strongly until it is running smoothly, then decentralize both responsibility and discretion.[16] Croker stabilized his organization by strengthening the AD Leaders, which in turn freed him of much of the burden of details and set him above the enmity of the unrewarded.

In a sense, Croker was making a positive virtue of what had become increasingly an established fact. The political machine of Tammany Hall—the Democratic Party of New York County—had its operational core in the Assembly Districts. Croker legitimized these lines of power and responsibility and split the decentralized *political* arm of Tammany off from the downtown fraternity, The Tammany Society. Since that time the Society has remained a place for rewards of Party honor without power.

In 1894 Croker went into voluntary retirement and left his deputy John C. Sheehan in nominal command. However, the loyalty of the AD Leaders was to Croker. In 1897, thirty-three of the thirty-five Leaders urged Croker's return[17] for the first campaign for control of the new Greater City, created in high hopes by and for the Republicans.

THE ORGANIZATION PATTERN:
MONOPOLY TO OLIGOPOLY

THE BEGINNING AND END OF MONOPOLY

The election of Robert A. Van Wyck as the first Mayor of the Greater City was a fitting climax to the political career of New York's least sensational and most ruthlessly efficient Boss. Van Wyck had been an uncorrupt, if undistinguished, Judge on the City Court for eight years prior to his nomination for Mayor. He possessed one of the hallowed old-family names and had no enemies. And he was a very regular organization man. As Mayor, he said of one of his minority appointments:

Q. How did you come to select Mr. Hess?

A. I had known Hess about 29 years. . . . He was a dyed-in-the-wool Republican, and never has been anything else. . . . He was a machine man, belonged to the regular organization . . . he was a thorough born organization man. . . .

   . . . I claim that when I picked out the Republicans, that I ought to consult with [the Republican leaders] to some extent. That is, I ought to get a machine man; some man that was really indentified. Not one of those mugwump fellows that run away as soon as the cloud comes over, but somebody that stood by the Republican party. I took the trouble to look up about Mr. Hess, to see that he had declared at the primary.[18]

Judge Van Wyck was Richard Croker's personal choice for Mayor. Brooklyn's Boss, Hughey McLaughlin, was persuaded because his organization, like Tammany, had been out of power at Albany and at Brooklyn City Hall during the three years of Mr. Croker's retirement. In return, McLaughlin's candidate for Comptroller was accepted by Croker.

Under Mayor Van Wyck every salaried cabinet member was an organization man, including the few Republican, minority

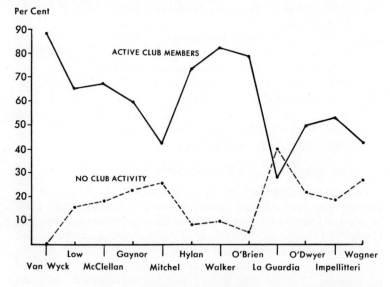

Figure 4.1   Per Cent of Salaried Appointees: Active Club Members and No Club Activity, by Mayor

appointees required by the Charter (Figure 4.1).[19] In the Van Wyck administration there were no independents, no mugwumps. In actuality, all of the salaried appointees bore Croker's stamp of approval; Croker was the unquestioned "grey eminence behind the imperial purple":

Q. Do you recall any member or an important officer [in the new City administration] . . . who was not discussed with you and your advice asked about him?

CROKER: No, I do not.

Q. These men were all agreeable to you, were they not?

CROKER: Yes, sir.

Q. And most of them were your personal selection . . . ?

CROKER: Well, no, they were not; not my personal selection at all.

Q. But the selection of yourself or of your immediate associates?

CROKER: Yes, sir.[20]

There were five nonclub members in the Van Wyck cabinet, all of whom were members of the nonsalaried Art Commission. The nonsalaried Civil Service Commission was filled entirely with organization men—including its Republican member Alexander T. Mason, an Assembly District Leader.

The political careers of Richard Croker and Robert Van Wyck ended in 1901, together with the party's monopoly position. In the 1901 Mayoral election, Croker tried to adjust to Consolidation by hasty acceptance of Edward M. Shepard, an insurgent with reformist leanings in the Brooklyn organization; but Democrats in the City were too hopelessly split. Croker's last act was one of loyalty to the organization: he retired as a result of the successful attacks on his leadership and the exposure of Tammany's methods. Leadership passed from Croker to his lieutenant, Louis Nixon, and then to a triumvirate. After four months of collective leadership, the Executive Committee, in September, 1902, recognized one of the triumvirate as the new "Boss":

Whereas, the experiment of the Committee of Three having proved the desirability of individual responsibility in leadership,

Resolved, That the powers and duties heretofore exercised and performed by the Committee of Three be hereafter exercised and performed by Charles F. Murphy.[21]

Contraction of the Party Domain

Mayor Seth Low, the idol of the reformers, made no vigorous effort during his two-year term to break the monopoly hold of the party system on the City government. Only thirteen of his ninety-three cabinet appointments were clearly nonorganization people, and most of these were appointed to the newly constituted forty-six-member Board of Education. Although his commissioners were undoubtedly of higher character than the party functionaries who headed Van Wyck's departments, they were hardly calculated to maintain the enthusiasm of the Fusion movement responsible for his election in 1901. His failure to break the party ties to government and his failure to reform the police force contributed to his defeat for re-election. But the factor of greatest importance was his adversary, Charles F. Murphy.

Murphy's first act as Tammany Leader combined brilliance with boldness. He secured the nomination of George B. McClellan, son of Lincoln's General, for Mayor over the objections of Boss McLaughlin, and the nominations of Edward M. Grout and Charles V. Fornes for Comptroller and Aldermanic President. The latter two had served in those offices as Fusionists under Mayor Low and had been dropped from Low's 1903 ticket after accepting the joint nominations. Murphy's ticket was swept into every important office in the City except the Richmond Borough Presidency.

McClellan was the Greater City's third Mayor, the third Protestant, and the third native-American. Like Van Wyck he was a product of the organization and, when elected, considered loyalty to the organization a prime virtue:

I have always been an organization man and have always believed in political organization. . . . I have always believed that in a democracy when a man is elected to executive office by the voters of one or other of the great parties, he owes it to those who have chosen him to surround himself as far as possible by officials of his own political faith. All things being equal the applicant for an office who belongs to the party of the appointing power should be preferred to the applicant who does not.

I was determined to appoint none but Democrats to office, and as Murphy was the official head of the party in the city I turned, of course, to him for consultation in the selection of my cabinet.[22]

During McClellan's first term as Mayor, lasting from 1904 through 1905, it appeared as though the monopoly established by Croker would be maintained by Murphy. McClellan was Murphy's cooperative protegé, and Murphy was never one to push his officials too hard. An obstinate and diffident man, Murphy depended largely upon organization loyalty and personal gratitude rather than open demands and sanctions. However, McClellan soon became disenchanted with the organization leaders, especially Murphy:

I believed Murphy to be absolutely honest. I had great respect for his judgment and felt perfectly sure that he would not "let me down." My disillusionment came later. . . . [23]

Almost all of Murphy's selections were District Leaders who were "as far as I knew perfectly respectable. I had no reason to object to the organization slate." [24] However, McClellan soon began to realize that these Commissioners were taking their orders from Murphy, not from the Mayor. Repeated protests by McClellan and repeated broken promises by Murphy, who continued in deep secrecy to issue his orders, led to the break. [25]

Mayor McClellan's disenchantment with the party leadership might have proved temporary had it not been for the campaign of 1905 for a full four-year term. [26] The moribund Republicans were no threat, but the new Municipal Ownership League, led by Citizen William Randolph Hearst was. In the face of Hearst's incessant campaign against the Tammany "plunderbund," McClellan made promises of independence which, in 1906, he felt obliged to honor.

McClellan's total appointments pattern shows him to have been only somewhat less regular than expected. Almost 20 per cent of his commissioners were nonorganization people, and less than 70 per cent were party functionaries. However, McClellan's contribution to the contraction of the organization's domain went beyond the withholding of a few appointments. In his second term he began appointing dissident members of the organization, party functionaries who were violators of the party's first commandment. John Purroy Mitchel was the most extraordinary case of McClellan's policy of political disruption. McClellan appointed the 28-year-old Mitchel, an unaffiliated Democrat, to the post of Commissioner of Accounts in 1907 and gave Mitchel a free hand in the investigations that led to the removal of the Borough Presidents of Manhattan and the Bronx. Both were Tammany District Leaders; one, Louis Haffen, had been the member of the Committee of Three to draft the resolution naming Murphy Tammany Leader. In 1907 McClellan vainly supported insurgent candidates for Assembly District Leader in an attempt to take over the party. McClellan's ally was Patrick McCarren, Brooklyn Leader from 1903 to 1909. McCarren followed McLaughlin's strict anti-Tammany policy and was largely responsible for Murphy's grudging acceptance of McClellan's renomination in the 1905 Convention.

The upshot of Mayor McClellan's actions during his second term was the irrevocable splitting up of the County organizations. He contributed mightily to the destruction of foundations laid by Croker and Murphy for the political consolidation necessary to gain continuing and exclusive party control of the consolidated City government. The Bronx, having no separate County status until 1914, was merely an adjunct of Tammany Hall when Murphy took the leadership. Immediately following McClellan's election in 1904, Murphy made a concerted effort to "cross the river" into Brooklyn, to consolidate the independent organizations in the new City as Tweed had done for Manhattan in the 1860s. The break with Murphy was a critical juncture in New York's political history precisely because McClellan did not reject the party system but tried instead to take it over. McCarren's death in 1909 brought on a period of Brooklyn-Tammany collaboration that was due to the friendliness of John H. McCooey and Charles Murphy. However, for eight years the mayoralty and control of the City were out of their hands.

Organization politics in New York remained strong inside the respective Counties; the parties held fast to their monopoly on County and Borough posts. Under the codirectorship of Murphy and McCooey the Counties could not create a solid front. In 1909, Murphy, with power enough to end McClellan's political career as punishment for McClellan's attempt to reorient party loyalty toward the mayoralty, could not name McClellan's successor.

Instead, the nomination went for the first time to a Brooklynite—worse yet, an irregular. William Jay Gaynor was a genuine reformer. As Supreme Court Judge he had exposed and imprisoned abusers of the ballot box, including the Coney Island

Democratic Leader. As Mayor, Gaynor followed an independent course, supported by the Fusionists who held the Comptrollership, the Aldermanic Presidency, and all five Borough Presidencies—therefore dominating the powerful Board of Estimate. Scarcely 40 per cent of Gaynor's cabinet were from the regular organizations, which meant around 60 per cent of his salaried commissionerships (see Figures 4.1 and 4.2). Gaynor's appointments pattern, his vicious attacks on "organization," coupled

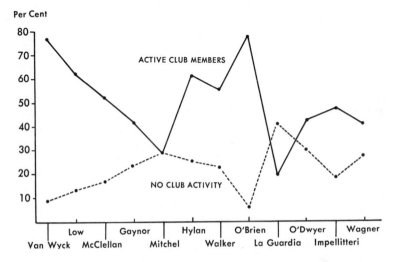

Figure 4.2   Per Cent of Total Cabinet: Active Club Members and No Club Activity, by Mayor

with Murphy's manipulation of Governor Sulzer's impeachment and the police involvement in the Rosenthal murder prepared the way for the second Fusion election and a further splitting off of the mayoralty and City administration from the party system. Mayor Mitchel carried on where Gaynor had left off, and by the end of his term had organization personnel in less than 30 per cent of his salaried commissionerships (Figure 4.2). An equal number with clearly no club affiliation were appointed.

A monopoly of party access had been prevented, but the parties had not been cut off from City Hall politics. When the County Leaders could fully agree on an organization candidate they were able to re-exert their considerable County-based power on the mayoralty—for example, John Hylan. During his eight-year tenure, over 75 per cent of all his Cabinet posts and over 60 per cent of his salaried commissions were given to organization personnel. Despite the breakup of the McCooey-Murphy-Hearst entente in 1924, the party grip on the mayoralty—a near monopoly—was maintained through Walker and O'Brien's terms of office.

These successes were, however, results of the *ad hoc* agreements of 1918 and the bitter primary of 1925, not a consolidation of independent organizations. Four months of collective leadership in 1903 were enough to convince Tammany of the need for Charles Murphy, but Murphy could never extend this principle across the river.

The party system never fully recovered from La Guardia's long rule. Nonparty entry into the cabinet rose from below 10 per cent of the cabinets of 1918–1933 to almost 30 per cent between 1946 and 1957. Party recruitment has now been stabilized to between 40 and 45 per cent of the salaried commissions, but in Van Wyck's day, cabinet selection from outside the clubhouse was exclusively for nonsalaried positions—the Art Commission. Since World War II, non-party appointees can be found in every type of office.[27] In fact, since 1926 all of the increase in non-party appointments has been in the salaried positions.[28]

The contraction of the party domain was not limited to cabinet politics. It involved the City administration generally. Party patronage in the lower "exempt" jobs declined from 1.9 per cent of the classified service of 1902 to 0.5 per cent in 1938 and 0.31 per cent in 1959 (Table 4.1). In absolute numbers, there was only a mild contraction—from 624 in 1902 to 1062 in 1930 to 465 in 1959—a fact suggesting *party stasis;* the parties held on to a hard core of good positions but were prevented by the civil service reformers from extending the patronage as the government service grew. To an extent, that was the case; but the true nature of the contraction was not reflected in the mere change of available exempt positions. In the early period, even the classified service was subject to a considerable amount of manipulation. A Civil Service Commission dominated by organization men often yielded to the demands for extension by the act of covering in patronage appointees or by so setting examinations as to give the advantage to the incumbent. Slowly the merit system was separated from the parties. Each reform

Table 4.1   Exempt Appointments in the Classified Service

Year	Number of Exempt	Total Employees in All Classes	Per Cent Exempt
1902	624	33,017	1.89
1906	728	43,009	1.69
1910	729	52,978	1.38
1914	805	55,570	1.45
1918	738	54,129	1.36
1922	705	60,451	1.17
1926	914	63,808	1.24
1930	1,062	89,501	1.19
1934	691	86,364	.80
1938	452	118,456	.40
1959	465	149,501	.31

SOURCES: Municipal Civil Service Commission, *Annual Report* for 1938, p. 20, and *Annual Report* of the Mayor, 1959. These figures are *only* for city employees under the jurisdiction of the Civil Service Commission. They do *not* include employees of the authorities, the public school teachers, county or judicial employees.

administration made a few changes; the State Civil Service laws were being strengthened until by 1922 the Commissioners were given six-year terms with removal only for cause, and each improvement had an exhilarating effect on the reformers. At least by the end of the Depression if not before, direct entry into government service had become the rule and entry via the party the exception. Where its own rights were concerned, the civil service had become a political force in itself with leverage both at City Hall and in Albany. Inside the departments, as well as at the top, party leaders had truly become one of several types of competitors for the stakes of government.

A LOOK INSIDE THE PARTIES

The contraction of the party domain and the development of several avenues of access rather than one has had little effect upon the internal processes of the party organizations. As recruiting agents, the parties continue to work in a traditional way, and the differences between the two major parties is not appreciable. In the clubhouses and committees there are pools of individuals who, by virtue of membership and activity, have displayed their eagerness for party and governmental affairs.

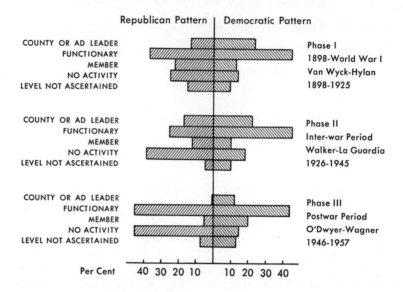

Figure 4.3   **The Pattern of Party Activity**
Party Backgrounds of Appointees Who Were Affiliated
Democrats or Republicans by Highest Level of Organiza-
tion Position Held Prior to Appointment to the Cabinet

The high proportion of functionaries in both parties indicates that most individuals recruited by the party are "groomed" for a considerable period before they receive important offices, such as cabinet posts (Figure 4.3).[29] To a great extent party recruitment in New York resembles the "ideal-typical" American party model: movement upward on the basis of seniority and service, the payoff not *necessarily* related to skill or talent but to a keen sensitivity to the needs of the organization. This does not automatically spell malfeasance of office; for often—and increasingly—a good appointment is good politics.

In a city of such strong Democratic predilection there are likely to be a few important differences between the dominant and the minority party, if only because membership in the former appears more promising to the ambitious. In the cabinet, Democrats have outnumbered Republicans almost three to one (Table 4.2). The most important difference is the extent to which mere party affiliates with no background of club membership or party activity can attain high office. The clubhouse

Table 4.2   Party Affiliation* in the Cabinet

Year	Democrats	Republicans	Major Third Parties	"Fusion"	No Party	N.A.	Total
1898–1925	300	103	6	12	3	200	624
1926–1945	130	60	3	15	5	97	310
1946–1957	127	23	3	2	4	98	257
Total	557	186	12	29	12	395	1,191

   *   Either national or local affiliation.

has not been nearly so important in the grooming of Republicans. The proportion of Republicans who were not active prior to appointment has risen steadily from 20 per cent to almost 45 per cent.

Nonactive Democrats amounted to about 20 per cent of all the Democrats only during the period between 1926 and 1945, and this was largely because of the many "Roosevelt Democrats" appointed by La Guardia. Being dominant most of the time in all five Counties, the Democratic organizations have a much larger active membership and keener competition for the stakes. In politics, supply *determines* demand; demand pushes up the price in loyalty and service which has not appreciably diminished with the contraction of the party's domain. The coalition character of the Republican-Fusion mayoralty has been more susceptible to newcomers. Nevertheless, it should be emphasized that over half of the Republicans *have* been club members, and the largest proportion of these were functionaries of some sort.

The decline of the party in New York has had at least one major impact on internal party processes, the gradual separation of AD and County Leaders from the cabinet (see Table 4.3; other changes will be described in Chapter 5). During his first month in office, Mayor Wagner announced that no Leader could expect appointment as head of a department unless fully qualified by training and experience.[30] Wagner held so rigidly to his rule that on several occasions Leaders who possessed very high qualifications were rejected.[31] Except for the Tax Commission and Board of Assessors, Leaders under Wagner were relegated to deputy commissionerships, clerkships, and the like.

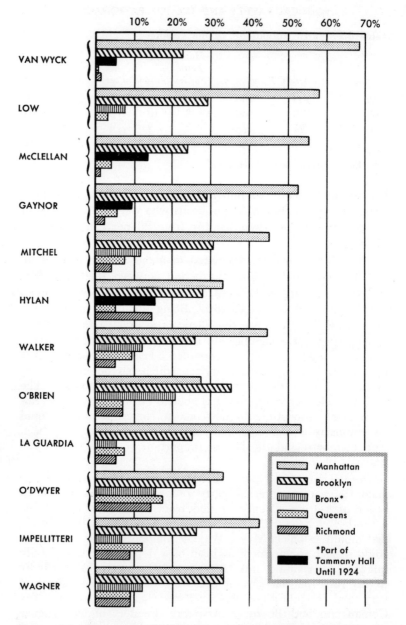

Figure 4.4 Geographic Distribution: Per Cent Party Members by Organization, for Each Mayor, 1898–1957

However, Wagner had made a formal rule of what had already become an informal practice. By 1946, no Republican Leader held a cabinet post. There were ten Republican Leaders in the cabinets of 1898–1925, three of whom were minority appointments by Democratic Mayors. From 1926 through 1945 there were also ten Republican Leaders in the cabinet, five of whom were appointed by Democratic Mayors. The three Republican-Fusion Mayors had received their nominations in spite of most of the seventy-odd Republican Leaders in the City, and felt no obligation to appoint them to any position, let alone a commissionership.

Table 4.3   County and AD Leaders in the Cabinet, by Appointing Mayor

Van Wyck	25	Mitchel	4	La Guardia	5
Low	3	Hylan	16	O'Dwyer	5
McClellan	19	Walker	18	Impellitteri	4
Gaynor	4	O'Brien	15	Wagner	5

Forty per cent of Mayor Van Wyck's entire cabinet were Democratic Leaders; during Mayor McClellan's six-year incumbency, nineteen Leaders held commissions. This is to be contrasted to the four or five Leaders in post-World-War-II cabinets. Like holders of great wealth, the personal bearers of great party influence have become a liability to the Mayor. County and AD Leaders retain the power to name many of the Mayor's top appointees, but less and less often can they name themselves. Like the early ethnic representatives in the cabinet, modern party Leaders are relegated to Boards and Commissions.

SUMMARY

The death of Boss Murphy in 1924 deprived the party system of the one man who might still have converted the temporary five-County coalition for electoral victory into a citywide machine. Throughout most of Murphy's rule, Tammany had dominated Democratic mayoralties even when it could not choose the Mayor (Figure 4.4). Until the selection of Ed Flynn, Tammany Hall included the Bronx, and together these two Counties under Murphy accounted for over 70 per cent of all the commissions given by Van Wyck, McClellan, and Gaynor to party members. As long as domination by a single organization lasted, there was always the possibility of consolidation under a single citywide Leader with recognition of County autonomy for all below the citywide offices. Instead, the City as a whole became an arena of varying degrees of intra-party competition, usually but not always along County lines. Each succeeding Mayor fell back upon the balancing of County accreditations along with ethnic and religious characteristics, and the County organizations became the more fully committed to their own political version of "separate but equal facilities."

A succession of weak Leaders followed Murphy; McCooey died an old man in 1934, and the Bronx under Flynn was no longer a Tammany field headquarters. Flynn quickly became the strongest Leader in the City but had no particular interest in the mayoralty, which was too much the property of Manhattan and Brooklyn. His extreme independence exaggerated the separatist tendencies of the Counties. In 1933, Flynn ran his own candidate for Mayor against the regular Democratic candidate, causing the split that elected La Guardia. Most of Flynn's own County and Borough candidates were elected, while Fusion captured nearly all of the offices in the other four Counties. After 1934 Flynn became a "modern Leader" with quite pronounced interests in national politics.

Meanwhile, the many towns and villages in Queens were consolidating under effective Democratic and Republican leaderships, which were making more claims for County recognition. Brooklyn had long since become the most populous Borough. All of this conspired to keep New York City a "county-unit" system. Borough representation on the Board of Estimate is both a reflection and a cause of continuing County political autonomy.

The party monopoly of pre-consolidation New York City rested on the identity of County and City. In the consolidated City the mayoralty was not attractive enough to overcome traditional County identifications. Democratic County Leaders have been unwilling to risk their Counties to the possible domination of an outsider; and their Republican counterparts have not had the incentive, for they have been essentially brigades in a State organization.

The breakup of machine domination in cities is often attributed to the end of immigration and the growth of governmental services. Indeed these factors are historically associated, but in New York they are hardly sufficient explanations in light of the continuing party monopoly of nominating and electoral instruments and the continuing Democratic dominance in the electorate—the very resources that had established and maintained the earlier monopoly. It appears quite clear that the party domain has contracted more directly because of the failure to break traditional boundaries. County autonomy—or, in the context of the entire City, *intra*party pluralism—prevented the capturing of the City's most prized office, the mayorality, by the party system.

Holding 40 to 50 per cent of the cabinet offices, the party remains the most important competitor for the Mayor's pleasure. Party leaders can veto the Mayor even when they have no command over his decisions. As an organization in which loyalty is still the first commandment, the party offers a source of organized partisan support if a Mayor uses his incentives wisely. But the relationship is one of competition, not monopoly. Party leaders today live in an increasingly pluralistic milieu, competing with each other and with non-party, autonomous group leaders for access to the City administration; and the relative advantage of each kind of leader and organization shifts according to Mayor (see Chapters 5 and 7) and according to area of governmental activity (see Chapter 6).

The weaknesses that have developed in the party system have given the Mayor a freer hand, when he wishes to exert it. Interorganization competition has opened up, for better or worse, new avenues of direct access to City Hall. There are not one but several power structures in community politics. But the price is paid in the difficulties a Mayor faces in getting organized partisan support. The separation of parties from the Mayor has made the relationship between the two uncertain and unstable. Party Leaders have resisted even temporary recognition of a *primus inter pares*, preferring to deal directly with the Mayor. Special recognition of one Leader courts alienation of others. And to exert direct leadership over the party is to risk disaster, like a McClellan or a Wagner, or dissolution, like the two Fusionists Mitchel and La Guardia and their movement. The Mayor's political role is all the more arduous because his office lacks the charisma of the Governorship and the Presidency.

NOTES

1. Quoted in M. R. Werner, *Tammany Hall*, Doubleday, Doran, New York, 1928, pp. 495-496.

2. Special Committee of the Assembly Appointed to Investigate the Public Officers and Departments of the City of New York and of the Counties Therein Included, *Hearings*, p. 325 (hereafter referred to as Mazet Hearings).

3. The Sachems constituted the "directing council" of the Tammany Society. According to Croker, they were like the trustees of the church, "charged with the temporalities of the church." Mazet Hearings, *op. cit.*, p. 326.

4. For excellent profiles of the power and personality of old-fashioned Bosses see: Richard Rovere, "The Big Hello," *The New Yorker*, vol. 21 (January 12, 1946), pp. 29-34; (January 19, 1946), pp. 26-30; Oscar Handlin, *op. cit.*, Chapter VIII; and James K. McGuire (ed.), *op. cit.*, vol. II, pp. 208-60. Also see Max Weber's classic essay, "Politics as a Vocation," in Gerth and Mills (eds.), pp. 77-128.

5. Gabriel Almond, *Plutocracy and Politics in New York City*, unpublished doctoral dissertation, University of Chicago, 1939, *passim*.

6. V. O. Key, *Politics, Parties and Pressure Groups*, Crowell, New York, 1958, p. 404.

7. Werner, *op. cit.*, 329.

8. *Ibid.*, p. 557. Cf. Gustavus Myers, *op. cit.*, pp. 310-311.

9. Quoted by Frank J. Goodnow, "The Tweed Ring in New York City," in Bryce (ed.), *The American Commonwealth*, Volume II, Capricorn Edition, p. 385. Dates and events reported above are also from Goodnow, *op. cit.*, and Myers, *op. cit.*, pp. 188 ff.

10. Croker was Tammany Leader from 1886 to 1901, except for a three-year interregnum between 1894 and 1897, during which time he ran his party's affairs from his estates in England. See M. R. Werner, *op. cit.*, especially p. 328.

11. Cf. Myers, *op. cit.*, p. 281.

12. Mazet Hearings, *op. cit.*, p. 329.

13. Myers, *op. cit.*, p. 273.

14. Mazet Hearings, *op. cit.*, p. 353. Emphasis added.

15. W. T. Stead, *Satan's Invisible World Displayed; or, Despairing Democracy: A Study of Greater New York*, Review of Reviews, London, 1898, *passim*.

16. Cf. James W. Fesler, *Area and Administration*, University of Alabama Press, 1949, pp. 64-70; and Fesler, "Field Organization," in Morstein Marx (ed.), *Elements of Public Administration*, Prentice-Hall, Englewood Cliffs, 1949, pp. 270-271.

17. Alfred Henry Lewis, *Richard Croker*, Life, New York, 1901, p. 342.

18. Mazet Hearings, *op. cit.*, pp. 955, 961-962.

19. No information on party background could be found on 12 per cent of the salaried commissioners. However, it is entirely likely that most of them were party members who moved out of obscurity into the cabinet and returned to obscurity afterwards.

20. Mazet Hearings, *op. cit.*, p. 328.

21. Quoted in Myers, *op. cit.*, p. 298.

22. Syrett, *op. cit.*, p. 181.

23. *Ibid.*

24. *Ibid.*, p. 183.

25. *Ibid.*, p. 198.

26. As an affront to the Democrats, the 1901 Charter reduced the Mayoral term to two years. Seth Low's victory, proving that Republicans could win under Consolidation, started a movement for return to the four-year-term—just in time for the resurgence of the Democrats.

27. During these years it was the *clubhouse* recruits who were becoming concentrated in one enclave. See Chapters 6 and 7.

28. In both the prewar and postwar periods, non-party people comprised 38 per cent of the nonsalaried posts. Between Walker and Wagner, non-party *salaried* commissions rose from 10 to 26 per cent.

29. This figure is based on percentages of clearly affiliated Democrats and Republicans, *not* on percentages of the entire Cabinet. All minor party affiliates and those Not ascertained on Table 4.2 have been eliminated. The term *functionary* refers to: (1) persons who held an office in the club or County organization below that of Leader—e.g., County committeeman, District captain, convention delegate, member of the law committee, etc.; (2) those who had been designated as regular candidates for elective posts; and (3) those who had held no formal position but were identified as important advisers, donors, and so on.

30. *New York Times* (January 24, 1954), Section 4, p. 11.

31. Reported in private interviews.

CHANNELS OF RECRUITMENT II:

CIVIC VIRTUE, PARTY,

AND THE CIRCULATION

OF ELITES

THE GROUP PATTERN

THE UNITED STATES is a nation of joiners. Madison's famous Federalist 10 attests to the spirit already apparent at the beginning of the Republic. Madison defined a "faction" as "a number of citizens . . . who are united and actuated by some common impulse of passion, or of interest, adverse to the rights of other citizens, or to the permanent and aggregate interests of the community." A generation later Alexis de Toqueville observed that "in no country of the world has the principle of association been more successfully used, or applied to a greater multitude of objects, than in America."[1] Still a generation later, Lord Bryce thought the phenomenon worthy of special mention, referring to the "expertness of Americans in using all kinds of voluntary and private agencies for the diffusion and expression of opinion. . . . In no country has any sentiment which touches a number of persons so many ways of making itself felt. . . ."[2]

Voluntary associations in cities are not entirely like those in Washington and the State capitols. Many local groups exist quite literally for the purpose of influencing government policy; and all groups, down to the obscure neighborhood associations, are involved at one time or another with the City agencies, the Mayor, the Council, and the Board of Estimate. However, local groups service the community in more direct ways: The public school system would be inundated if suddenly there were no more parochial schools. Calamity would strike the community if the civic and philanthropic groups operating private hospitals decided without notice to cease operations, or if the various community service and welfare operations abruptly disappeared. In fact, many voluntary activities have become so important that they receive substantial subsidies from the City treasury to continue and to expand their good works. The "special cause" interest groups sometimes provide vital services to City government agencies while trying to influence them. For example, the Citizens Budget Commission—manifestly devoted to local government efficiency and reduction of public expenditure—spent almost half a million dollars on a "Little Hoover Commission" study for Mayor O'Dwyer. During the ten years prior to the establishment of the City Planning Commission (1938), the Regional Plan Association was providing the City with regional land-use and ecological studies. RPA helped create the City Planning Commission and now serves as the Commission's major constituency.

While there were always many voluntary associations in the City, the large civic, economic, and professional groups with paid staffs and resources large enough to exercise a continuing influence on government and civic problems were phenomena of the turn of the century and after. The City Club was founded in 1892, the National Municipal League in 1894, the Citizens Union and the Merchant's Association—predecessor of the Commerce and Industry Association—in 1897. All were a response to the reform ferment of the period, and more or less reflected the final separation of the older governing class from direct governmental control:

Leadership in the struggle for municipal reform, in the absence of any solid working-class support had to come from the old governing class. Unfortunately many of the most talented members of that class were now absorbed in the scramble for gain, while the majority had drifted into political apathy. . . . [3]

A somewhat later phenomenon, except for the Commerce and Industry Association, are the "peak associations" whose memberships are other, smaller groups and corporations. The Citizens Budget Commission, established in the financial crisis of 1932, includes many of the City's largest taxpayers. The United Parents' Association is a coordinating board for the many P.T.A.'s in the City. The Community Council of Greater New York is supported by the many religious and nonsectarian health and welfare groups. Each major religious group also has a coordinating council that sometimes supports and often competes with the Community Council. Many of these later-day associations were founded by officials and founders of earlier groups, and all of the constituent smaller groups at times strike out for their own political influence.

Like the parties, local interest groups are run by a relatively small core of activists or functionaries. The Citizens Union, one of the most influential groups in the City, has approximately 3 thousand members, about 250 of whom are active on the Union's Executive Committee and on its committees on Legislation, Local Candidates, City Planning, and so on. The Commerce and Industry Association, a "peak association" of 4 thousand corporations and individuals, is run by about 400 leaders and staff.[4] There are a great many interlocking directorships among groups, and leadership tenure tends to be very long.

Holding public office has never been the principal means by which groups have sought to influence public policy; in this they differ by quite a large degree from parties. But one of the "latent functions"[5] of all groups is leadership recruitment. Parties and groups can be compared from the standpoint of community leadership recruitment. Like the parties, groups groom talent for collective activity, aid in recognizing ability and status outside the private career world, and define availability for public affairs. As Peter and Alice Rossi observed in their Bay City study:

The functions of status allocation and recognition, which were once performed by public office-holding, have been shifted . . . to a relatively new set of institutions, the community service organizations. Beginning around the turn of the century, a number of private organizations came into being which were dedicated to the provision of social services to the community under private financing and control.[6]

To apply this description to New York City, one needs only add to these civic-philanthropic groups the various economic associations—trade, realty and manufacturing groups—and professional associations.

The numerous offices on the governing boards of these organizations have replaced public office as the channels through which the functions of public recognition and status allocation operate. . . . Control over the membership of these boards can be maintained by the (economic and status) elite leaders through their heavy donations. . . . Such positions carry with them an entree into certain social circles, publicity and recognition of financial worth. . . .[7]

With the parties, local groups are channels of recruitment for higher public office. The Mayor turns to them for able and popularly supported commissioners. *Ex officio,* they are "men

Table 5.1   Per Cent Appointees in Each Cabinet Who Were Functionaries in a Party or Officers in at Least One Local Group

Mayor	Per Cent	Mayor	Per Cent
Van Wyck	100	Walker	96
Low	99	O'Brien	96
McClellan	94	La Guardia	93
Gaynor	100	O'Dwyer	90
Mitchel	96	Impellitteri	97
Hylan	97	Wagner	94

with a following." In no cabinet were more than 10 per cent of the commissioners without some form of grooming—typically, less than 5 per cent. In a city the size of New York the strictly self-made man is a rare phenomenon. By its nature, politics is a collective existence; in the urban environment practically every aspect of business, social, and civic life is also collective. The group is a means of discovering a community, and it is also the typical means of escape from obscurity.

Civic-philanthropic groups have been the most important non-party channel of recruitment for the cabinet (Figure 5.1).[8]

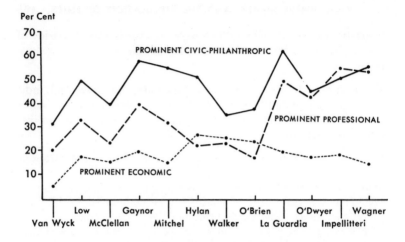

Per Cent

70 —
60 —
50 —
40 —
30 —
20 —
10 —

PROMINENT CIVIC-PHILANTHROPIC

PROMINENT PROFESSIONAL

PROMINENT ECONOMIC

| Van Wyck | Low | McClellan | Gaynor | Mitchel | Hylan | Walker | O'Brien | La Guardia | O'Dwyer | Impellitteri | Wagner |

Figure 5.1   The Pattern of Group Activity: Per Cent of Appointees Who Were Leaders of Civic-Philanthropic, Economic, or Professional Groups Prior to Appointment to the Cabinet

Well over 40 per cent of the commissioners were civic officials of one kind or another prior to appointment. A very noticeable rise in professional group recruitment is recent years is largely the result of a practice of delegating the actual choice of a commissionership to a professional society. However, despite the increase of professional group recruitment, the general tendency has not been toward displacement of party by group recruitment. *The decline of party has not been accompanied by an equivalent rise in the appointment of nongovernmental group leaders.*

Cabinets composed over 45 per cent of civic leaders and, in recent years, about the same proportion of professional group leaders at first blush appear to be excellent examples of "interest representation." However, in order to assess the true role of nongovernmental groups in the cabinet, it is first necessary to control for overlapping, to control for the possibility that civic, economic, and professional group leaders are typically party functionaries as well: To what extent do nongovernmental groups function as channels of recruitment *alternative* to the party?

In the aggregate, it is quite clear that groups have not replaced the party. Between 1898 and 1957, party recruitment declined from over 90 per cent of all cabinet posts—every commissionership except those on the Art Commission—to little more than 40 per cent. In the same period, independent entry of

Table 5.2 **Alternative Routes to the Cabinet: Non-Party Commissioners Who Were Leaders in at Least One Local Interest Group**

Mayor	Number of App'ts	Per Cent of Cabinet	Mayor	Number of App'ts	Per Cent of Cabinet
Van Wyck	5	8	Walker	8	9
Low	12	13	O'Brien	—	—
McClellan	20	12	La Guardia	57	34
Gaynor	21	22	O'Dwyer	20	19
Mitchel	23	24	Impellitteri	10	16
Hylan	14	12	Wagner	18	21

group leaders increased, but only by a few percentage points. Independent entry is associated almost entirely with anti-organization mayors. Mayors Hylan and Wagner had extensive group support in their elections. Hylan's nomination was very largely secured by Hearst-led groups, and in the 1953 primary contest Wagner banked heavily upon groups when only parts of each County Democratic organization supported him. Nevertheless, there was no great influx of non-party personnel from the boards and committees of interest groups. The stronger tendency was to appoint party-affiliated group leaders.

Under conditions of joint recruitment or overlapping membership, there is always the question of where the greater influence lies, with the party or the group. Without evidence from extensive interviews the question cannot be answered. However, it can at least be said that loosening the party monopoly has led to greater permeability of the party organizations themselves, as well as to greater direct access to government. The party functionary who can "point with pride" to his civic service has a better bargaining position with appointing authorities than the pure professional functionary. And the civic leader without party connections usually finds himself at a considerable distance from the appointments arena. Overlapping memberships improve the power position of a group, but at the same time reduce its maneuverability outside the party system. A Fusion movement depends very largely upon the groups with the least amount of overlapping (see Chapter 8). A Fusion movement is a rejection of the party system, and only occasionally are many groups willing or able to do this.

Some types of groups have been more independent of, and competitive with, the party than others. Thus it becomes necessary to separate the groups into the three major types in order to assess their influence. Prior to the 1930s, only the two "reform" cabinets of Gaynor and Mitchel contained over 15 per cent of civic leaders who were not also party functionaries. Except for La Guardia, the same was true of more recent cabinets (see Figure 5.2). Within rather extreme variations, related to the reform cycle (see Chapter 8), there has been no increase in independent, non-party, civic group recruitment. Except for Mitchel and La Guardia, the old alliance between economic groups and party has remained quite strong, so that in no other cabinets were there more than 6 or 7 per cent non-party economic group leaders. The only observable increase in recruitment alternative to the party has been the professional groups, a matter deserving separate analysis.

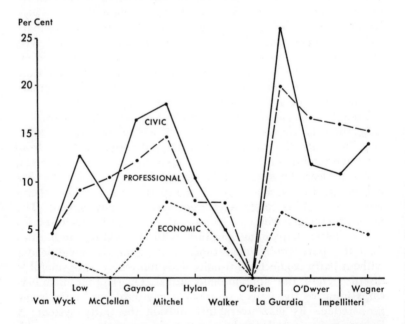

Figure 5.2   Civic, Economic, and Professional Group Leaders in the Cabinet Who Were Not Members of a Party Organization

For the entire sixty years joint recruitment by party and group has been the norm, independent group recruitment the exception. For most of the civic and economic group leaders party and group were highly compatible (Figure 5.3). The personally

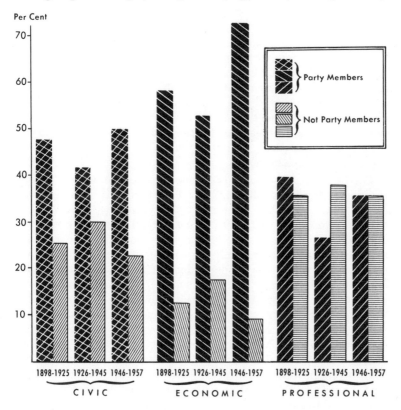

Figure 5.3   Civic, Economic, and Professional Group Leaders in the Cabinet: Comparison of Those Who Were Members of a Party With Those Who Were Not Members

ambitious community leader often seeks a role in several local activities, the party organization being one means of extending his range. Of equal importance is the fact that the groups themselves often seek a party balance on their boards and committees. This practice insures a modicum of access to City Hall regardless of the party in power. For instance, two of the most prominent leaders of the Citizens Budget Commission are Harold Riegelman, an important City Republican and 1953 candidate for Mayor, and Robert Dowling, one of the Democratic Party's most important money raisers.

The compatibility of groups and parties, as measured by the proportion of joint and independent recruitment, has varied over the years, usually directly with the reform cycle. The three Fusion Mayors tended to sever the connection between groups and parties. Following each reform administration, group leaders tend to gravitate back toward working relations with the party organizations, and tend also to lose their identity as independent channels of recruitment (see also Chapter 8). The reform coalition attracts groups hostile to the party system and group leaders who had been unable or unwilling to find a place for themselves in the clubhouse.

The decline of the party in cabinet politics has indeed meant the increasing possibility of direct transactions between the Mayor and local interest groups. Between 1946 and 1957—twelve Democratic years—59 per cent of all cabinet appointees were either non-party recruited or had been too obscurely so to be counted. However, only a small proportion of the 59 per cent were group leaders independent of party. The true influence of local groups has not been their displacement of the party and the provision of entirely new pools of personnel. These groups, acting as new constituencies for the Mayor and selected agencies, have attempted, with varying degrees of success, to narrow the Mayor's range of choice. They do not often offer candidates to the Mayor; they press standards upon him. The increasing opportunities available to group leaders to bargain directly with the Mayor are being used to create a "job image" and to enforce it.

CHANNELS OF RECRUITMENT AND THE
CIRCULATION OF ELITES

American history and folklore are bountiful with illustrations about the role of the political Party as an instrument of status improvement for the lowly born and the new ethnic minorities. Usually part of a segregated subcommunity, the upwardly and outwardly mobile perceived that that very characteristic, which had been a liability, could, in politics, be converted into assets:

... many of the youngsters growing up in the confused decades after 1850 came to understand that the state might also be the means of their own personal advancement. As the sons of immigrants, without the inherited advantages of capital or family connection, not many roads to success were open to them. In politics, any office was available to him who could command the support of numbers; and in many places, the immigrant who had no other assets had at least the weight of numbers. The connection with a community of the foreign-born might be an impediment in other endeavors; in the quest for office it was a positive aid.[9]

As the Irish did it, so might other depressed persons, perhaps with Irish aid. The vulnerability of the urban political party to numbers made it perhaps the one apparent channel to power

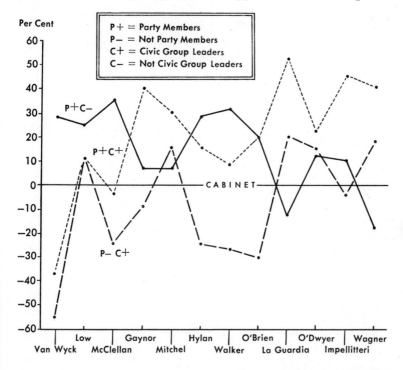

Figure 5.4   Party vs. Civic Groups: Degree of Mobility in Each Recruitment Pattern Compared to the Degree of Mobility in the Cabinet

and respectability to all working classes, which before the turn of the century were largely immigrant.[10] If the urban party was the channel of social mobility, then the businesses, professions, and the groups emerging from them presumably tended toward the maintenance of class relationships. Assuming this to be an accurate picture of urban society before 1900, to what extent does mid-century New York depart from it?

Perhaps the most surprising discovery coming out of this study is that *the political party is no longer the clear channel of social mobility.* In the earlier part of the century, political parties were very clearly associated with high mobility, but the passage of years has brought alternative routes for movement out of the

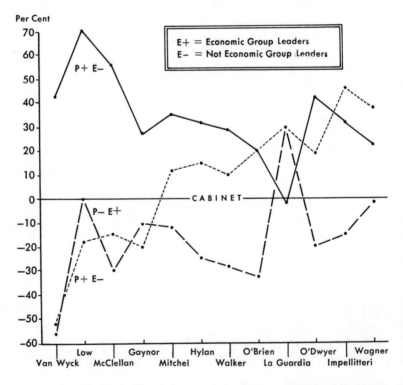

Figure 5.5   Party vs. Economic Groups: Degree of Mobility in Each Recruitment Pattern Compared to the Degree of Mobility in the Cabinet

lower classes (Figures 5.4, 5.5, and 5.6). Civic-philanthropic groups and economic associations are still controlled by some of the most important businessmen in the community. However, both the businesses and the groups they control have broadened their social base. Where once the appointment of a civic or economic group leader was a net reduction of mobility in the cabinet, the reverse is now more often the case. Note on Figures 5.4 and 5.5 how the tendencies of the party in relation to mobility (P+C— and P+E—) have been downward, and the pure civic and economic relationship (P—C+ and P—E+) have been upward. The difference between the earliest and latest periods is quite extreme.

Nor would the history of recruitment be different if I had separately analyzed recruitment in the Democratic and Republican organizations. The changes that have been observed are for the most part parallel in both parties. For the entire sixty years there has been a higher degree of mobility among Democratic Leaders and functionaries than in the cabinet. However,

Table 5.3   The Proportion of Democratic Party Leaders and Functionaries Who Were High-Mobility Commissioners, Compared to Degree of Mobility in Each Cabinet

| | PER CENT HIGH MOBILITY | | | PER CENT HIGH MOBILITY | |
Mayor	In Cabinet	Among Democratic Leaders	Mayor	In Cabinet	Among Democratic Leaders
Van Wyck	55	74	Walker	29	50
Low	17	38	O'Brien	30	45
McClellan	31	50	La Guardia	13	—
Gaynor	21	50	O'Dwyer	21	38
Mitchel	16	20	Impellitteri	16	32
Hylan	27	55	Wagner	18	36

the rate of decline has been about the same for both, and at present almost two thirds of all party-groomed commissioners come from middle- and upper-middle-class origins.

The party continues to show a stronger affinity only for the highly mobile *ethnic* type. Between 1898 and 1925, 81 per cent of the highly mobile ethnic commissioners were party functionaries; between 1926 and 1947, almost 70 per cent of this group were receiving some form of Party grooming. However, in the entire recent period, there have been only forty such commissioners and 67 per cent of them (twenty-seven in all) have also been officials in some kind of civic group.

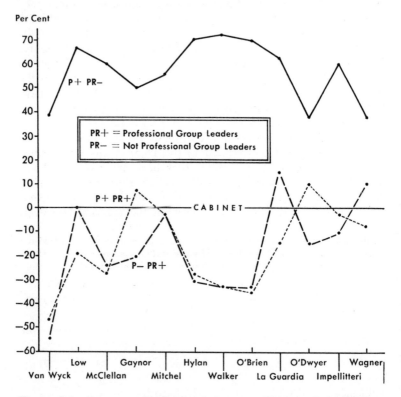

Figure 5.6 Party vs. Professional Groups: Degree of Mobility in Each Recruitment Pattern Compared to Degree of Mobility in the Cabinet

The only strong confirmation of our hypothesis lies in comparing mobility rates of party and professional groups (Figure 5.6). Here the difference is extreme and consistent, the degree of mobility of pure party-recruited commissioners deviating from 40 to 60 points above the cabinet norm and even more so above joint party-professional and pure-professional group recruitment. That the party appears to favor high mobility only when compared with professional associations bears directly upon the plight of the party. The need for professional backgrounds in top executive posts will never be abated, and parties will be further removed from cabinet politics if men seek mobility through the party only when they have no outstanding skills. Unlike businessmen, to whom wider contact means greater profit, professional leaders must be sought or coopted by the party. Except for the bar association leaders, professional leaders are increasingly attractive for their professional accomplishments alone.

PARTIES, GROUPS, AND THE RECRUITMENT OF SKILLS

New York City Mayors have shown increasingly strong preferences for specialists, candidates for the cabinet whose training and careers have equipped them specifically for the posts they seek. If the Mayor cannot find these *job-oriented* skills in his party, he is strongly pressed to turn elsewhere; moreover, in many cases he gets "good press" when he rejects all party candidates and solicits professional associations and clientele groups for their "best man." As skill values grow in importance, the mayor whose cabinet is short on specialists is increasingly likely to feel a net loss in his own administrative power. Such an important change of values inevitably affects relationships of the major recruitment channels with the cabinet and their relationships with each other.

The parties have not kept pace with the increasing need for skills in the cabinet. Mayor Van Wyck took thirteen of his twenty job-oriented commissioners from the party; Mayor Low took eleven of his eighteen specialists from the party. In contrast, only seven of Mayor Impellitteri's thirty-three and six of Mayor Wagner's forty-five job-oriented commissioners were party-recruited. Compared with group recruitment of skills, this presents a pretty sorry picture for the future of the party in cabinet politics.

Prior to La Guardia, the largest proportion of skilled commissioners in the cabinets of regular Democratic Mayors were either party functionaries or both functionaries and group Leaders. Recruitment of independent group leaders (P—C+, P—Pr+, P—E+) was a practice primarily of Mayors McClellan, Gaynor, and Mitchel (Figures 5.7, 5.8, and 5.9). Largely

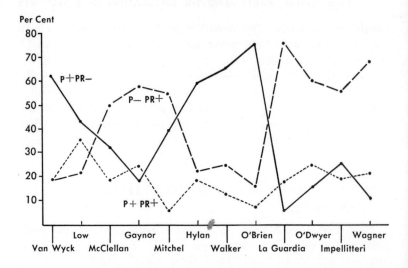

Figure 5.7 Party vs. Professional Groups: Proportions of Job-Oriented Skills From Each Recruitment Pattern

as a result of their struggles with the organizations, they turned for support to groups or leaders hostile to the party system. Access of groups to City Hall in Democratic Administrations depended upon the Mayor's relations with party leaders. But even when party and Mayor were united, access opened up for groups when control of the mayoralty itself was in peril: Mayor O'Brien was elected in 1932 to finish the final year of Walker's second term. Mayor Walker's resignation had been largely due to revelations of mismanagement by poorly selected commissioners, and the 1932 special election and O'Brien's entire twelve-month incumbency constituted a mere preparatory maneuver for the big election of 1933. O'Brien tried his best to propitiate the groups that were to become the foundation of the Fusion movement. He did so by appointing a goodly number of skilled personnel, many of whom were both party and group leaders.

The impact of La Guardia was to polarize parties and groups in the extreme. While earlier reform mayors had appointed some party leaders if they had the requisite skills, La Guardia turned almost exclusively to groups for his commissioners, particularly the specialists. It was as though party leadership was a *prima facie* disqualification. Prior to La Guardia the party had provided a fair share of skills to the Cabinet. However this was a fair share of a rather small total number of skilled appointments (see Chapter 3). As cabinet specialization intensified, the

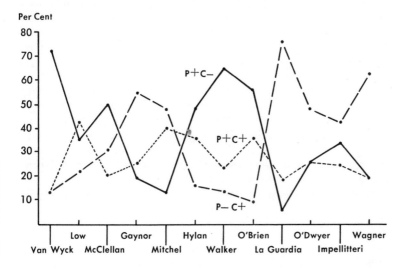

Figure 5.8   Party vs. Civic Groups: Proportions of Job-Oriented Skills From Each Recruitment Pattern

increase was provided by non-party groups and leaders completely independent of party grooming. That professional groups compare extremely favorably to the party is to be expected since these groups are virtually organized around skill. It is worth noting, however, the degree to which professionally recruited skills enter the cabinet independently of the party. Except for the bar associations, which have special affinities for politics and party organization, very few professional groups have any relations with the party at all (see Figure 5.7).[11] By and large they remain insulated from the party and, in the context of Cabinet appointments, competitive with the party.

The role of civic groups in the recruitment of skills has been considerably more variable than that of professional groups. Of all types of groups, the civic and good government groups appear to be least concerned with providing actual candidates to the Mayor. Their role in cabinet recruitment of skills followed the reform cycle, but it was a significant role only under La Guardia. Mayors Low and Mitchel chose group leaders who were affiliated also with the Republican party. But La Guardia selected his skilled personnel from party-hostile groups.[12] Civic leaders joined the reform movement, and many agreed to take a commissionership for a short period after La Guardia's election. But quite soon thereafter they returned to the more accustomed role of "veto groups" outside the governmental and party apparatus.

There are seldom more than ten or fifteen economic leaders in the cabinet, but it is remarkable how weak the party ties with economic groups are where the recruitment of skills is concerned. The traditional affinity of parties with economic groups, as shown dramatically in Figure 5.3, might well have developed into an important source of skills for the party. A few specialist commissioners do enter the cabinet by way of joint party and economic group recruitment, but just as often economic leaders are independent of the party (see Figure 5.9). That party cooption

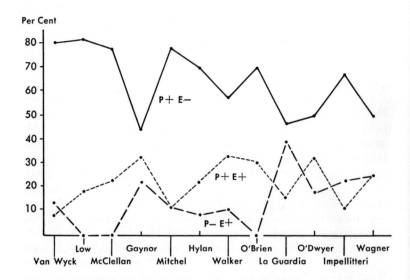

Figure 5.9   Party vs. Economic Groups: Proportions of Job-Oriented Skills From Each Recruitment Pattern

of economic group activists has not developed is another harsh blow to the future of party participation in cabinet politics.

There are personal pressures on the Mayor that his party seldom feels, at least not until it is too late. Once in office the Mayor's perspectives change from the broad base of party morale and support to the problems of administrative control. This is a shift from the general to the particular, a direction that puts party leaders in the least favorable position. When the Mayor requests a man specifically to run the Police Department, the Health Department, or the Welfare Department the parties are equipped only to answer that they can provide him with a total slate that nicely balances all of the symbols of identification. In contrast, the Mayor sees interest groups virtually organized around departmental affairs; interest groups are particularistic along lines precisely appropriate for the Mayor's needs. Parties have declined in cabinet politics not because of a weakened electoral position but because they do not yet run the right kind of employment agency.

It was earlier observed that the decline of the party in the cabinet was not accompanied by the rise of alternative interest group channels of recruitment. Now, however, it is equally clear that in the recruitment of specialists for the cabinet, non-party groups *have* become an alternative channel and here have very largely displaced the party. Party recruitment has become limited very largely to a few selected Departments in which specialization is not yet paramount (see Chapters 6 and 7).

If urban political parties are to survive, they must keep pace with the changing needs of the governments they seek to service. If the available job-oriented skills in the community are possessed by non-party groups, then the party must seek to collaborate with them and in some manner coopt some of their leaders. Special skills are increasingly the basic need of departmental administration. Perhaps they were always basic, but mayors have only recently begun to discover the need. The Mayor must calculate his decisions with the aim of making a net gain in power for himself. In doing so, he draws on any source he can find. If the parties hold tightly to their present composition, there will be an even stronger tendency for future Mayors to ignore the party offhand on the expectation that the key characteristics will not be found there. Further transferance of power from the parties to interest groups would be inevitable.

A large influx of professionals, upper salaried technicians and the like would transform the party and its leadership, but that would not necessarily destroy the organization itself. Political parties were strongest when the amateur ruled and the values of the *bund* and the brotherhood prevailed. But they are now weakened to the extent that they remain nineteenth century in a twentieth-century world.

SUMMARY AND THEORETICAL NOTE

Thorough examination of New York City's cabinet officials has suggested a number of propositions concerning urban politics. The decline of the party was not a result of direct displacement by any alternative channels of recruitment. However, these alternative structures have displaced the party in regard to certain relevant characteristics. The old distinction between the role of party and interest group in the circulation of elites is becoming less and less meaningful. Only those of lower class *and* ethnic origins continue to be in any way significantly associated with party recruitment. However, this is a mere vestige of the nineteenth century. There is still a relationship between commissioners of lower-class ethnic origin and party activity; but, as was shown in Chapter 3, this is a small and ever-dwindling segment of the cabinet.

Interest groups have tended to gain in power precisely because of the limited scope of their interests. To organize around the business of an agency or two is to attract those with a special stake in the agency's decisions, but it also tends to develop informal and professional expertise in departmental problems and technology. The staff of the Citizens Committee on Children is relatively small but probably has more experts on problems of juvenile delinquency than all party organizations combined. The Community Council—formerly the Health and Welfare Council—is a "peak association" of "do-gooder groups" with a wealth of professional and semiprofessional welfare personnel. Many members of the Boards of Correction, Health, Hospitals, and Education had been groomed for years in the Council or one of its constituent organizations. The old Bureau of Municipal Research and its parent organization, the Citizens Union, provided many mayors with officials for overhead agencies. John Purroy Mitchel, McClellan's Commissioner of Accounts, was one of many so recruited.

As adjuncts of the party these groups can be a source of strength to the party because of their capacities for attracting and grooming specialized talent. Independent of the party, they have managed to isolate and capture many of the City's departments and to exercise considerable veto power over the appointments in still other departments. While groups have not shaken the party loose from its monopoly of the nominating and electoral arena—although entry of insurgents with group support has become easier and the average tenure of party oligarchies is not so great as in earlier years—group access and group personnel resources have managed to shorten the party's span of influence. Nowadays, it is the exceptional party leader whose influence at City Hall continues for long after an election, and even then such influence is limited to a certain few agencies (see Chapters 6 and 7).

Study of types of decisions other than appointments might reveal an entirely different relationship between the party, the scope and span of its influence, and interest groups. Such research would, however, be predicated on an extremely important change in our present theories of community power: that there may be not one but several structures of power in the community. It will be the burden of the next two chapters to demonstrate the great importance of control for "arenas of power."

Finally, the data of this chapter and Chapter 4 ought to have demonstrated the importance of the time factor in studies of community power, and that the role of the party is highly dependent upon who holds the mayoralty and the circumstances of his election. The relationship of party to each type of group has also been seen to be highly variable and explicable only in terms of certain timely, critical events. Several definite secular or constant tendencies and relationships could be identified, but rather extreme variations within these trends suggest another important caveat in present studies of community power: Sampling "across the board" in a single cross-section of time does not, in any sense, constitute a study of power *structure*. Without history, how is one to know what phase of community trend he has captured? Chapter 8 will be devoted to analyses of two important phases in New York politics: reform and consolidation. In Chapter 6 the reader will also find a case study on the consequences for party and group access of two bitter, but entirely different, types of mayoral primary contests. If "community power structure" is to be identified at all, it requires a careful identification of arenas and a careful assessment of these in an historical context.[13]

NOTES

1. *Democracy in America*, Mentor edition, p. 95.
2. Bryce, *op. cit.*, p. 336.
3. Harold U. Faulkner, *Politics, Reform and Expansion*, p. 26.
4. Figures from Sayre and Kaufman, *op. cit.*, pp. 497, 502. In the following analysis only the group leadership is included; i.e., cabinet appointees were treated either as prominent group activists or as nonmembers. A three- or fourfold distinction of levels of activity—as in the analysis of party—would have been preferred, but such data were not available.

The groups have been arranged according to the three most important areas of voluntary activity: (1) civic-philanthropic (hereafter referred to as civic or C+); economic (E+; all business, trade, etc., groups. Trade unions were not included; and there were too few trade unionists in the cabinet to warrant separate treatment); and professional (Pr+).

5. Cf. Robert Merton, *Social Theory and Social Structure*, Free Press, New York, 1957, Chapter I.
6. Peter H. and Alice S. Rossi, "An Historical Perspective on the Functions of Local Politics," revision of a paper presented at the 1956 meeting of the American Sociological Society (mimeo) in Detroit, p. 15.
7. *Ibid.*
8. The three categories are not cumulative because of the high degree of overlapping.
9. Oscar Handlin, *op. cit.*, p. 209.
10. Another, although more restricted, alternative has been sports—the prevailing value of which is not personal *following* but personal *well-being*. Just as the Irish and Jews once dominated boxing, for instance, so now is it dominated by Negroes and Puerto Ricans. In fact, in the earlier days there was a close affinity of values between the two fields. A great many of New York's local bosses were prominent both in gang warfare and on the playing field.
11. The fact that more skills are recruited through the joint party-professional group channel (P+Pr+) than by party alone (the horizontal line in Figure 5.7) is attributable almost entirely to the bar associations in the City. Generally speaking, the P+Pr+, P+C+, and P+E+ lines on Figures 5.7, 5.8, and 5.9 are a rough measure of party-group compatibility. In this particular case, however, it is already known that the one type of professional group, the bar association, accounts for practically all of the apparent compatibility.
12. La Guardia also required his commissioners to sever all party (Republican or Fusion) connections, if any, prior to taking the oath of office.
13. These methodological points will be elaborated still further in Chapter 9.

PART THREE

Political Change

CHAPTER 6

ARENAS OF POWER I:

PERSONAL CONTINUITY

COMMITMENT

Two Primaries and After: A Case Study

JAMES J. WALKER came to the mayoralty over the wreckage of the Hylan administration. The struggle between the two men resulted in the first bitter Mayoral primary contest in the City's history. The great 1925 primary was not in the usual sense an intra-party struggle. Walker had the support of practically all the Democratic Leaders in the City; Hylan was fighting this with the last vestiges of the "Hearst organization," which, operating under several banners and labels over the previous twenty years, was essentially a collection of local business and union leaders. The Hearst organization enjoyed a political bite because its bark was fearsome; it had two mass-circulation daily newspapers and was willing to use them for partisan purposes. In 1917, Charles Murphy purchased the Hearst papers' support by an agreement to let Hearst name the Democratic mayoral nominee. As Mayor for eight years, John Hylan had used Hearst's support to counterbalance the claims of organization Leaders; but by 1925, Hearst's support was not enough. With Walker, the party was again in control.

The aftermath of the primary had almost everything to do with the respective power positions of the participants in City

Hall politics. The vulnerability of group leaders in Walker's administration was extreme. None of the interest group leaders (except those in fixed-term positions) survived the transition. The few group Leaders appointed by Walker stayed in the cabinet for very short periods (Figure 6.1).[1] The average Tenure Ratio for non-party group leaders was almost 30 points below the Walker cabinet's average and almost 40 points below

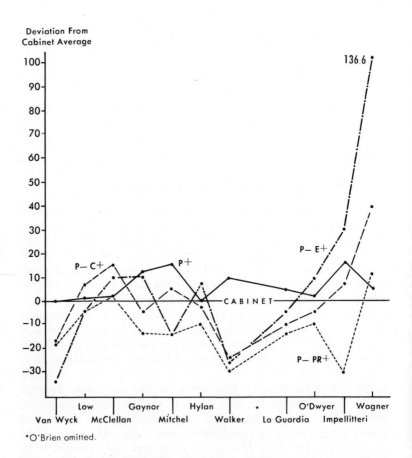

*O'Brien omitted.

Figure 6.1   The Contributors to Cabinet Stability: Tenure Ratios of the Channels of Recruitment Compared with Mean Tenure of the Cabinet (Zero)

that of party functionaries in the cabinet.[2] Most of the party functionaries in Hylan's Cabinet survived the primary and kept their jobs under Walker.

The second great primary contest for the Democratic Mayoral nomination was between Mayor Vincent Impellitteri and Robert F. Wagner, Jr. In contrast to the first, the 1953 primary was strictly an intra-party affair. Large blocs of party Leaders within each County organization were pitted against each other, and the survival of each was at stake. Brooklyn and Queens were fighting Manhattan and the Bronx, and there were district defections within each County.

This time it was the party that suffered the consequences. Interest group leaders strengthened their positions spectacularly, whereas the party's overall position was weaker. Party functionaries dropped from 53 to 42 per cent of the cabinet; and those who became commissioners were most vulnerable. The life expectancy of party functionaries in the Wagner cabinet of 1954–1957 was far lower than that of group leaders, many of whom were actually held over by Wagner from the O'Dwyer and Impellitteri cabinets (see Figure 6.1 and Table 6.1).

Table 6.1   Net Changes in Mean Tenure Ratios of Recruitment Types Resulting from the Transition from Impellitteri to Wagner

Recruitment Type	Tenure Ratios: Impellitteri	Tenure Ratios: Wagner	Net changes
P +	19.7	4.6	− 15.1
P–C +	10.3	38.6	28.3
P–E +	31.4	136.6	105.2
P–Pr +	− 30.8	13.2	44.0

A struggle for leadership in the party usually results in the breakdown of bargaining among party factions. A hotly contested primary between party factions signifies the final breakdown, the temporary "balkanization" of the party organization. The primary usually settles the question of leadership for a while, sometimes by *rapprochement,* more often by exile of the losers. A clearcut victory tends to strengthen the hand of the victor over his own District and with other Districts, County Leaders, and City Hall; but for a while after a primary the relations between the party organization in the involved District and the outside world are weakened. During this period, and perhaps beyond it, interest group access to government becomes stronger. A mayor whose election has been preceded by an intense intra-party struggle usually finds himself committed very strongly to interest groups, and less bound by his party. However, his appointment of interest group candidates and his retention of them for longer periods are not necessarily evidence of personal weakness. Party weakness may for a time be a source of strength for him. Mayor Wagner's relative independence of the Party may have been due to the mortgaging of offices for group support. But it may also have resulted from weaker claims on him by the victorious, as well as the defeated, party faction. Party control over governmental access and the life expectancy of all party leaders in government positions vary considerably according to the degree of consensus among party leaders concerning the Mayor. This is also the turmoil that cabinet stability and instability are made of. But the *specific* sources of stability or instability are not fixed; they too are dependent upon the *nature* of the struggle. If yesterday party appeared as a stabilizing force, today may be otherwise. If today party appears in a state of weakness, tomorrow may be a day of strength.

Differential Commitment in the Cabinet I: Tenure

Every appointment is a commitment. The pattern of appointments directly commits the Mayor to a stable or an unstable administration because some types of appointees are better suited for survival—perhaps "success"—than others; there are differences in the life expectancies of appointees. In a more indirect fashion, every type of appointment is also a *commitment in kind:* commitment to the appointees themselves and to the *attributes* of the appointees. The social balance, the pattern of group representation, and the nature and degree of cabinet specialization are only partly the result of the Mayor's pleasure. He is limited in his choices by the appointment pattern of preceding mayors because the expectations and demands of his constituencies are based upon the established pattern. And, in turn, his own appointments become part of a pattern that is difficult for him and for succeeding mayors to break.

Functionally, *commitments* are the power relations between the Mayor, his commissioners, and his and their constituencies.

Commitments can be roughly measured in any number of ways. Case studies, interviews, memoirs, panels of participants, and so forth have all been used separately and combined with varying degrees of success. But no matter how objectively and exhaustively the data have been collected, they still require interpretation according to personal insight and theory and subjective judgment.

By now it should be apparent that considerable historical depth is necessary in order to identify prevailing power relations, to discover any of the underlying conditions of community power structure. The study of long-run trends and variations sacrifices many of the delicious nuances of the political struggle. But if an advantage is gained in the overall picture of trends, the sacrifice may be worthwhile. The aftermaths of the two primaries have illustrated several things: First, that relations among participants in the political struggle are highly variable despite long-run trends. Second, that the access of groups to the mayoralty may have little to do with their own activity or efficacy. Third, that these conditions of access are susceptible to rough measurement and control, or that it is possible to reveal important power factors with quantitative data. And finally, that data on length of service or "life expectancy" can, with careful interpretation, be used for those purposes.

A second measure—not length of service, but personal continuity (the survival of a change of administration)—will also be used. And the next chapter, still a third measure will be employed: attribute continuity, the pattern of replacing one commissioner by others with identical characteristics. The purpose of all three measures is to identify and describe several significant political arenas and to contrast and compare hypotheses about elements of the power structures of each.

Life Expectancy: Cabinet stability is political stability. Spectacular policy changes and reorganization may well be the events by which history judges mayors, but on the job the Mayor's fundamental need is for equilibrium. Only then is he free to select the policies he wants and the changes he desires to make. The Department head serves the Mayor well if, and only if, his Department is run smoothly. Cabinet instability is very demanding of mayoral attention. During Mayor Wagner's second term, for example, the greatest portion of his time and energy and political profit was devoted to the simple matter of ending departmental crises. Turmoil in housing, markets, real estate, and purchasing left him with the passive role of receiving complaints and smoothing tempers.

The life expectancy of political executives in New York City has been relatively high[3] and steadily on the rise since 1902 (see Table 6.2, column B, which follows).[4] Average tenure of cabinet appointees rose to its highest points prior to the La Guardia administration, then dropped and started a new incline afterward. The decline of service under O'Dwyer was not due to a sudden injection of instability but to the fact that he was a Democrat starting with a fresh slate after twelve years of Republican-Fusion rule. O'Dwyer's cabinet was in fact much more stable than La Guardia's; for, relative to O'Dwyer's *own* length of service, his commissioners served longer than La Guardia's. Cabinet stability is not simply a matter of average length of service; rather, it depends upon the relationship of the average length of service of the appointees to the tenure of the appointing Mayor. Twelve months was full service under Mayor O'Brien, 20 per cent service under O'Dwyer, and only a brief encounter under La Guardia. A tenure *ratio* between cabinet and mayor is the proper index of cabinet stability (see Table 6.2, column D).

Cabinet stability has been increasing somewhat over the years, but the variations in the trend are of greater interest. Part of the variation is due to differences in mayoral tenure; for example, short mayoral terms like Low's (24 months) and O'Brien's (12 months) exaggerate the tenure ratio. But that does not affect the overall pattern.

Democratic cabinets by and large are more stable than Fusion cabinets. And cabinet stability tends to increase rather sharply during periods of long Democratic rule. This was especially striking in the period from Hylan to O'Brien. When one "organization" Mayor succeeds another he is strongly committed to the existing commissioners. A few holdovers from earlier cabinets, having built up long service in the job, raise the average tenure ratio—thus, the stability—of succeeding Democratic mayors. This was true even of Walker and Wagner, who fought their predecessors Hylan and Impellitteri in bitter primaries. Despite the great residue of animosity, both Walker and Wagner reappointed Hylan and Impellitteri commissioners

Table 6.2   Life Expectancy of Political Executives: Average Tenure
and Average Tenure Ratio for All Appointees Serving at
the Pleasure of the Mayor, 1902–1957

| | AVERAGE TENURE IN THE CABINET | | TENURE RATIO IN THE CABINET | |
| Mayor | Number of Appointees | Average (in months) | Tenure of Mayor (in months) | Average Tenure Ratio |
	A	B	C	D (B/C)
Low	37	24.2	24	100.1
McClellan	96	29.1	72	40.4
Gaynor	51	39.4	48	82.1
Mitchel	53	39.7	48	83.0
Hylan	98	46.4	96	48.3
Walker	75	64.3	84	76.5
O'Brien	47	57.5	12	479.2
La Guardia	115	54.7	144	37.3
O'Dwyer	81	36.2	60	60.3
Impellitteri	51	51.4	36	142.8
Wagner	60	50.5	48	105.2

in considerable numbers. Wagner reappointed Impellitteri men
to such a degree, and retained them for such a time, that average service in his first-term cabinet exceeded his own tenure
(see Table 6.2, column D, above).[5] Mayor Wagner's tenure ratio
was lower than Impellitteri's because Impellitteri had been an
O'Dwyer protégé and was very strongly committed to O'Dwyer's
commissioners. The same was true of O'Brien's relation to
Walker's commissioners.

Stability in the La Guardia cabinet was at an all time low.
And his own long tenure is only partly the answer. Many early
commissioners, following the reform pattern, resigned according
to plan after the short period of consolidation was over. A number of others resigned or were transferred because their work
was not to La Guardia's liking. In fact, the cabinets of strong
mayors like McClellan, La Guardia, and O'Dwyer, tended to be
the most unstable.[6] The exceptional case was John Purroy
Mitchel, perhaps the model reform leader, who was also a strong
mayor. Unlike La Guardia's policy orientation, Mitchel's interest was in honest administration by talent. Of all strong
mayors, stability in Mitchel's Cabinet was the highest because
he ruled "not by intervention and close supervision, but by a

generous encouragement of his appointees and strong support for them against any attack."[7]

The Contributors to Cabinet Stability: Average tenure ratios for the entire cabinet mask a number of interesting variations because some types of appointees are better suited for survival than others. Differences in the Mayor's commitment to the various types of appointees affect the stability of his administration. Subject to the exception of an intra-party struggle for the mayoralty, the party types have tended toward cabinet stability (see Figure 6.1 on page 126). Although the non-party channels of recruitment are highly variable, they have tended toward a lower life expectancy than that of the party or the cabinet average. The variations of all three types of non-party recruitment have been parallel almost all of the time. That they have been "out of phase" with party variations is again suggestive of an incompatibility of the types. However, it is clear that the consequences of every type of alliance are largely determined by the circumstances surrounding the nomination and election of each mayor. The so-called "pluralist pattern" is associated with the secular weakening of party organization, but the degree of party power continues to vary according to the amount of consensus the Mayor has among party Leaders. Group and party affiliations are related both to the selection and the survival of commissioners; but an asset today may be a liability later.

Job-oriented commissioners tend to resist the many vicissitudes of the ordinary group Leader in the cabinet (Figure 6.2). Until

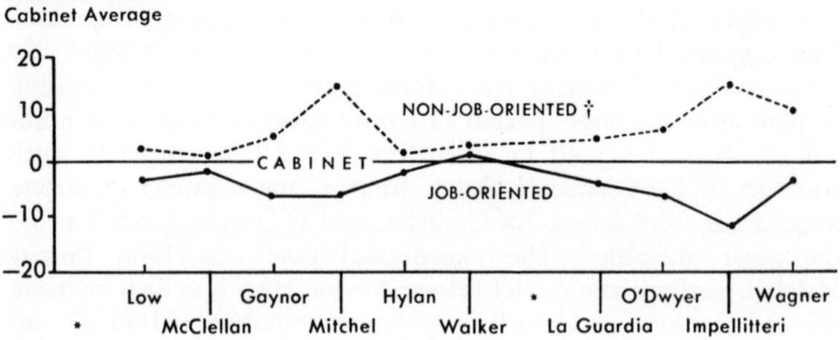

Deviation from
Cabinet Average

*Van Wyck and O'Brien omitted.
†Also includes "job-experienced" commissioners.

Figure 6.2   Contributors to Cabinet Stability: Tenure Ratios of Job- and Non-Job-Oriented Commissioners Compared with Mean Tenure Ratio of the Cabinet (Zero)

O'Dwyer, the life expectancy of these commissioners was higher that that of any channel except the Party. This suggests that their place in cabinet politics was determined by factors outside the realm of group politics. Generally, the nonjob-oriented commissioner needs some form of party or group support, and his survival value changes accordingly. The life expectancy of the job-oriented commissioner resists the ups and downs of group access because the commitment of the Mayor is more to the skills, much less to the groups supporting them. Group or party support is almost always necessary for recognition and for successful candidacy for appointment; but once in office the survival of the specialized commissioner rests somewhat less on continuing support. The Mayor becomes personally committed to the skilled commissioner or to his one most outstanding attribute.

Differential Commitment II: Personal Continuity

The stability of a cabinet is of prime importance to the Mayor, and changes in the degree of stability are intimately associated with overall political conditions. However, the degree of stability *between* administrations is of equal importance, for continuity of personnel has a great deal to do with continuity of policy and administration.[8] One of the outstanding features of politics in the history of the Greater City is the personal continuity in the Mayor's cabinet. *There was never a complete break between Administrations* (see Table 6.3).[9]

In spite of the bitterness generated both by changes of Party and by changes of factions within the dominant Democratic party, there was always some degree of continuity. Even Seth Low, the first reform mayor, reappointed three nontenure commissioners who had served under Van Wyck. McClellan, who followed Low, reappointed four Low commissioners and also brought five of Van Wyck's cabinet members back from cold storage.[10]

Mayor Mitchel, the second Fusion Mayor, drew eleven nontenure appointments from preceding Democratic cabinets and contributed three in turn to his Democratic successor. And, despite La Guardia's great break with the past, seven former Democratic commissioners were included in his Cabinet. Six additional Mitchel commissioners returned, after a fifteen-year

Table 6.3 Personal Continuity of Appointees Serving at the Pleasure of the Mayor: Pattern of Reappointment in the Cabinet, 1902–1957

APPOINTED BY	REAPPOINTED BY										
	Low	*McClellan*	*Gaynor*	*Mitchel*	*Hylan*	*Walker*	*O'Brien*	*La Guardia*	*O'Dwyer*	*Impellitteri*	*Wagner*
Van Wyck	3	5	2		2	1	1				
Low	37*	4									
McClellan		96*	8	3	3	3	1				
Gaynor			51*	8	2	1					
Mitchel				53*	3		1	6			
Hylan					98*	19	10	1			
Walker						75*	29	2			
O'Brien							47*	4			
La Guardia								115*	9	2	1
O'Dwyer									81*	28	11
Impellitteri										51*	17
Wagner											60*

* Total appointments at the pleasure of the Mayor.

interval, to service under La Guardia. Nine (11 per cent) of these men were retained by Impellitteri and Wagner.[11]

Personal continuity in the cabinet is greater still among the fixed-term commissioners (Table 6.4).[12] Larger numbers of fixed-term appointees are reappointed and they reach further out into more and more administrations. Counting both the tenure and nontenure officials, Mitchel drew twenty-six (27 per cent) and La Guardia nine (5 per cent) of their cabinet appointees from prior Democratic regimes. In turn, Hylan and O'Dwyer drew seven (6 per cent) and sixteen (15 per cent), respectively, of their commissioners from Fusion cabinets.[13]

Due to the relatively long cabinet life of commissioners serving fixed terms,[14] there is a general presumption of reappointment when the term expires. This is particularly true when the term of a Democratic appointee expires during the term of a Democratic mayor other than the one who appointed him. And the presumption is strengthened by the fact that many terms expire after the succeeding Mayor's first year—after political pressures have subsided and after many of the Mayor's strongest commitments have been honored.

Cabinet continuity has been increasing over the years. Personal continuity drops extremely with Fusion mayors, but they do not break the link altogether. And with each new period of long Democratic rule, the personal link with the past gets stronger.[15] Well over half of all Impellitteri's and Wagner's commissioners had served in earlier cabinets.

Although there are no comparable data on other communities, the political science and public administration literature would lead one to conclude that continuity in New York politics is relatively high.[16] Party responsibility and the chief executive's own personal position would dictate the search for political executives free from competing loyalties. At first blush, it would appear that the Mayor of New York does not perceive any necessary incompatibility between service under earlier mayors and loyalty to himself. Otherwise, the search for sufficient executive power would dictate at the very least a clean slate for each new Mayor. If the Mayor were a completely free agent, he might well choose to make a fresh start. However, his commitments often extend to existing commissioners.

Social types, recruitment patterns, and skills are all associated in some degree with length of service in the cabinet. Under

Table 6.4 Personal Continuity of All Appointees: Pattern of Reappointment in the Cabinet, 1902–1957

APPOINTED BY	REAPPOINTED BY										
	Low	McClellan	Gaynor	Mitchel	Hylan	Walker	O'Brien	La Guardia	O'Dwyer	Impellitteri	Wagner
Van Wyck	3	5		1	2	1	1				
Low	93*	16	10	1	1						
McClellan		160*	30	10	7	6	2				
Gaynor			95*	15	4	2					
Mitchel				94*	6	3	1	5	1		1
Hylan					119*	33	11	2	1		
Walker						90*	30	2			
O'Brien							50*	5	1	1	1
La Guardia								170*	15	3	6
O'Dwyer									108*	31	23
Impellitteri										62*	19
Wagner											86*

* Total Cabinet appointments.

varying conditions, the characteristics of commissioners contribute to their life expectancy in the cabinet and, in turn, to
the stability of the cabinet. However, in the transition from one
mayor to the next, these personal characteristics are apparently
irrelevant. *No particular characteristic is better suited than any
other to survive the transition of administrations.* Personal continuity is neither reduced nor increased by differences in the
composition of the cabinet. Reappointment was no greater
among ethnics than among native-Americans, and neither status
group departed more than five percentage points from the reappointment pattern of the total cabinet (Table 6.5, row 3).[17]
Professional group leaders tend to have a small advantage with
incoming mayors for reappointment, but the difference is quite
small. Similarly, the skilled commissioner is at no particular
advantage.

Recognizing that the differences of percentage points and
ranking are slight, if there is a relationship at all between length
of service and the probability of reappointment, it is an *inverse*
one. On the average, ethnic commissioners have a higher life
expectancy than native-Americans. Yet, between 1934 and 1957,
the reverse was true of personal continuity. The tenure ratio
of Party commissioners was higher than non-Party group commissioners (see Figure 6.1 on page 126). The reverse, though
mild, was repeatedly true of personal continuity. This suggests
that the resources best suited for survival within an administration may prove to be poorer bases for an effective claim on the
succeeding Mayor.

What, then, is the nature of the Mayor's commitment? Where
does he have a free hand, where do group and party claims
encumber him? Variations in the Mayor's commitment, the relative power of those competing for his pleasure, are to be 'explained by the nature of the conflict at a given time and the
composition of constituencies of each area of governmental activities. *To control for area of governmental activity is in reality
to expose the differences in the nature of the political conflict.*

ARENAS OF POWER

Political scientists, sociologists, journalists, and others often
refer glibly to *the* political process or *the* power structure, revealing an assumption that there is only one of each in any

Table 6.5 Personal Continuity of Appointments Made at the Pleasure of the Mayor: Pattern of Reappointments for Status Groups, Recruitment Channels, and Skills 1902–1933 and 1934–1957

	I (1902–1933)			II (1934–1957)		
	Total Nontenure Appointments	Number of Reappointments	Per Cent Reappointments	Total Nontenure Appointments	Number of Reappointments	Per Cent Reappointments
Cabinet	455	106	23	306	78	25
1. Pattern of recruitment:						
a. Party	233	56	24	83	21	25
b. Non-Party:	131	32	24	117	31	26
(1) P–C +	69	18	26	56	15	26
(2) P–C −	62	14	23	61	16	26
(3) P–E +	20	4	25	17	5	29
(4) P–E −	111	28	25	100	26	26
(5) P–Pr +	66	16	24	69	20	29
(6) P–Pr −	65	16	25	48	11	23
2. Skills:						
a. Job-oriented	211	53	25	188	45	24
b. Non-job-oriented	229	53	23	112	33	29
3. Status:						
a. Ethnic	177	45	25	132	26	20
b. Native	181	39	22	103	28	27

political system. Some recent studies have rejected this assumption; they have investigated community leadership in a variety of "issue areas," such as education, urban development, and so on.[18] Peter Rossi argues that " . . . the best way of characterizing communities for the purpose of understanding fluoridation controversies in principle may be different from the best way for understanding some other community process." [19]

However, the problem with issues is that they are transitory and unique. If the study of the entire community as a single political process is too general, the study of power and leadership through issues is too specific. What I propose here and in the following chapter, by way of hypotheses that seem to explain the observed patterns, is that events, issues, and leadership be studied within defined areas of governmental activity. These areas are, in effect, the functions of government defined more broadly than a single agency, more narrowly than government with a single political process.

Much of the tone of City politics is set by conflicts between "money-providing" and "service-demanding" groups. However, the weight and intensity of their claims, the degree of cleavage between them, and the amount of consensus among groups on both sides vary greatly because the impact of government decisions varies. Groups tend to specialize around these subject-matter areas—one or several related Departments. And the types of alliances among groups and relationships among them, the party organization, the officials, and the Mayor depend upon the organization of Departments and the different kinds of access that are available. Except in very small and undifferentiated communities, action involving the whole community takes place in a governmental context. Those who hold formal positions in government do not hold all or necessarily most of the decision-making power. But since they must make the formal decision, if it is to be legitimate, their offices provide the focus for political activity, and the nature of the decisions made there ought very largely to determine the political process.

The First Arena: Services and Welfare[20]

This arena affords the greatest opportunity for stable, organized squabble (Table 6.6). Bankers, large property owners and developers, and all other owners or controllers of great

Table 6.6 Departments Arranged According to Area of Governmental Activity*

Regulation and Property Protection	Services and Welfare	Governmental Inputs	Overhead
Police Department	Department of Education (*Board*)	Tax Department (Commission)	Deputy Mayor
Fire Department	Parks Department	Finance Department (Treasurer)	City Administrator
Board of Health (after 1936)	Hospital Department	Board of Assessors	Budget Bureau (Director)
Corrections Department			
Buildings Department†	Welfare Department		*City Planning Commission*
	Sanitation Department		Law Department (Corp. Counsel)
Board of Standards and Appeals (after 1936)	Department of Water, Gas and Electric		Department of Personnel†† (Civil Service Commission)
Licenses Department	Department of Marine and Aviation		*Art Commission*
	Health Commissioner		
Markets Department			*City Records Supervisor*
Department of Air Pollution Control			*City Register*
City Sheriff (1942)			Department of Labor
Chief Medical Examiner (1918)			Department of Public Works

* *Italicized* departments are headed by fixed-term personnel and are not included in the earlier tables.
† Earlier known as Tenement House and Housing and Buildings.
†† Only the new Commission President included. After 1922, Commission members were given fixed terms and were excluded from analysis in this section.

amounts of capital employ every possible resource to hold the line on city expenditures. Many of the largest groups in town, the "peak associations," are mere fronts for these interests. Against them, the health and welfare councils, religious associations, unions, and the welfare bureaucracies themselves are constantly pushing for more and better schools, broader and more lenient categories of welfare assistance, and in every way a stronger commitment of City government to the redistribution of the City's great wealth. The battle is constant, the battle lines are relatively clearly drawn, and each side is well-organized and ably led. Under these conditions, the Mayor, in trying to fill executive posts, is in that uncomfortable position of "damned if you do and damned if you don't." Sayre and Kaufman describe this position with unusual sympathy: "To the extent that the appointment may involve him in the risks of greatly displeasing some groups while pleasing others, the [Mayor] may . . . regard it as a painful choice . . . and perhaps as more of a liability than advantage." [21] Welfare politics is class politics *par excellence*. The political struggle is almost institutionalized. [22] In the rooms where policy is made there is probably seldom space for any but the wealthiest or the best organized.

What better way to start a new administration with equanimity than to continue in office a Welfare or Health Commissioner whose peace with the hostile elements has already been made? "Good Administration" and "continuity of policy" become handy defenses for the Mayor, who helps himself by not upsetting the equilibrium. At whatever sacrifice to hoped-for policy changes, the Mayor can manage to keep pariah politics at arm's length, perhaps to attack the area later after he has his job a little better under control. And, incidentally, many of the large peak associations that dominate this area have resources that the Mayor has drawn upon for his election and on which he hopes to depend for legislative support in the Board of Estimate, in Albany, and in Washington.

Personal continuity has clearly been highest in this area. Well over half the Services and Welfare Commissioners since 1934 have been reappointed at least once (Table 6.7). In the first thirty years of this century continuity was not quite so high. However, it should be recalled that most service functions were quite new at that time and were undergoing the painful period of consolidation and the search for "roles and missions." The

Table 6.7 Total Nontenured Appointments and Per Cent Who Were Reappointments, by Area of Governmental Activity

Area of Activity	I (1902–1933)			II (1934–1957)			Net Change, I:II
	Total Nontenure Appointments	Number of Reappointments	Per Cent Reappointments	Total Nontenure Appointments	Number of Reappointments	Per Cent Reappointments	
Regulation and property protection	99	29	29	58	15	26	−3
Service and welfare	112	37	33	55	32	58	15
Governmental inputs	96	34	35	64	29	45	10
Overhead	148	17	11	131	13	10	−1

large nongovernmental associations were also in a period of consolidation.

The life expectancy or Tenure Ratio of these commissioners is not so high and has declined on the average in more recent years (Table 6.8). All of which suggests that the establishment

Table 6.8   Mean Tenure Ratios for Areas of Governmental Activity, 1902–1933 and 1934–1957 (Nontenure Offices Only)

Area of Activity	I (1902–1933)	II (1934–1957)	Ranking
Regulation and protection	106.6	65.7	3
Service and welfare	107.2	88.2	2
Governmental inputs	163.1	109.2	1
Overhead	74.3	54.2	4

of political peace with his constituency is extremely difficult for a commissioner. But once that is accomplished all the forces conspire to retain him. He becomes indispensable to the new Mayor.

Services and Welfare policies are or threaten to be *redistributive* policies, largely because of the available methods of financing. By that very fact the impact of most decisions in this area hits the community in a most crucial way, along class lines.[23] "Welfare state" decisions cut the widest possible swath across the community and are extremely likely to affect the political process accordingly.

REGULATION AND PROPERTY PROTECTION

As line agencies, Departments like Police, Fire, and Buildings would naturally be involved with nongovernmental groups and leaders, including many of those involved in the Service and Welfare arena. But significant differences between regulatory and welfare policies can be found in the *nature of the conflict* and in the composition of the groups and types of leaders. An interview study that identifies leaders by name and reputation alone is not likely to reveal such differences unless they are anticipated in the beginning.

If ever there is agreement between the money-providing and service-demanding groups it is in the need for more protection of life and property. Differences do occur over the "best" commissioner. Extreme differences often develop over the optimum pattern of protection, as for instance over a decision to saturate

high-crime areas with policemen to the detriment of "silk stock-
ing" neighborhoods. But there is seldom disagreement about
whether there should be more of it.

Conflict generates as a result of the highly differential impact
of regulatory policies, which tend to cut across every possible
alliance. It is the nature of regulatory decisions to pluralize their
environment because they hit individual businessmen and citizens
individually. A health regulation sets food producers and dis-
tributors against all other businessmen *qua* consumers. Merchants
who act as one to resist a new welfare activity are split asunder
over a new one-way street pattern that sets the immediately
affected merchants and transportation companies against those
"disinterested" many whose only care is in smooth traffic flow.
Large property owners split with large property users. Thus,
while the money-providers can agree on principles of less government, more efficiency, or protection of public credit, they
tend to part company over rules and orders that are too specific
for alliance-making. Peak associations melt into their constituent
units.

There is yet another reason why the regulatory arena is so
highly pluralistic: The patterns of access to regulatory decisions.
In general, services and welfare activity is highly "ministerial."
Most of the important shifts in policy come from increments of
change at the center; the welfare employee, for instance, has
very little discretion, if any, in the applicability of the categories
of public assistance. In contrast, a great deal of regulatory activity can be subjected to influence, for the ordinary regulatory
employee has considerable discretion; and formal proceedings
of all sorts are handy for exploitation. In the regulatory arena,
it is largely a matter of every man for himself.

In the regulatory arena, conflict may follow economic lines,
but seldom, if ever, class lines. The nature of the conflict is
therefore unstable. Establishment of group alliances and peace
pacts between commissioner and clientele are extremely rare.
It is a fortunate commissioner who enjoys anything like a consensus in his constituency. Many of New York's mayoral campaigns have been fought over alleged corruption in these Departments, and most mayors have been committed to at least
some housecleaning here.

The consequences are clearly apparent in our data. Life expectancy was far from the highest of the four arenas and

dropped precipitously between 1902–33 and 1934–57 (see Table 6.8). Personal continuity has also been low, exceeded only by overhead commissioners (see Table 6.7). Actually, in absolute terms personal continuity is almost as low for regulatory as for overhead commissioners. The *percentages* are higher because fewer appointments in all are made in this area. The extreme pluralism of the regulatory arena provides conditions that few incumbent commissioners can ride out from one mayoralty to the next. Extreme pluralism, plus a continuous suspicion of corruption—probably a symptom of the former—have freed, if not obliged, each new Mayor to provide new commissioners.

In the Services and Welfare arena, one might have confidence in the results of a power structure study of a single issue. In the regulatory arena, one study would very likely be most inadequate. And one would expect the respective *roles* of leaders in each arena to be different.

GOVERNMENTAL INPUT

The stable cleavage between money-providing and service-demanding groups is manifest here as in the welfare arena. Local business is deeply involved in the sales taxes and even more particularly in the form and degree of property assessment that affects private revenues and long-run land use patterns. Their stake in assessments is all the greater because the amount of City government indebtedness for capital expenditures is geared to the total assessed valuation of property. The so-called "constitutional debt limit" that holds the City's debt to a fixed percentage of property valuations was a victory won by bankers and merchants in 1894 and has been jealously guarded by them ever since.

As in the welfare arena, Governmental Input is a holding operation for the money-providing groups. However, the cleavage does not parallel the welfare arena in all respects; revenue politics is not the mirror image of spending politics. Individuals are constantly trying to shift the burden of taxes and assessments. And opportunities are available because not all revenue decisions take the form of county- or citywide policy. If there is a "power elite" in the City, it would include those who have perpetual influence over the thousands of individual assessments on individual pieces of property.

As a consequence, the tenure of commissioners in this arena consistently has been extremely high (see Table 6.8). Average tenure has dropped off in all four arenas, but it remains highest here. Personal continuity has also been relatively high, highest of all in the early period. Part of this is a result of the fact that this is the last party enclave (see Chapter 7), and that several Democratic administrations have succeeded each other. But that cannot explain the high continuity of the more recent period with its one Fusion-Democratic transition and one bitter primary battle between Democrats. Despite Mayor Wagner's animosity toward the Impellitteri faction, he reappointed City Treasurer Sarafite and retained a goodly number of Tax Commissioners and Assessors. Elaboration awaits the data of Chapter 7.

OVERHEAD

The overhead agencies are the most important instruments of policy development under the Mayor. In 1954, this function was more formally recognized by the establishment of a "cabinet" composed, not of line officials, but of officials of the overhead agencies. According to Sayre and Kaufman, the "heads of overhead agencies have both broader responsibilities and greater opportunities for advice to the Mayor and to the Board of Estimate than do the heads of line agencies." [24] The Mayor can actually count on reliable advice from only a few overhead agencies, and "information and advice from the others he must recognize as intended primarily to influence him, to bring him into agreement with the Board of Estimate or with a particular overhead agency constituency." [25] However, the fact that the overhead agencies can themselves become special pleaders makes it all the more necessary for the Mayor to place personally loyal men at the top. The overhead agencies' authority over the line agencies gives them supra- or multi-departmental power. Usually the best possible way for a mayor to see his policies become realities is through his overhead agencies.

Interest-group and party backgrounds are not absent from overhead agencies, but their composition and nature are distinctively different from the other arenas. In the overhead arena, the most effective constituencies are the other agencies, the heads and organized bureaucracies of Service, Regulatory, and Input departments. Line agencies in particular are often forced to come as supplicants to overhead officials, and this has a tendency to lead to competition and animosity. Officials of the line are likely to become deeply involved with the overhead appointments. Nongovernmental groups must in large part depend on their access to the line agencies for any influence with overhead officials. Otherwise, influence can be exercised only at the very top through the Board of Estimate, which has final say on both the Expense and Capital Budgets, through the Mayor himself, or—especially on personnel policy—through Albany. One group, the Citizens Budget Commission, enjoys special direct access to the Budget Bureau (Expense Budget) and City Planning Commission (Capital Budget), but this is largely because of the CBC's reputation for activity only on behalf of efficiency, economy, and rationality of government structure.

Of all areas of governmental activity, overhead was lowest by far in personal continuity, and the survival value of these commissioners within an administration was also the cheapest (see Tables 6.7 and 6.8). No more than 22 per cent of the overhead commissioners ever survived a change of administration. In the later period, of the thirteen reappointments recorded, six are accounted for by only two men.[26] Budget Director Thomas J. Patterson (1943–1952) survived one Fusion-Democratic transition and one Democratic one. Frederick Zurmuhlen, appointed Public Works Commissioner in 1947, survived one relatively peaceful and one stormy transition of Democratic mayors. Thus, in actuality only eight individuals in overhead posts survived their appointing Mayor. Those who have survived have ordinarily done so through protective alliances with the Board of Estimate.

The constituencies of some overhead agencies are complicated by strong governmental as well as nongovernmental participants.[27] And personal continuity of overhead commissioners varies according to which type of participant is predominant: (1) Overhead agencies with strong *line* functions develop strong nongovernmental constituencies, and these overhead commissioners have extremely high personal continuity. (2) Conversely, in overhead agencies with predominantly overhead functions and, therefore, *intra*governmental constituencies, the commissioners are associated with much lower personal continuity.

On the City Planning Commission, for instance, continuity has been extremely high. Since its inception in 1938 the terms of very few of its members have been allowed to expire without at least one reappointment. Personal continuity on the Art Commission has been even higher. Both agencies deal primarily with nongovernmental groups—for example, real estate developers, architects, and artists—even though their decisions are essentially overhead—the Capital Budget and the aesthetic clearance of all public works, respectively. In contrast, the Civil Service Commission, with its intragovernmental constituency, is at the very bottom of the continuity scale.[28] During the early parts of the century, continuity on the Civil Service Commission was quite high, despite the fact that until 1922 the commissioners could be removed at the pleasure of the Mayor. This was a period of civil service consolidation as well as services and welfare consolidation. The Mayor and commissioners were beset from all sides by the parties and the reformers. Once the merit system was established and the bureaucracies themselves became the most important participants in civil service politics, the fight became internalized.[29]

Continuity dropped to virtually zero. Between 1933 and 1957, only one commissioner succeeded himself in office, and his reappointments were by the same Mayor. This was Ferdinand Q. Morton, the Negro member, who was reappointed once by La Guardia in 1938 and again in 1944.

NOTES

1. The Tenure Ratio is computed by dividing accumulated months of service in the same job for a commissioner or the average of a class of commissioners by the months of service of the appointing Mayor. For example, Robert Moses served a total of 286 months (through 1957) as Parks Commissioner. His tenure under La Guardia was 144 months; under O'Dwyer, 204; Impellitteri, 250; and Wagner, 288. His Tenure Ratio was 100, 340, 694, and 600 respectively.

2. The Walker Administration lasted 84 months. The average tenure in his Cabinet was 64.3 months, average tenure ratio 76.5 per cent. For non-Party group Leaders in the cabinet the average tenure ratio was between 43 and 49 per cent.

3. See Second Hoover Commission, *Report on Civil Service and Personnel*.

4. All fixed-tenure posts have been eliminated from Table 6.2 because the longer life-expectancy associated with them is due to legal protections, not politics. For the same reason, the Van Wyck Administration (1898–1901) had to be eliminated because the 1897 Charter granted the Mayor power of

removal at pleasure only for the first six months of his term, after which no Department head could be removed without cause.

5. The average Tenure Ratio of Wagner's cabinet was 105.2 in his first term.

6. Cf. Sayre and Kaufman, *op. cit.*, p. 691: "[La Guardia] made the fewest concessions to administrative autonomy, viewed his department heads with a skepticism bordering on suspicion, breathed down their necks with his close supervision, and was ferociously impatient with default. . . . the administrative agencies were his mere instruments." McClellan's instability was a result of his second-term break with Tammany Hall. McClellan "made the strongest effort of any Democratic Mayor to assert his dominance over the party leaders" (p. 696).

7. *Ibid.*, p. 693.

8. The Tenure Ratio is to a certain extent an index of continuity, for appointees who serve even longer than their appointing Mayor raise average Tenure Ratios of future cabinets in which they serve. However, the cabinet *average* masks the full extent of continuity because the long-tenure holdovers are averaged in with the short termers. Thus, in this section I deal *only* with the holdovers, the nature and extent of *reappointment*. This is *personal* continuity.

9. This table includes *only* those appointees serving at the pleasure of the Mayor. Continuity is, of course, much greater when the fixed term offices are included: Compare Table 6.3 with Table 6.4.

10. Actually there is some double-counting in Table 6.3 and later tables on continuity. For example, if a man served under Van Wyck, Low, *and* McClellan, he was tallied under Low as a holdover from Van Wyck and from Low. This was necessary to get a full profile of continuity, and is not inconsistent since we are using the appointment, not the individual, as the unit.

11. Proportion of nontenure appointees who were reappointed after service under previous mayors (from Table 6.3):

Mayor	Number of Nontenure Appointees	Per Cent Reappointments
Low	37	8
McClellan	96	9
Gaynor	51	20
Mitchel	53	21
Hylan	98	10
Walker	75	32
O'Brien	47	89
La Guardia	115	11
O'Dwyer	81	11
Impellitteri	51	50
Wagner	60	48

12. Here all cabinet members are included, those serving at the pleasure of the Mayor *and* those whose terms are fixed by law with removal only for cause, the "tenure" posts.

13. Proportion of *all* appointees who were reappointed after service under previous mayors (from Table 6.3) :

Mayor	Number of Appointees	Per Cent Reappointments
Low	93	3
McClellan	160	13
Gaynor	95	42
Mitchel	94	29
Hylan	119	17
Walker	90	50
O'Brien	50	90
La Guardia	170	8
O'Dwyer	108	16
Impellitteri	62	56
Wagner	86	58

14. E.g., Board of Education members serve for seven-year terms and cannot be removed before then without legal proceedings; members of the Civil Service Commission and the Board of Standards and Appeals serve under the same conditions for six years.

15. Mayor O'Brien is an exceptional case, his one-year term being merely a holding operation.

16. Cf. Second Hoover Commission, *op. cit., passim.*

17. The distributions on Table 6.5 are not materially changed by different periodization. Presentation for every cabinet would have been too complicated, and the small numbers in each category produce highly variable percentages. However, several different time periods were experimented with, and the resulting distributions were very close to those presented on Table 6.5.

18. Cf. George Belknap, "A Plan for Research on the Socio-Political Dynamics of Metropolitan Areas," SSRC paper (mimeo.), August 1957; Nelson W. Polsby, "The Sociology of Community Power: A Reassessment," *Social Forces,* vol. 37 (1959), pp. 232-236; and Robert A. Dahl, *Who Governs?,* Yale University Press, New Haven, 1961.

19. "Power and Community Structure," *Midwest Journal of Political Science,* vol. IV (1960), p. 393.

20. Departments were categorized according to what appeared to be their primary function. Except for the Health Department—in which case the Commissioner was classified under Services and Welfare and the Board under Regulation and Property Protection—each Department was placed in a single category. For example, the Department of Markets directly operates a number of enterprises, but its primary function is regulation of all City markets. The new Labor Department performs both regulatory and overhead functions under the "Little Wagner Act," but the weight of its activity falls heavily upon the latter. (Cf. Sayre and Kaufman, *op. cit.,* pp. 387-390.)

21. *Ibid.,* p. 212.

22. The development of the neutral, professional administrator in this arena, as shown in the next chapter, is roughly analogous to the emergence of the neutral Speaker in the British House of Commons, a position that developed along with disciplined Government and Opposition parties (Cf. Carl Friedrich,

Constitutional Government and Democracy, Ginn & Co., Boston, 1950, rev. ed., pp. 309-311).

23. Cf. Peter Rossi, "Power and Community Structure," *op. cit.,* p. 396.

24. Sayre and Kaufman, *op. cit.,* p. 351.

25. *Ibid.,* p. 393.

26. Due to the double counting explained in a note to Table 6.3. For example, Budget Director Patterson, having served under three Mayors, was tallied as follows: Reappointment No. 1—O'Dwyer from La Guardia; No. 2—Impellitteri from La Guardia; and No. 3—Impellitteri from O'Dwyer.

27. Of course this is a matter of degree, but to heads of overhead agencies the distinction is important (Cf. Sayre and Kaufman, *op. cit.,* pp. 354-355).

28. The three agencies mentioned above are headed by commissioners with fixed terms and, hence, are not included in Tables 6.7 and 6.8. However, even here great differences emerge when we control for type of constituency.

29. Cf. Sayre and Kaufman, *op. cit.,* p. 385.

CHAPTER 7

ARENAS OF POWER II:

ATTRIBUTE CONTINUITY

WHAT IS PUBLIC HEALTH, ANYWAY?

ON MARCH 4, 1946, Mayor William O'Dwyer announced the choice of Dr. Edward Bernecker for Commissioner of Health, ignoring the report of a special committee he had named to recommend candidates to succeed Dr. Ernest Stebbins, the outgoing commissioner. The Chairman of this special committee was Dr. Thomas Parran, United States Surgeon General, and the committee was made up of prominent public health people from all over the country. O'Dwyer had objected that their recommendations did not have any City service experience, and to find an alternative he had consulted with representatives of the five County medical societies of the City, who had hailed Bernecker's candidacy.

Dr. Stebbins, who had agreed to stay on until July 1, resigned immediately in protest, and several civic and public health groups joined him in damning Bernecker's appointment as a violation of the City Charter.[1]

Although Bernecker was installed on March 4, the protest continued. All parties praised Dr. Bernecker's long career as a hospital administrator and his service under La Guardia and O'Dwyer as Hospital Commissioner, but the public head groups found him unacceptable as a Health Commissioner. The City Board of Health, with Bernecker presiding for the first time, adopted a formal resolution condemning his appointment. The Board was led by former (Mitchel administration) Health Commissioner Haven Emerson. The public health relations committee of the New York Academy of Medicine also formerly protested on the grounds that hospital administration in no way qualified a man in public health.

On March 12,[2] O'Dwyer, "visibly upset" after a long conference with Emerson and other members of the Board of Health, defended Bernecker and informed the press that his Corporation Counsel had found the appointment legal. He added, however, that the appointment had been understood to be temporary. Quietly, copies of the biography of Deputy Health Commissioner Israel Weinstein were being widely circulated around City Hall.

On March 13, nine days after his appointment, Bernecker submitted his letter of resignation in which he said that he did not want "public confidence to be undermined in one of the most important departments of city government such as resulted from the statements issued yesterday by the Board of Health and the public health relations committee of the Academy of Medicine, *for the purpose of establishing the principle of administration on behalf of the professional public health groups of the country.*"[3]

Following Bernecker's resignation[4] many statements were made pro and con: James J. Lyons, a Democratic Leader and Bronx Borough President, announced that he had planned to get a Board of Estimate resolution endorsing Bernecker and condemning the "unfair criticism or hysteria on the part of the organized professionals."[5] On March 19th, the Coordinating Council of Medical Societies "representing 15,000 practicing physicians" in New York City, praised Bernecker and deplored "the activity of any special groups or interests which would seek to obtain an appointment which might be to their own advantage."[6]

The story of Bernecker is worthy of detailed treatment because it so well illustrates the existence and workings of the participants in the appointment process. For long periods interests and claims on their behalf may remain either dormant or hidden from public view. But their quiescence is often related to their success. Mayors anticipate the interests of other leaders much of the time; but just when a mayor might begin to feel he is on

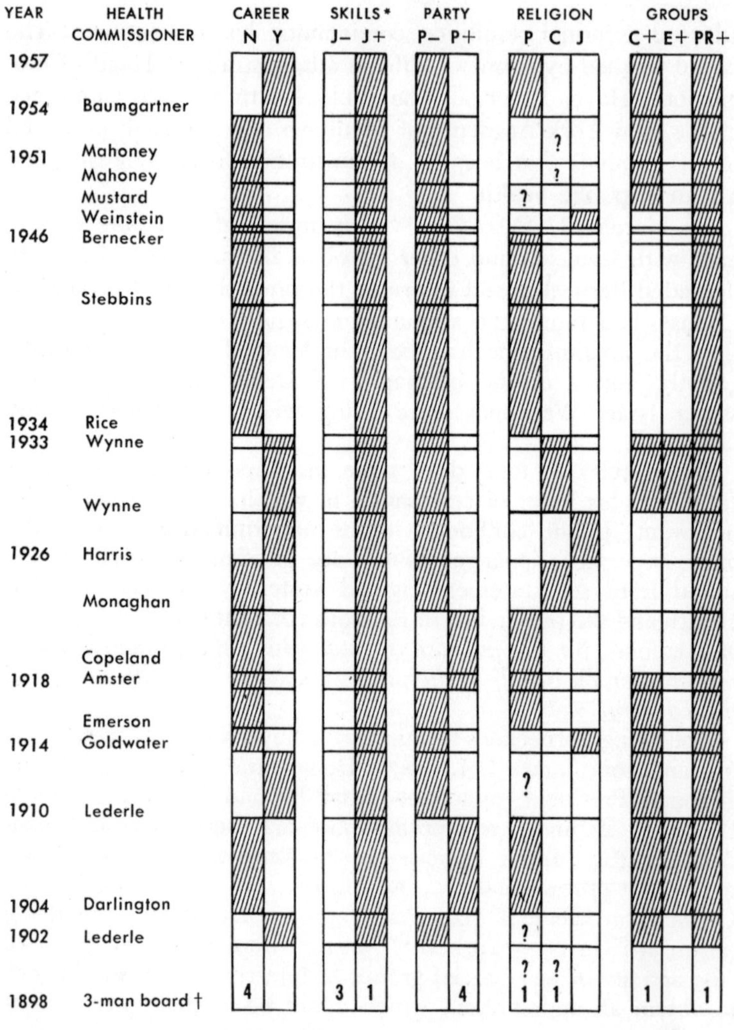

YEAR	HEALTH COMMISSIONER	CAREER N Y	SKILLS* J– J+	PARTY P– P+	RELIGION P C J	GROUPS C+ E+ PR+
1957						
1954	Baumgartner					
1951	Mahoney				?	
	Mahoney				?	
	Mustard				?	
	Weinstein					
1946	Bernecker					
	Stebbins					
1934	Rice					
1933	Wynne					
	Wynne					
1926	Harris					
	Monaghan					
	Copeland					
1918	Amster					
	Emerson					
1914	Goldwater					
1910	Lederle				?	
1904	Darlington					
1902	Lederle				?	
1898	3-man board †	4	3 1	4	? ? 1 1	1 1

*Job-oriented skill required after 1938.
†Four commissioners served 1898-1902.

Figure 7.1 Attribute Continuity of Health Commissioners, 1898–1957

top of things, he violates expectations and activity begins again. Indeed, the Bernecker case shows how nice the distinctions can become; egregious departures from the norm are not always necessary. Also, the Bernecker case shows how close to complete has been the capturing (i.e., the establishment of the "job image") of the Health Commissionership by the professional public health groups.

To many groups, the *attributes* of commissioners are more important than the commissioners. And all participants in the appointments process identify candidates by the characteristics most salient to them. Participants lose very little in transactions with the Mayor if "their man" is replaced by another who bears the identical stamp.[7] One of the familiar strategies of participants is the "creation of a 'job image.'"[8] The "capturing" of a post—restriction of the field of candidates to one exclusive type of person—results in an enormous and continuing advantage in access to a department's decisions. The prevailing attributes vary from one arena to the next and depend largely upon what types of leaders have the best access. The degree of attribute continuity—with "capturing" the limiting case—depends upon the stability of the coalitions of support.

ARENAS AND ATTRIBUTES

ATTRIBUTE CONTINUITY IN THE SERVICES AND WELFARE ARENA

There is no hard-and-fast pattern among commissioners in this area, but some strong similarities do appear. Of these, perhaps the most conspicuous is the absence of party recruitment. Prior to La Guardia, party appointees held these posts once in a while; since La Guardia the party attribute no longer appears (Figures 7.1–7.4, Party column). One exception, Benjamin Fielding, was transferred from his License Commissionership for a temporary, five-month stint as Welfare Commissioner. Afterwards, he returned to his post as License Commissioner, relieving the acting Commissioner there.

Skill is certainly a predominant value in this area, but it is remarkable how few commissioners have been recruited from the departmental career ranks. All of these Departments are highly professionalized; even the Sanitation Department has a kind of professional ritual at the management level.[9] In the past

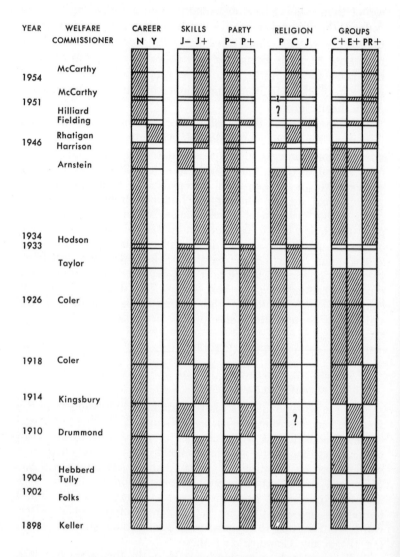

Figure 7.2 Attribute Continuity of Welfare Commissioners

generation, Health Commissioners have come primarily from University Public Health schools and Welfare Commissioners from welfare societies and State or Federal welfare positions. Perhaps there has been more career recruitment in Sanitation and Hospitals because there the accent is on the management of publicly owned enterprises, whereas in the former, the accent is on the dispensation of funds.

Table 7.1 Balancing of Religions in Three Service Departments: Religious Affiliations of Commissioners, 1934–1957

	Welfare	Health	Hospitals
Wagner (1954–1957)	C	P	P, J
Impellitteri (1951–1953)	C	C?	J
O'Dwyer (1946–1950)	C, J, P?	P, J, P?, C?	P, P, J
La Guardia (1934–1945)	P, J, P	P, P, P	J, P, P

One further reason why it has been so often necessary to go outside the departmental bureaucracies, or even outside the City, is the special stake that local religious groups have in this area, again particularly Health and Welfare. The religion pattern strongly suggests "capturing" not by a single religious group but perhaps "capturing" by religions (see Figures 7.1–7.4 and Table 7.1).[10] Except for the Hospitals Department, there has

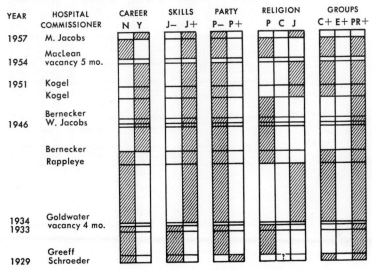

Figure 7.3 Attribute Continuity of Hospital Commissioners

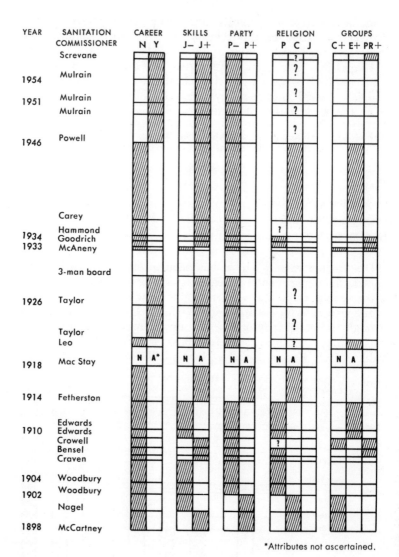

*Attributes not ascertained.

Figure 7.4 Attribute Continuity of Sanitation Commissioners

been a considerable amount of equal alternation and exchange between incumbent and replacement in each Department. Second, there seems to have been an attempt to strike a balance of major religions in the Welfare, Health, and Hospital Departments. Apparently, if a Catholic is appointed Welfare Commissioner, Protestant and Jewish interests have a somewhat stronger claim upon the other two commissionerships. Of course, the pattern is not as precise or as stable as that on the Board of Education. But a minimum of balance at least is maintained. Only once were all three of these Departments headed by men of the same religion, and that situation existed just for a brief period at the end of La Guardia's last term. Sanitation is almost completely a Catholic property, but if so, it is probably due to the willingness of Irish and Italian laborers of the 1930's and before to use that Department as a channel of mobility. Except for Sanitation, almost all commissioners were prominent in their respective professional societies. The only ones who were not were the party commissioners during the Walker period.

REGULATION AND PROPERTY PROTECTION

In the uniformed Departments the organized career bureaucracies play a vitally important role. However, they have far from succeeded in capturing the commissionerships (Figures 7.5, 7.6). Capture of the Police Commissionership might well be an established fact at this writing, with the replacement of Commissioner Kennedy by another police careerist. But another scandal of the order of that in the O'Dwyer period might break this continuity. A sudden increase of public scrutiny has a tendency to throw a commissionership out of the hands associated with the scandal and back again closer to the Mayor. Murphy, Monaghan, and Adams were experienced law enforcement officials but had not been policemen. They were drawn from the immediate followings of Impellitteri and Wagner.[11]

In the entire sixty-year period, only three Fire Commissioners have been careerists in the Department. Also, only five were specialists $(J+)$; two of these served under La Guardia. In contrast, practically every Police Commissioner was a specialist, most of them having served in the Police Department or a District Attorney's office. Group recruitment is rare in both Departments.

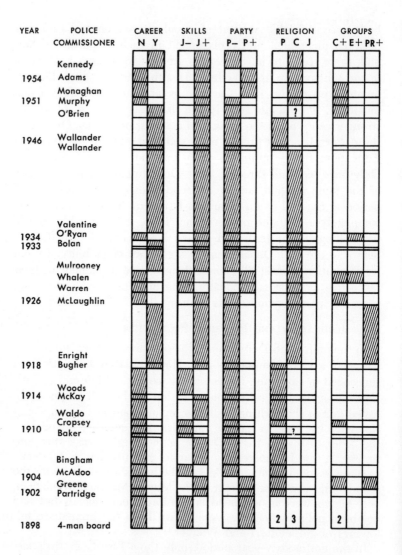

Figure 7.5 Attribute Continuity of Police Commissioners

In many respects, Sanitation and Fire Commissioners have a great deal in common, probably because both Departments have thousands of employees who can be used for party purposes and because Fire is more a service agency than Police. With the exceptions of La Guardia and Impellitteri, whose Fire Commissioner was installed in the aftermath of scandal, there has been a fairly strong tradition of political Fire Commissioners. Political backgrounds are indeed scarce in the Sanitation Commissionership, but many of them have been coopted for political purposes once in office. This was true of Mulrain, who was a strong contender for the Queens County Democratic Leadership after retirement, and of Screvane, who became a 1961 running mate of Wagner—perhaps because of Wagner's desperate need for an organizational arm in his insurgent battle for renomination. Even Grumet, Impellitteri's "nonpolitical" Fire Commissioner, became close to the inner core of City Hall not long after his appointment. In contrast, the Police Department was long ago insulated from overt political activity by a "Little Hatch Act."

There is little "lateral entry" in any of the uniformed Departments. The lines of promotion extend from the lowest rank clear to the top. However, the discrepancies that can be found among commissioners, and the particular similarities that can be found, strongly suggest that at the top *the similarities of attributes that follow from like forms of organization are not so many as the variations deriving from differences in activities and constituencies.* In many respects, for example, Sanitation Commissioners follow Service Department patterns; in other respects, Sanitation and Fire belong together in a separate category.

Two nonuniformed regulatory Departments, License and Buildings, are clearly illustrative of the relationships of the appointment pattern to the functions and constituencies of Departments. Prior to La Guardia, the party held a tight grip on the commissionerships of both these Departments (Figures 7.7, 7.8). In recent years, the party hold on the Buildings Department has been completely broken. From 1933 to 1957 the only party-recruited Buildings Commissioner was Robert F. Wagner, Jr., who held the post for a few months early in O'Dwyer's first

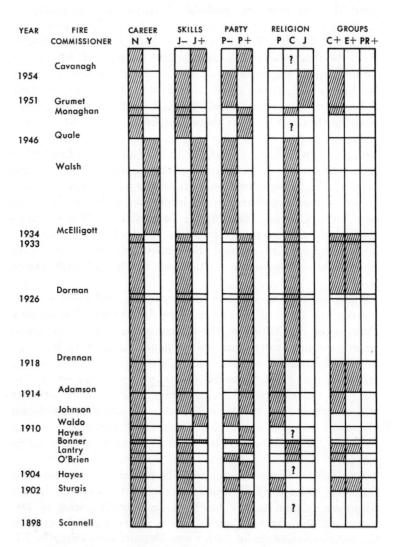

Figure 7.6   Attribute Continuity of Fire Commissioners

term. Career recruitment has become a pronounced attribute, and skill values have prevailed for all but a few years. In contrast, party control of the License Commissionership has been unbroken, even during the La Guardia period. Career recruitment is entirely absent, and specialists held the office for about half the time only.

What of the comparative functions of the two? The Departments of Buildings is responsible for enforcing the State Multiple Dwellings Law and City's Building Code, which set the standards of building and maintaining all dwellings above one- and two-family houses. This requires constant and highly skilled surveillance, and most deputies and inspectors are required by law to be trained for the tasks. Constantly, the commissioner and his assistants must be prepared for appeals to the Board of Standards and Appeals. In contrast, licensing under the Department of License is primarily a one-shot affair. If a barber or restaurateur shows evidence of reliable character and has the wherewithal to file a surety bond (as he does in most cases), the matter is settled. Licensing involves large numbers of small, relatively obscure decisions, and the dispensation of this form of low-liability patronage has become more and more important as the parties have lost patronage in jobs. A license is a permit to do what is otherwise prohibited, and a license means money to the recipient. Since licenses are susceptible to manipulation, they make good currency for political transactions. Party organizations have a great stake in the License Commissionership, so great that they have held on here despite retreats in many other areas.

Overhead

When the Budget Bureau and the Department of Purchase were still new agencies in the 1920s, the heads of both agencies were party functionaries. After the earliest appointments, the bureaucracies became professionalized and the top posts were captured by skill groups. Party recruitment in the overhead agencies has been almost eliminated. Long-time Budget Director Abraham Beame became active in Democratic affairs after his appointment, but it cannot be said that he was party-recruited. Such cooptation of sitting commissioners like Beame,

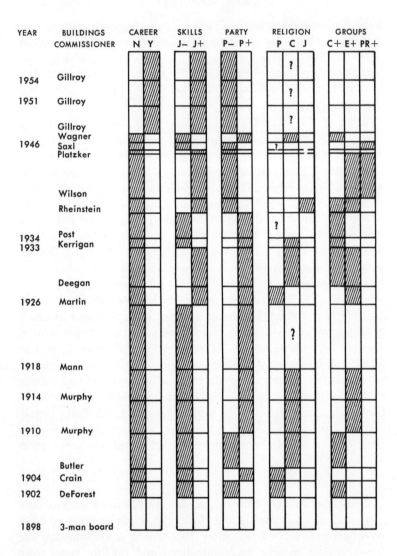

Figure 7.7 Attribute Continuity of Buildings Commissioners

Mulrain, Grumet, and Screvane is probably not a regular occurrence, but there are some known and probably more unknown cases.

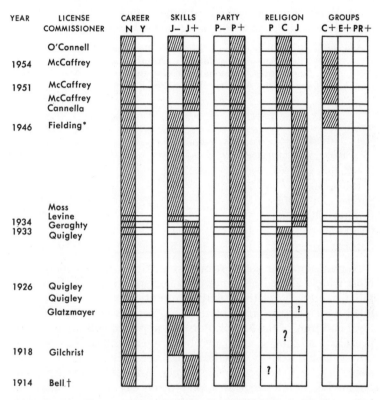

*Fielding left the office vacant five months while serving as Welfare Commissioner.
†Created by state law early in 1914. Commissionership filled June 1914.

Figure 7.8 Attribute Continuity of License Commissioners

Very few overhead commissioners were departmental careerists, but almost all were specialists in the work of their Department (Figures 7.9–7.11). Corporation Counsels are typically
party functionaries and, far more than the others, prominent in
civic, economic, or professional groups. Other overhead commissioners have not been so deeply involved in community affairs.
As in Washington, it seems least important for overhead officials
and advisers to bring a following to their jobs.

Table 7.2   **Appointees Known to Have Personal Relationship with
Their Appointing Mayor: Number and Per Cent of All
Nontenure "Personal" Appointments, by Area of Gov-
ernmental Activity, 1902–1957**

	1902–1933		1934–1957	
Area	Number of Nontenure Personal Appointments	Per Cent of All Nontenure Appointments	Number of Nontenure Personal Appointments	Per Cent of All Nontenure Appointments
Regulation and Protection	26	26	9	16
Service and Welfare	13	12	7	13
Government Input	9	9	5	8
Overhead	16	11	18	14
"Strictly" overhead	12	18	16	38

Notwithstanding some strong similarities already noted, the
most widely shared attribute does not appear on the Figures in
this Chapter: A relatively large proportion of overhead posts is
filled with *personal appointments,* appointees who were friends,
loyal and true, of the Mayor. Personal appointments are especially
prevalent in the "strictly" overhead agencies.[12] Of all areas of
governmental activity, overhead has been highest for a generation. In the O'Dwyer and Wagner Administrations, personal
outnumbered nonpersonal appointments six to four. This pattern, of course, varies with the commissioner's ability to make
alliances in aid of his resistance to changes of Administration—
reappointments are seldom, if ever, "personal" appointments.
Budget Director Beame's tenacity, for instance, derived in large
part from his skill in playing the Board of Estimate against the
Mayor.

GOVERNMENTAL INPUT

Governmental Input is the party enclave. In every administration this area had the highest proportion of party functionaries.

While the party was suffering an extreme decline in the other three areas, the proportion of functionaries and Leaders in this area stayed at the three-quarter mark (Table 7.3). Shifting the definition of party recruitment to include club *members,* the

Table 7.3 Party-Recruited, Nontenure Appointments by Area of Governmental Activity (Leaders and Functionaries Only)

Area	I (1902–1933) Per Cent	Ranking	II (1934–1957) Per Cent	Ranking	Net Per Cent Changes
Regulation	65	2	40	2	— 25
Services	65	3	24	4	— 41
Input	83	1	71	1	— 12
Overhead	48	4	38	3	— 10

party decline in three of the areas is even more extreme; but in the Input area, party recruitment accounted for over 90 per cent of all appointments in both periods (see Table 7.4).

Table 7.4 Party-Recruited, Nontenure Appointments by Area of Governmental Activity (Leaders, Functionaries, *and* Club Members)

Area	I (1902–1933) Per Cent	Ranking	II (1934–1957) Per Cent	Ranking	Net Per Cent Changes
Regulation	77	3	41	3	— 36
Service	80	2	29	4	— 51
Input	91	1	90	1	— 1
Overhead	59	4	44	2	— 15

On the Board of Assessors, party recruitment has declined slightly, very slightly relative to other areas. Party recruitment of Tax Commissioners has actually increased. Finally, the Treasurer, heading the third Inputs agency, was captured by the party after La Guardia's initial nonparty appointment.[13] Many new agencies tend to start out in party hands and then tò fall away from the party into the hands of the clientele groups;[14] but this is a pattern resisted by the Department of Finance, an Input agency.

Governmental Input is an area of party monopoly because it is an area in which small favors to the loyal constituents and donors can still be granted. The stakes in this area are similar to those in the Department of Licenses. Unlike welfare activities, the assessment of property for taxes cannot be precise and ac-

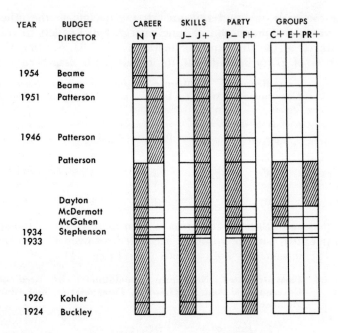

Figure 7.9   Attribute Continuity of Budget Directors

cording to established formulas. Input decisions remain *ad hoc*, unsystematic, and discretionary. Under the Charter, the Tax Commission appraises the value of real property and reviews and corrects assessments. Its decisions are subject to review only by costly court procedures. The Board of Assessors controls most assessments for public improvements and settles claims for damages caused by public improvements. Literally thousands of valuations and assessments are made every year. A little slack here, a little more sternness there—all this is possible with so many variables to manipulate. Patronage opportunities here are of great importance to the party—all the more so because of the capturing of jobs by the merit system from below, interest groups from above, and new, hostile values all around.

FOUR POLITICAL PROCESSES: A SUMMARY

Tenure, personal continuity, and attribute continuity or discontinuity among commissioners reflect some real differences in the four areas of governmental activity. In effect they constitute four arenas of politics, each possibly having a distinct power structure. These differences are determined very largely by the great differences in the impact of the types of decisions made in each area. From these patterns at least two general hypotheses can be proposed:

1. The nature and form of the political process is related to the degree to which the typical decision in the arena approximates class cleavages in the total community. In this, for example, we found a plausible explanation of the observed differences in personal continuity—the probability of reappointment—between the Services and Input arenas on the one hand and the Regulatory arena on the other. A similar difference in the structure of arenas might be noted at the national level between the redistributive area and the distributive ("pork barrel") area,[15] or between regulatory and fiscal activities.

2. The nature of the political process is related to the amount of discretion available to officials in a Department: Where *policy* values prevail, continuity tends to be low; the Chief Executive tends to choose his commissioners from his own immediate cadre. Where *administration* values are dominant, personal continuity, skills, and professionalism tend to be high.[16] Access tends to be more centralized and more formal. Every effort is made to "objectify" policy in formulas and general rules.

These two hypotheses are of course interrelated. Service and Input agencies become so involved with their highly organized constituencies that political peace often demands administrative continuity over policy considerations. This is perhaps why most welfare policies have emanated from Albany and Washington, where a multiplicity of groups with dispersed geographical bases might tend to neutralize each other. Groups with favored access to an incumbent commissioner attempt to maintain that access by maintaining that commissioner. In the *redistributive* agencies, Services and Welfare and Input, large groups and stable alliances make this possible to so define the needs of the job that reappointment of the incumbent, *or a man just like him,* becomes the Mayor's most satisfactory alternative.

In the *Services and Welfare* arena, party recruitment suffered its most precipitous decline. There was an equivalent rise in personal continuity. Skills and religious attribute continuity were pronounced. There are not yet any tendencies toward depart-

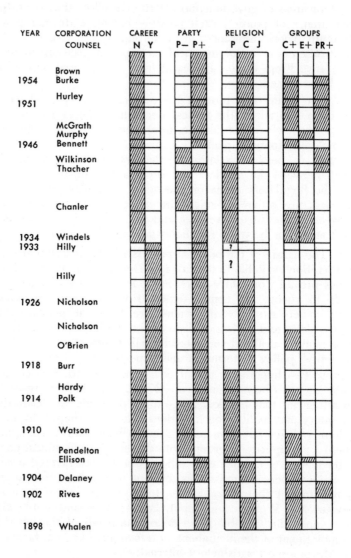

Figure 7.10 Attribute Continuity of Corporation Counsels

mental career recruitment, but New York is perhaps fortunate
in having developed quite early a tradition of professionalism
in these agencies.

Governmental service and welfare on a mass scale is a relatively recent phenomenon. The dispensation of these services,
especially because of their redistributive nature, led to the establishment of new clientele and, as it were, anticlientele groups,
and the situation quickly stabilized as an arena of large and effective group alliances and peak associations. During the early period
of consolidation of these agencies, personal continuity was low.
At present, as a matter of defense, Mayors typically turn to
"administration" values as the *sine qua non* of good appointment
strategy.

In the *Regulatory* arena, party leaders learned after great trial
and greater error that political control involved quite as many
liabilities as assets: Reform has had a way of spreading especially
from police scandals. Variation has been the rule, but it is a
type of variation associated with the nature of the stakes involved and with the kind of leadership and group structure of
the arena. In this arena, discretion tends to be highly decentralized and widely shared. This, combined with highly specific
rules and orders, tends to particularize the political struggle.
As a result, the steady insulation of the Party from the upper
reaches of this arena was accompanied by the rise of departmental career and/or skill attributes. Tenure and personal continuity are both low. Following scandal, commissionerships are
more likely to be drawn from the Mayor's immediate cadre.
Because of the special stakes involved, the License Department
is a special case.

The *Overhead* arena was characterized by low tenure and
personal continuity and the prevalence of "personal" appointments. Most of these commissioners are specialists; except for
Corporation Counsels, they are seldom prominent in party or
civic circles. "Policy" values prevail. The relationships between
agencies and constituency organization—the tendency toward
development of distinct arenas—appeared especially clear by the
differences between strictly overhead agencies and those exposed to nongovernmental leaders through the performance of
line functions.

The *Governmental Input* area, because of the susceptibility
of its decisions to manipulation, showed itself to be the last

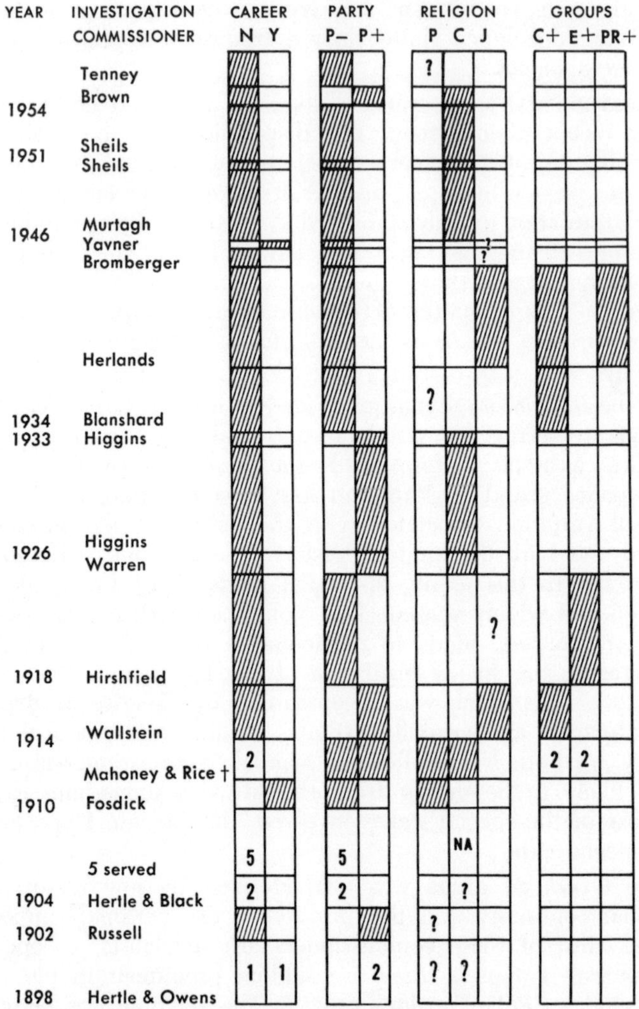

Figure 7.11 Attribute Continuity of Investigation Commissioners

*Known earlier as Commissioner of Accounts.
†The Mayor was empowered to appoint two commissioners
to serve simultaneously.

enclave of Party. Like the Regulatory arena, great discretion is possible, but unlike Regulatory decisions, Input decisions, like pork barrel, can more often be indulgences rather than deprivations. In such a case, decisions are more likely to be obscure; opposition groups are less likely to organize for purposes of exposing these transactions.[17] Continuity is high, but this more than likely results from long periods of Democratic rule. However, Wagner's re-election in 1961 is likely to alter this temporarily.

Political history and process take on much more precise meanings in the context of governmental functions, activities, and arenas. Indeed the party monopoly has been broken, perhaps forever. However, the concomitant developments of professionalism and pluralism have been uneven and specialized.

Trends are not steady; the positions of the participants vary. A sampling of leadership at any one point in time, regardless of rigid controls and good theory, does not reveal power structure. Trends are also specialized, so that both history *and* control are necessary. In three of the arenas examined, the development of pluralism has been clear but at different rates and with greatly different consequences. In one the field is limited to giants, in effect the executive committees of the bourgeoisie and proletariat. In another, everyman is a group unto himself. In still another, the power structure is contained, although not hermetically sealed, within the governmental structure, with bargaining primarily among formal power holders. In the fourth area, party monopoly remains very much as it was in the days of Van Wyck.

NOTES

1. "The Commissioner (1) shall be a doctor of medicine or the holder of a degree in public health. . . ., and (2) shall have had at least eight years' experience either in public health administration or in college or university public health teaching or in both" (Section 551).

2. *The New York Times* (March 13, 1946), p. 31.

3. *The New York Times* (March 14, 1946), p. 1. Emphasis added.

4. He was reappointed Commissioner of Hospitals.

5. *The New York Times* (March 14, 1946), p. 26.

6. *The New York Times* (March 20, 1946).

7. Since no two men are exactly alike their "identity" becomes a matter of the observer's definition. The terms and conditions of identity in this chapter are those characteristics employed all along. I have taken these characteristics as the ones most typically involved in appointment transactions. A successful transaction involves, if not a specific person, the characteristic(s) most salient to a given participant.

8. Cf. Sayre and Kaufman, *op. cit.*, p. 225.

9. Job-oriented skills are represented by J+, departmental career recruitment by "Y" in the Career Column.

10. In several cases guesses had to be made, which are signified by question marks in the appropriate box. These were not wild guesses but approximations based on fairly good circumstantial evidence in the absence of explicit identification.

11. It is also worth noting that the career commissioner tends to last a good deal longer than the others.

12. "Strictly" overhead refers to agencies whose constituencies are almost exclusively governmental; i.e., Budget, Personnel, Deputy Mayor, City Administrator, Law, and Investigations. The figures on Table 7.2 are on the low side because they are expressed as percentages of a total in each area that included "nonpersonal" and "relationship not ascertained." Appointments were not counted as "personal" unless biographies and reports so stated.

13. Three of the City Treasurers since 1946 were prominently associated with the Party prior to appointment.

14. E.g., The first Chief Medical Examiner, Budget Director, and Commissioners of Purchase and Hospitals were party-recruited.

15. Cf. especially Arthur Maass, "Congress and Water Resources," *American Political Science Review*, vol. XVIV, no. 3 (1950); and Steven K. Bailey, *Congress Makes A Law*, Columbia University Press, New York, 1950.

16. I do not intend to deny the assertion of Appleby and others that policy and administration are inseparable in practice. But it is possible to separate the two for analytical purposes. Policy and administration are independent functions, and they are combined in different degrees depending on the amount of supervision, specificity of command, and so forth. Those who insist that the two functions are inseparable usually accept the legal distinction between "discretionary" and "ministerial" responsibility.

17. Cf. Arthur Maass, *op cit.*, *passim*.

CHAPTER 8

THE REFORM CYCLE

THE RHYTHM OF REFORM

SETH LOW

BETWEEN 1898 AND 1902 politics had come to such a pretty pass in New York City that Boss Richard Croker could run the City's business from his estates in England. City Democracy had survived Consolidation and the new Charter, and Croker had chosen an ideal puppet Mayor. Robert Van Wyck possessed superb family credentials, an irreproachable if unspectacular career, and an absolute loyalty to the organization. Republican State Boss Platt had failed in his attempt to inundate Manhattan's Tammany with hostile Brooklyn and independent Queens votes. The new City did not go Republican according to Platt's plans.

But what the voters of the new Greater City would not do, the State Legislature could and would do. In 1899 a Special Committee of the Assembly was formed to investigate City and County offices in New York. The Mazet Committee's underlying purpose was the destruction of the Croker machine. Boss Croker's testimony before this committee, unrivaled in its confident cynicism, served the committee's purposes very well:

MR. Moss: So we have it then, that you, participating in the selection of judges before election, participate in the emolument that comes . . . at the end of their judicial proceeding, namely, judicial sales.
MR. CROKER: Yes, sir.

MR. MOSS: And it goes into your pocket?

MR. CROKER: I get—that is part of my profit. . . .

MR. MOSS: Then you are working for your own pocket, are you not?

MR. CROKER: All the time, same as you.[1]

Another source of discontent came from the pulpit. Dr. Charles Parkhurst, minister of the Madison Square Presbyterian Church from 1880 to 1918, was a constant attacker of "Tammany." His evidence may not have been particularly reliable at times, but he was most effective in dramatizing those evils that were widely known and generally accepted. His sermons during the Van Wyck administration gave the Mazet findings special urgency.

None of the Mazet and Parkhurst revelations were new, and alone they would probably have altered the situation very little. But one new discovery made all the others suddenly more damning. The Mayor himself was revealed to be corrupt. Van Wyck was one of many Tammany politicians involved in the spectacular "ice scandal." [2]

By the summer of 1901 reform successes in getting a new Charter made Croker realize that defeat in the 1901 mayoral election was virtually certain.[3] In desperation, he accepted the nomination of Democratic independent Edward M. Shepard, a corporation lawyer from Brooklyn. But the die was cast. Croker's last strategem availed him little. City politics burst open with activity around the incorruptible former Brooklyn Mayor, Seth Low. The Republican-Fusion coalition was formed, bringing together all hitherto potential, widely dispersed opposition to the Democracy.[4] Reform was on its way in.

JOHN PURROY MITCHEL

The second reform wave swept in under extraordinary conditions. Progressivism was running rampant all over the country. The merit system and short ballot, the city manager, the direct election of Senators, and direct primaries were going to set public men on the straight and narrow path of public interest and resurrect a government by the people. More directly important to reform in New York in 1913 was Woodrow Wilson. As has happened so often, Tammany had backed the loser, Wilson's opponent Champ Clark, for the Presidential nomination. As a result, Wilson made every effort to inspire Boss Murphy's removal. This was one of many attempts by Presidents to dabble in New York City politics.

Without these national events it is certain that the second reform wave would have come somewhat later. For New York between 1910 and 1914 was enjoying one of its better Mayors, William Gaynor. In many respects, the pesky, unpredictable Judge Gaynor was already giving the City another taste of reform. Gaynor made extreme reductions in party appointments, broadened the merit system everywhere, and his appointments in the key posts were generally enlightened. In normal times his behavior could have sapped the strength of reform groups, but New York City was in the grips of a national, irresistible reform wave.

John Purroy Mitchel, New York's youngest Mayor, made his first headline as a Democratic appointee.[5] He had been elected President of the Board of Aldermen on the Democratic line and had served with Gaynor until his resignation in 1913, at which time he accepted a Wilson appointment as Collector of the Port of New York. The nomination of this young "independent Democrat" for Mayor was virtually forced upon the Republican party by the Fusionists.

Morale had never been higher for the elements of reform. And the Democracy was equally demoralized. Murphy's position was extremely weak (to be revived later, of course). The sensational murder of Herman Rosenthal and the later implication and execution of Police Lieutenant Charles Becker in 1911 and 1912 brought forth the formation of a New York Citizens' Committee, a step that typically precedes a City Fusion movement. Finally, in 1913 Murphy exposed himself by engineering the impeachment and conviction of Democratic and Tammany Governor William Sulzer. There were several futile attempts to depose Murphy;[6] and Gaynor, too, attempted to sever his relations completely from the Manhattan organization. Gaynor would have thrown the party into a bitter primary struggle[7] had not death, by a timely compliance, prevented him.

FIORELLO LA GUARDIA

New York's greatest mayor was also a product of reform; and, like Mitchel, his nomination was forced by Fusion upon an unhappy Republican organization. He was the personal choice of Samuel Seabury whose 1930–1931 investigations had rallied the third reform wave. Agitation for reform began soon after Mayor Walker's re-election in 1929. Walker's care for things other than the Mayoralty provided plenty of the grist so necessary for the reform mill. And the New York democracy had not yet recovered from Murphy's death in 1924; at the City level, the party was leaderless.

Men in power inevitably become associated with the ups and downs of the business cycle. And Walker, who enjoyed his celebrity but had no real will to power, made no effort to create an impression that he was fighting for solvency. Two years of legislative investigation, even more spectacular under Samuel Seabury than the 1900 Mazet Committee, administered the *coup de grace* to Walker. The Democrats won the 1932 special election, thus filling out the remainder of Walker's term; but, as Fusion grew, the Democracy began to crack. When Bronx Leader Ed Flynn deserted the party in 1933 and instead ran his own man on the Recovery Party line, he guaranteed a Fusion victory to save himself.

THE TWO SYSTEMS

Cyclical phenomena are not peculiar to economics. Some types of political and electoral behavior also move cyclically, sometimes related, sometimes unrelated, to the business cycle.[8] Political cycles may occur because " . . . the unlimited prosecution of group interests may meet a counter movement from people adversely affected."[9] When individuals and groups find the direction of public activity diverging increasingly from their preferences, " . . . there is increasing stress toward action on the part of the inactive participants [to redress the balance], and the cycle is completed."[10]

The political cycle in New York's history has been composed of alternations of two broad but distinctly identifiable systems: the traditional party system and the reform system. Were it not for long-range secular changes in political structure and complexion—the description of which has been a major part of this study—it might be said without qualification that the traditional party system and traditional political style are the norm, the reform system a sporadic exception. In fact, it is the sporadic nature of the reform movement that has given New York politics a most pronounced cyclical pattern.

No political activity better demonstrates the cyclical aspects of American politics than the urban reform cycles.[11] In it, one can observe many of the most important aspects of political behavior: the political generation, the alternating patterns of exhilaration and apathy and of issue orientation versus party orientation, the effects of charisma and habit, and so on. There is a continuing preference for the Democratic party in New York. No elaborate sample survey of the electorate is necessary to demonstrate the high Democratic "index of political predisposition." However, from time to time, a majority of voters shows preference for an *alternative to the party system itself*, in which case the choice is not between Democrat and Republican candidates but actually between organization and nonorganization government. A sample survey *that takes cycles into account* is likely to reveal a shift in the usual class, ethnic, religious, and other relationships to voting. And studies of community power that do not incorporate enough political history to control for cycles are most likely to uncover some quite misleading "structural" patterns. Political values and political power are not the same in reform as in party periods of control.

The purpose of this chapter is first to identify and contrast the salient features of the two types of political control. Second, since these two types are but phases in the history of the overall political system, and since party control is for all practical purposes the norm, it will be desirable to assess the effects of the reform periods on party government. This assessment is particularly important because of the significance of the reform movement for innovation in a City dominated by one party with strong tendencies toward conservatism both in political structure and recruitment and in public policy.

TRADITIONAL POLITICAL STYLE

The style of machine or organization politics in the City has been set by the immigrant, especially Irish, and that of Reform by the Yankee. These differences of style have been captured so well by Hofstadter that one can do no better than to quote him at length. Hofstadter found that two distinct political traditions have emerged in America:

One, founded on the indigenous Yankee-Protestant political traditions, and upon middle-class life, assumed and demanded the constant, disinterested activity of the citizen in public affairs, argued that political life ought to be run, to a greater degree than it was, in accordance with general principles and abstract law apart from and superior to personal needs, and expressed a common feeling that government should be in good part an effort to moralize the lives of individuals while economic life should be intimately related to the stimulation and development of individual character. The other system, founded upon the European backgrounds of immigrants, upon their unfamiliarity with political action, their familiarity with hierarchy and authority, and upon the urgent needs that so often grew out of their migration, took for granted that the political life of the individual would rise out of family needs, interpreted political and civic relations chiefly in terms of personal obligations, and placed strong personal loyalties above allegiance to abstract codes of law or morals. It was chiefly upon this system of values that the political life of the immigrant, the boss, the urban machine was based.[12]

There is more accuracy than invective in references to "Irish-Catholic in-group" control of the Democratic County organizations in the City. However, there are two important shortcomings to the appellation. First, of course, is the share of control enjoyed by leaders from other ethnic groups. Second is the only slightly lesser degree to which an in-group of quite similar composition and values also controls the Republican organizations. All traditional party organizations in the City have in common an in-group, communal, *gemeinschaft* basis of integration.[13] Through long-standing neighborhood contacts (although this is weakening), through the local political clubhouses, through the operational core of the party, and through a vague sense of common destiny that developed out of ethnic minority status, old-line party leaders, and functionaries, activists and fellow-travelers are held together by a set of personal, nonrational bonds. Many District organizations are in actual fact *bunde*, or at least fraternities, modern vestiges of the fraternal-convivial origins of Tammany Hall, the neighborhood gangs, the ghettos, and the self-defensive societies of new national groupings.

Some writers would offer the political party as an example of a *rationalistic* group. Schattschneider, for one, defines parties as "an organized attempt to get power . . . control of the government. The life of the parties revolves about the present possession of power or the bid for power, a bid made with the reasonable expectation that it will be successful at an early date." [14] Unquestionably this rationalistic element is present in the traditional system of New York, but it is only part, and not necessarily the largest part, of the cohesive stuff of the machine. Heberle has found a better approach in his argument that American parties are "combinations of texture types"—the spiritual community or fellowship, the *following* with its charismatic leaders and the rational association. That is, the "fellowships of friends" have a strong utilitarian tinge.[15] Much of the resiliency of parties in New York lies in the amoral, entrepreneurial bias of the Party Leaders that enables them to serve both licit and illicit interests in both licit and illicit relationships to the agencies of government. Holding the organization together and winning elections is put above any single policy or person. But there is more.

Communal or emotional identifications and rationalistic purposes are not incompatible. On the contrary. In the clubhouse they have proved to be mutually reinforcing. As cohesive forces, the sense of common past and common destiny has served better than the best ideology, policies, and formal organizational structure. These emotional and traditional ties have made the parties efficient instruments of conflict resolution and discipline. Bargaining among the fuedal chieftains, including bargaining *between* Democratic and Republican Leaders, has settled far more disputes over candidates than primaries and elections. For a regular to become an insurgent is to refuse to bargain in good faith; to take to the primaries is to take the dispute literally outside the family, which is virtually to leave the family forever through self-exile or ostracism: " . . . once a person who has been a member of the organization turns against it in a primary election, that person is forever barred from any political preferment." [16] Mr. Flynn is, of course, exaggerating. There are many cases where the successful insurgent, like Carmine DeSapio, is able to make his peace with the organization in-group. There are fewer, but still probably numerous, cases where even the defeated insurgent is allowed to return to the fold. In fact, a show of strength even in defeat can sometimes accelerate promotion in the party hierarchy. Nevertheless, Mr. Flynn was accurately describing what appear to be overall tendencies.

Ties to the local party organization are far stronger than those in organizations with more strictly rationalistic identifications. Clubs do not dissolve because of temporary deprivations; in fact electoral defeat, the indictment of a Leader, or exile from the higher-ups often makes them more cohesive. Identification with the club, furthermore, extends to large numbers of voters in each District—the "captive vote"—few of whom have gotten anything directly as a result of their loyalty. Honest members maintain fealty to the dishonest ones. The young and ambitious among them, the most rationalistic, are often willing to defer demands for many years without loss of morale because the corporate organization has a life quite distinct from its members. Being both fraternal and entrepreneurial, party leaders can as easily support irresponsibility in a Jimmy Walker as it can statesmanship in an Al Smith. Max Weber, during the heyday of American bosses, observed that although the boss is socially detested and without "principles," he does not run the same old party notables for office again and again, as in Germany:

Thus the structure of these unprincipled parties with their socially despised power-holders has aided able men to attain the presidency— men who [in Germany] never would have come to the top. To be sure, the bosses resist an outsider who might jeopardize their sources of money and power. Yet in the competitive struggle to win the favor of the voters, the bosses frequently have had to condescend and accept candidates known to be opponents of corruption.[17]

There are times, and increasingly so, when "honesty is the best policy."

Histories of New York tend to stress the unsavory quality of its politics. The evidence itself is incontrovertible, but the interpretations are based largely upon comparisons with some ideal of popular government, all too seldom contrasting machine politics with other real systems. One could, for instance, make an excellent case for the superiority of machines over the no-party, multi-factional systems in the southern states. In Alabama, for example, electoral efforts are made by *ad hoc* organizations; they are essentially contests among personal followings. As a result, all political transactions are personal, and all payoffs must be immediate. There are few opportunities to amortize the deals over time or among many leaders. Thus the pressures for corruption are at their greatest. It is very likely that the corruption associated with machine politics is better known and more fully documented not because there is in fact greater corruption, but because *an organized opposition is a more efficient means of discovering it.* The traditional political system in New York is too easily denounced. Corruption is an index of the level of public morality, but *awareness* of corruption may well be the sign of a healthy system.

The Democratic party has dominated City politics for years, but it has not been able to eliminate all organized opposition. Its success is largely due to its cohesion as a large minority in the face of dispersed opposition. The Republican organizations can alone win nothing but a few small, gerrymandered Districts. They can win the big stakes only by mobilizing all of the hostility to the party system itself. This they can do through the control they share in the State legislature, by bringing forth the investigating committees that precipitate the reform movement by revelations of corrupt practices and then by "waiting for unorganized citizens clamoring for change to come to it for the machinery needed to win elections." [18] Very few campaigns in the City are fought out over alternative policies. By and large, the choice for the electorate lies between machine government and its alternative. From year to year the majority of decisions are fought out within the Democratic party in wide open primary contests when internal bargaining has broken down. But since the overwhelming force of intra-party settlement is toward consolidation, innovation, if there is to be any at all, is likely to come from the outside. It is here that "corruption" plays an important role. Discovery of corruption is both a function of the reform system and a cause of its formation.

THE NATURE OF URBAN REFORM:
ORGANIZATION AND IDEOLOGY

The three reform waves were made up of the Republican party and a congeries of local interest groups coming alive to the full promise of political action. All elements of the fragmented Democratic opposition coalesced into a temporarily effective weapon. *Fusion* is a most accurate label for the past reform movements in New York, if it is understood that the resultant alloy was most unstable. Although a reform movement does attract many hundreds of hitherto apathetic individuals, it does not in general signal the transformation of the inchoate into the irresistably active—the interest-group components of reform are hardy perennials in New York politics. Rather, the reform spirit in each instance transformed the strategies and tactics of interest groups. For the time being they nominated candidates and sought votes. They were transformed into elements of a new political party.

In the years between reform waves, many of these interest groups worked through the established party-political system. The struggle for the stakes of politics took place within that system; interest-group influence was exerted on parties and the government from the "outside." Interest groups in effect accept the established political system when they act strictly as interest groups. The onset of reform is the beginning of a temporary rejection of the system, the establishment of a channel for making innovations in the established order of things. Their rejection of the system takes the form of direct participation; they attempt to control outright the governmental apparatus.

As we shall see, the reform movement of the late 1950s was not ideologically distinct from the earlier periods of reform, but in personnel and in strategy there were some important differences. The personnel of the present reform movement, the young middle-class intellectual and the professional and skill groups, were the work horses at about the middle levels of the earlier movements. Now they appear to have been the leaders, although it is inevitable that they will draw considerable financial support from typical reform interest groups. But it is in strategy that the present movement is most distinct. Rather than reject the party system from the beginning, the modern reformers have attempted to take over from the inside, through insurgency rather than reform in the strict sense. This shift in strategy is in very large part due to a single change in party rules: the direct election of Assembly District Leaders. Until 1952, a successful insurgency within the dominant party in Manhattan required the election of hundreds of County committeemen who in turn selected the District officers. This system of indirect election was subject to so many forms of manipulation that insurgency, especially in several Districts simultaneously, was extremely difficult.[19] The lag between population change and leadership change was enormous. This simple reform in New York County Democratic rules attracted most of the liberals who in earlier times were repelled by party politics. In democratizing the rules of his organization, Carmine DeSapio very clearly planted the seeds of his own defeat.

The rules change in Manhattan is significant because the leadership of earlier reform movements came from Manhattan.

The Brooklyn Democracy, after all, has always allowed for direct election by making the State Committeemen *ex officio* Leaders of their Districts. Fusion might have appeared again in 1961 except for the fact that so many of its potential leaders were absorbed in an intra-party struggle in Manhattan.

The democratization of the rules of the dominant party in Manhattan might in the long run destroy the reform cycle by removing its most important condition. However, that possibility does not reduce the need to assess the phenomenon that has been a major dynamism of politics up to now. The following sections analyze the common elements of the past three reform movements as though the reform cycle remains an important potential factor. It must also be noted that there have been insurgent movements within the Democratic party before, and the present movement may be more comparable to those than to the earlier reform movements. In any event, given the fact that the ideology of the reformers of today is so similar to that of the earlier reformers, it might turn out that the present reform movement, regardless of strategy, is itself merely a phase of the political cycle. If the dictates of party politics are such that new "bosses" emerge, the disillusioned reformers will again create a reform system.

THE ORGANIZATION OF REFORM

The most outstanding feature of the reform movement in New York has been its short life. In every respect it has been a coalition, or alliance, of previously existing groups. A pervasive hostility to party organization has prevented the Fusion groups from becoming absorbed by the Republican party; and in turn, Republican leaders—having made their peace with the dominant Party—have never sought the role of vanguard of permanent reform. The coalition is held together by its animosity toward the *local*[20] Democrats, and the interest-group components of the City Fusion party quickly disperse and return to their accustomed roles once they turn the Democrats out.

Once in office, Fusion Mayors have no true organization arm. While this alone may or may not spoil the implementation of their policies, it has made their re-election difficult, if not impossible. The patronage necessary to ingratiate them with Republican leaders was not forthcoming because it violated reform tenets. As a consequence, the Republicans in 1917 abandoned

Mayor Mitchel, who was defeated for re-election in a three-cornered race against a Democrat and a Republican candidate. This ephemeral quality of reform organization—not really an organization at all—was just as true of their last great victory as of the earlier ones, in spite of the fact that La Guardia served three terms as compared to one each for Low and Mitchel. By 1937 the City Fusion party was past history. For one thing, La Guardia would not allow Fusion leaders to hold government and party offices jointly. To the Republican party he gave little and expected a lot. In return, the Queens and Bronx County Republican organizations tried to block La Guardia's renomination by running conservative Democratic Senator Royal S. Copeland against him in the 1937 primary. Thus, in less than four years Fusion had again become a shambles. La Guardia's genius was simply not to depend on his original base of success. By 1937 he and Franklin D. Roosevelt had set up a viable tool in the American Labor party. It was this *party* organization that gave the La Guardia mayoralty its long duration. As Table 8.1 demonstrates, the reform movement, the Republican-Fusion coalition, had spent itself long before.[21]

The reform movement in New York has indeed been cyclical. Each time its onset was widespread, energetic, irresistible. But as soon as there was a partial redress of the Democratic imbalance of power the components dispersed. There has been no club core and no central bureaucracy; thus, the reform system has not been institutionalized.

Table 8.1   Votes for La Guardia, by Party and Year

	Defeat 1929	Election 1933	Re-election 1937	Re-election 1941
Republican	367,675	446,833	674,611	668,485
Fusion	———	421,689	159,556	63,367
ALP	———	———	482,790	435,374
Other	———	———	27,673	19,292
Margin of victory	−319,847	259,469	453,874	129,383

The traditional party organizations have been conservative and consolidative. Once party leaders adapt to a given legal structure of government and a given set of activities and policies, they have a strong tendency to prefer them over any changes.

Why change something if it is paying off? On taking office, Mayor Hylan wrote to the Civil Service Reform Association that "We have had all the reform that we want in the city for some time to come." [22] Hylan did not prefer bad government, he was simply reflecting the organization politician's preference for keeping the whole system *as is*.

By contrast, the reform system is the major channel of innovation. Given its ephemeral quality, perhaps it would be best if the reform movement became a permanent part of one of the parties. This may become the case if the reform clubs take over the Democratic County organizations. But more than that will be required. As long as New York remains a "modified one-party" system, the *dominant* party—Democratic or Republican—will probably remain a conservative force, especially in matters of government structure and organization. Reformers have a curious way of becoming conservatives once they have succeeded in instituting what they consider the major remedies. Dominant parties in local government probably tend toward conservatism regardless of their national affiliations. Until such time when the two parties in New York are more evenly balanced, innovation will probably depend upon temporary alliances of groups hostile to party organization *per se*, but especially the dominant one.

THE IDEOLOGY OF REFORM

As proposed before, the style of reform is based largely upon Yankee traditions and values, upon beliefs in abstract principles of law, objective application of rules, and "a common feeling that government should be in good part an effort to moralize the lives of individuals." [23] It is a style based essentially upon "old-middle-class" orientations, orientations akin to those of Riesman's "inner-directed" type. According to Riesman, the inner-directed type, always a "moralizer," displays entirely different political styles according to whether he is in or out of power. In power, he sees politics as a "field of work"; as such his activity is aimed toward protecting his vested interests, "and whether these are of a 'practical' or an 'ideal' sort, he feels little ambivalence about them." [24] The "moralizer in retreat" is quite a different fellow; he alternates between "curdled indignation" or "passive, frustrated resistance" on the one hand and on the other the enthusiasm of the crusader.[25] Hofstadter and Riesman are describing traditions and orientations clearly manifest in reform ideology.

Their words are not used here to describe the reform ideology but the tradition and temperament on which it is based.

The Democratic and, to a large extent, the Republican machines have been dominated by the immigrant or ethnic style. Many Yankees became part of the organizations after their establishment in the last half of the nineteenth century, but they remained in the organizations only by accepting organization norms. Most of the old stock withdrew into economic activity and depended on indirect means of shaping politics. Perhaps persistently hostile, they alternated between alliances with and active hostility toward the new style of urban politics. In our own day the young professional and skilled men and women, either far removed from their ethnic origins or actually from "WASP" families, cannot feel at home in the fraternal atmosphere of the old club. He who would live, at least temporarily, "for" politics does not rest easily with those who would live "off" politics.[26] And even when the "outsider" is willing to go along, he receives little encouragement from old-line leaders who classify any attempts to bring practice closer in line with the ideal as "do-gooder" or "goo-goo" activities. Theorizing and moralizing about politics is a means of self-exile in the eyes of those to whom politics is a business as well as a vocation.

Many of the reformers are "conservative" in the strict sense of attitudes toward expansion of governmental activities, civil rights, and internationalism. This is to suggest that "liberalism" and "reform" are quite distinct doctrines. Reformers differ among themselves about policies at the national and local level, but they are as one on the tenets of reform.[27] All reformers are "liberal" in terms of attitudes toward party and governmental structure and political leadership, regardless of difference in attitudes toward government policy.[28]

The central tenet of urban reform is the assumption of the intrinsic evil of the dominant party. In this tenet is the cohesive stuff of the movement—and one of the reasons for its recurrent dissolution. Inevitably this tenet generalizes into a hostility toward party organization *per se*.[29] La Guardia saw no inconsistency in identifying all politicians as "punks, tinhorns and cheap crooks." To him "bosses are bunk";—in other words, he thought it possible to "depoliticize" politics. The fact that he did not do this did not in the least alter his and others' belief in the possibility. La Guardia created "the paradox of a machine that was anti-machine." [30]

One perennial reformer judged an earlier Mayor in a manner that reveals this belief:

[McClellan was] anxious to break the grip of [Tammany] on the city government; but he never seemed to be sure about the kind of system he was going to establish in its place. Many of his appointments were admirable, but he had been brought up in an atmosphere of machine politics, and the conception of the "machine" as a necessary part of a city administration he could never escape. He wanted to make the existing system as effective as possible, but he had no inclination to change the system itself. At heart he was not a fighter. . . . [31]

Mayor McClellan provides his own answer:

I have always been an organization man and have always believed in political organization. That the wrong men only too often control our local politics is due to the fact that the right men refuse to do their duty. If those who spasmodically take part in so-called reform or fusion movements would join the organizations of the parties to which they profess to owe allegiance and would devote the time they spend in their clubs to the practice of the profession of politics . . . , they could acquire the control of the machinery of politics and bring forth works meet [sic] for repentance. [32]

Juxtapose these two quotes and you have a key to the difference between the honest reformer and the honest organization man. The hostility to the system is not based entirely on the association of party with corruption. The reformer is not so naive as to believe that corruption can be completely eliminated or that parties are responsible for it all. It is the party's commitment to *material interest,* its entrepreneurial character, which galls the reformer most. The political calculus weighs every decision according to the net gain or loss of power. This to the true reformer has always been anathema.

The positive side of reform is, of course, its commitment to merit, to the principle of "efficient business administration." There is no "Democratic way to lay a sewer and no Republican way to pave a street." The reform movement has not offered *programmatic* alternatives to the machine but has eschewed those along with the material goals of the party. According to

Adrian, reform movements have "placed a misleading over-emphasis upon the *forms* and *structures* of government."[33] The city manager, the direct primary applied to all nominations and party offices, nonpartisan local elections, and the independent commission are some of the antiorganization devices basic to reform. These devices would "change the system" by removing most of the opportunities and incentives for corruption. But since the overriding tenets have been elimination of corruption and the introduction of efficiency, the most important goal for political action has been merit—alterations in personnel. Place the governmental apparatus in the hands of persons trained specifically for the job and you can eliminate corruption and achieve efficiency at one and the same time. Expand the civil service system. Professionalize political executives.[34] Get the "best men in the field," promise them "no political interference," and departmental administration will take care of itself. Then we can all return to our private pursuits.

This has been the goal of reform: No integrated program, no concept of public interest to which all Departments and agencies would be devoted, but an instrumental view in which responsible programs and the public interest would emerge from elites of skill. Even La Guardia "left few permanent institutional assets to the office of Mayor."[35] On the credit side of the ledger, reform has helped equip City government with the skills necessary to keep pace with the problems of growing complexity. Reform onslaughts have forced a partial change of values upon the parties, which remain entrepreneurial but with a broader concept of "good politics."

THE SOCIAL CONSEQUENCES OF REFORM

PLOTTING POLITICAL CHANGE

The alternating currents of reform and machine, of ideological and entrepreneurial leaders, of innovative and consolidative forces, ought to manifest themselves in the characteristics of the top political personnel. What kinds of changes are associated with each form of Mayoralty? To what extent do reform cadres in power change things at all? If changes do occur, are they *cyclical* like the reform wave that caused them, or are they *structural?* In other words, do the reforms survive the reformers?

The data of this study have proved to be particularly useful for trend analysis. And the same technique is most appropriate for plotting political change at any given point in time. For, to assess the degree and type of change, we must know the pattern before we can assess the departures. Operationally, cyclical change is simply a "blip" in a secular trend, a clear, discontinuous departure from the established pattern and then a return shortly thereafter to the established pattern. Conversely, a *structural* change is one that departs from the pattern and does not later return to it; i.e., a departure that begins a new pattern. See Figure 8.1 for the "ideal-typical" model.

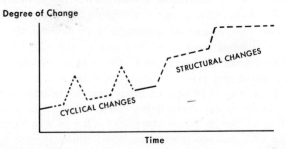

Figure 8.1   Cyclical vs. Structural Change: An Ideal-Typical Model

Naturally some changes are ambiguous. Without an *a priori* standard, the one or the other type of change is impossible to determine in any but the clearest cases. However, inspection will serve well for the present purposes because the impact of reform means nothing unless the departures are unambiguous. That is to say, reform is hardly a "channel of innovation" unless the changes are clear and unmistakable.

Social Mobility and the Reform System

The "Committees of One Hundred" or "New York Citizens Committees" that have preceded the formation of the reform system have been essentially gatherings of the most important economic, civic, and social leaders in the community. In one way or another they become the inner core of the reform system. Because of their community status, wealth, and institutional position, their cooperation, if not initiative, has been prerequisite to any coordinated, non-party political effort. The so-called "coalition" of interest groups in City Fusion has been to a great extent simply a working agreement among these leaders. In each reform movement a different set of groups may appear dominant, and the spokesmen of reform, perhaps thought popularly to be the leaders of reform, may come from lower strata. For example, La Guardia and such popular reformers as Norman Thomas and Paul Blanshard were important to the reform success of 1933. But the reform system would never have become organized around these types. The inner core requires popular leaders and ideologies, but the popular leaders would not be a sufficient condition for the formation of the reform system.

The inner core of the reform system can be identified among those famous New York names responsible for the founding of the big civic and economic associations of the *fin de siècle*. The Citizens Union, formed in 1897 out of the City club and a congeries of Good Government Clubs, was a conscious effort to create a municipal political party. Its first "leader" was Seth Low, but Low was only one of many real founders—Theodore Roosevelt, William Jay Schieffelin, Carl Schurz, Jacob Schiff, and members of the House of Morgan. Failing to win alone with Low in the 1897 mayoralty election, the Citizens Union leaders sought and got a Republican joint nomination in 1901. Thus, the practices of status dominance of reform and collaboration with the Republican machines were both established at the very beginning of Greater New York's history as soon as it was clear that the Republicans could no more easily win control of the new City than of the old.

Other merchants and financiers not included in the Citizens Union became a part of the reform coalition through their membership in the Merchants Association, reorganized as the Commerce and Industry Association in 1942. This is an association of individuals and corporations and, through these, somewhat of a coordinator of all manufacturing, financial, real estate, and a number of other interests in the City. When the Board of Directors of the Merchants Association aligned itself with other status leaders in a Committee of One Hundred, then and only then could a reform system be built; then and only then did the reform movement have a solid base of support. Because of the stability of economic, civic, and status leadership in the community, many founders of the reform system participated in all three major reform movements. Those who did not have such longevity were succeeded in the inner core by essentially the same types of community leaders.

Specifically in this sense, the reform system has been a coalition of money-providing interest groups. And because the constituent interest groups are so oligarchic, the reform system itself is oligarchic, despite the large number of participating enthusiasts. If there were a power elite in the City, the inner core of the reform system would be a central feature of it. However, the fact that the reform movement is a manifest attempt to create an overt power elite strongly suggests a low probability that there is a covert power elite in the City.

The inner core of the reform system is thus composed of individuals who control resources sufficient for large-scale, *ad hoc* collective effort. The particular composition of the leadership group and of the larger numbers near this group deeply affects the complexion of the reform mayoralties; and, paradoxically, some of these unanticipated social consequences of reform seem to take hold while most of the elements of the reform *program* tend to disappear with the reformers.

The reform system is not only strongly oligarchic, it is also essentially an upper- and upper-middle-class reaction. With each wave of reform the low-mobile Social Registerites return to government. The steady disappearance of the upper classes from direct participation in politics is halted. This is one of the cyclical aspects of the reform movement that makes the relationship of the upper classes to reform all the more clear (see Table 8.2, "Low Mobility"). As seems to be the case with one-party politics, *nonorganization reform politics tends to favor people who already have high economic or status position.*[36]

Along with the return of the upper class to government leadership one finds an equally clear increase in the entry of upper-middle strata, educated business, and professional people. Some of these men were part of the inner core of the reform leadership, others had simply been activists in the movement— very often younger men completely new to political activity— and still others who had not been associated with reform at all but who were coopted by reform as outstanding men of talent whether residents of the City or not. This increase of upper-middle-class (medium-low mobility) personnel is probably the most important influence of the reform movement on the political system because it tends to bring about a structural change. The proportion of top political executives recruited from these upper-middle business and professional strata increases in reform may-

Table 8.2   Changes in Degree of Mobility Accompanying Reform Mayors: Comparing Social Origins of Reform Cabinets with Their Democratic Predecessors and Successors

Mayor	Mobility	Net Per Cent Change over Predecessor	Net Per Cent Change by Successor
Low	High	− 27	6
	Medium-high	− 11	8
	Medium-low	12	2
	Low	17	− 15
Mitchel	High	− 1	6
	Medium-high	− 4	5
	Medium-low	− 1	4
	Low	4	− 17
La Guardia	High	− 7	− 1
	Medium-high	− 10	9
	Medium-low	23	3
	Low	18	− 11

oralties and never returns to earlier levels or earlier rates of increase (see Table 8.2 and Chapter 3). Data from earlier chapters suggest that eventually these middle strata will take over top governmental administration almost entirely, that the educational system and the large business bureaucracies are the true channels of mobility, and that government and politics are becoming more and more ancillary to the true career in occupations requiring special skills. These trends are clear even during periods of party organization rule; but the reform system tends strongly to accelerate the take-over.

REFORM AND THE GROUP PROCESS:
A SHIFT IN RECRUITMENT PATTERNS

In some respects, the reduction of the degree of social mobility associated with reform is peculiar because of the dependence of reform upon interest groups. As was shown earlier, in recent decades groups display on the average a higher degree of social mobility than the parties. Yet, here we have observed that the degree of mobility in the cabinet is considerably reduced during the group-based reform periods. To explain this apparent discrepancy is to expose some of the most significant differences between the reform and traditional systems. Our earlier analyses of social-mobility patterns in parties and groups did take the reform cycle into account; but when we do take it into account, we will find that the high-mobility groups and group leaders are those associated with the traditional system, whether they are affiliated with the parties or not.

The reform system, in other words, temporarily shifts the sources of political leadership and governmental power. The "group alliance" structure of reform shows up clearly in the backgrounds of the cabinet executives, but these are different types of groups and different types of group leaders from those associated with the traditional system. The outstanding feature of group representation in reform cabinets has been the civic-philanthropic groups. While the large economic associations are the core of the reform elite, civic associations have been the operational arm, and civic leaders more often than economic leaders have accepted governmental roles (Table 8.3).[37] Civic group leadership indeed seems to be an important criterion

Table 8.3 Changes in Group Recruitment Accompanying Reform Mayors

Mayor	Group	Net Per Cent Change from Predecessor	Net Per Cent Change by Successor
Low	Civic	20	− 12
	Professional	13	− 9
	Economic	13	− 2
Mitchel	Civic	− 2	− 4
	Professional	− 10	− 6
	Economic	− 5	11
La Guardia	Civic	21	− 14
	Professional	30	− 5
	Economic	− 5	− 4

SOURCE: Figure 5.5.

standing between the leaders of the big economic associations and public office under a reform Mayor. For example, well over 90 per cent of all economic leaders in the three reform cabinets were also office holders in one or more civic or philanthropic groups. The top leadership of professional groups is also a far weightier factor in the reform cabinet; however they appear by

and large to be coopted members rather than instrumental factors in the reform coalition itself. Many professional group
leaders had not even been residents of the City before appointment to the La Guardia cabinet.

The reform system not only favors the large civic groups and
economic "peak" associations, it tends to select from those groups
and leaders the ones least associated with the traditional system.
Reform tends to polarize parties and groups. Under reform
mayors, considerably larger numbers of civic and professional
group leaders enter the cabinet without any party grooming
at all (Table 8.4). Of greater significance is the fact that party-

Table 8.4   Changes in Group-Party Relations Due to Reform: Group
Leaders Who Were *NOT* Members of Party

Mayor	Type of Group	Net Per Cent Change over Predecessor	Net Per Cent Change by Successor
Low	Civic	12	− 10
	Professional	6	4
	Economic	− 4	− 2
Mitchel	Civic	2	− 18
	Professional	4	− 18
	Economic	4	− 4
La Guardia	Civic	48	− 26
	Professional	42	− 10
	Economic	12	− 8

group compatibility never returns to earlier levels; this is a
structural change. Independent entry increases sharply with each
reform Mayor and declines only slightly in the succeeding
Democratic regime. Reform has indeed been the spawning
waters of pluralism.

The sharp drop of average mobility accompanying reform
periods is thus simply one factor in a general shift of recruitment
channels. The reform system is based on distinct types of groups
and types of group leaders. Groups and leaders identified with
parties or who enjoy particularly good access during traditional
periods become committed to the traditional system, and to that
degree can become *persona non grata* to reform. These groups
may become part of the reform coalition, but it is unlikely that
their leaders become cabinet officials.

Special economic interest groups provide the best illustration of the problem. One of the strategies of economic interests is to use a *special* interest group for certain purposes and one or more general interest groups or "peak associations" for other purposes. For example, real estate operators might use neighborhood associations and local real estate boards for defense against land-use regulatory activities, in which case friendly relations with leaders of both major parties will be cultivated. On the other hand, in matters of taxation, in the broader aspects of city planning, and in general defense against expansion of government the same real estate operators, either as individual corporations or through their special-interest organizations, seek membership and influence in the Commerce and Industry Association, Chambers of Commerce, and Citizen Budget Commission. All the special constituent interests in the peak association will find that their leaders are rough equals among the hundreds of other special group leaders, and that leadership in the peak associations is generally restricted to leaders of the highest status among them. It seems that reform draws a high proportion of its active personnel from the higher-status leaders, especially those who have never been prominently identified with local party affairs. The reform system thus appears to be more oligarchic and more "upper class" than the traditional system. In extremely oversimplified terms, there appear to be at least two "power elites" in the City, a party-centered one and a "status-centered" one.

REFORM AND ETHNIC CIRCULATION

Reform politics is Yankee politics. Not only is this manifest in style and ideology, but also in the ethnic composition of the top political personnel. Taking all three Fusion administrations together, the native-American stock outnumbers the Irish about six to one.[38] However to stress this dominant relation only is to overlook one of the most important features of the reform system, namely its influence on the representation of newer ethnic minorities.

The integration of new ethnic minorities appears to be a function of the minority party. Just as they are conservative on matters of governmental structure and, for that matter, on local government policy, *dominant* local parties, regardless of national or State affiliation, display a strong tendency toward conservatism in their social policies as well. Not only is an expanded electorate to the advantage of the *minority* party; its position makes it more permeable by new groups of every sort. When one adds to this the extremely loose structure of the reform system, of which the minority political party is simply one factor, the capacity for absorption of new groups appears all the greater.

Reform mayoralties are strong reflections of this tendency. The aristocratic Seth Low did much better by the Jews than his predecessor did, and he also made the first Italian cabinet appointments (Figure 8.2). Mayor Mitchel added another increment to the Jewish share and appointed the first Negro to a cabinet post. All three groups, but particularly the Jews and Italians, fared better under La Guardia than at any time before.

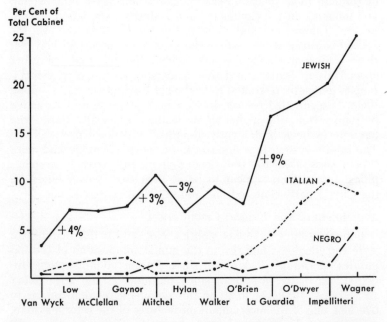

Figure 8.2   Per Cent of Jewish, Italian, and Negro Appointments (1898–1957)

And these are for the most part *structural* changes. The gains made by the new groups in reform periods were not lost with succeeding Democratic regimes. Wooing and winning new and weakly committed voters has always been a major part of the activity of political clubs, and one of the strongest magnets has been the symbolic recognition of minorities through appointments and nominations. But it appears that that is an over-simplified view of the process of integration, at least in New York City. Apparently, new groups tend to stake their first claims on the minority, and each such appointment becomes a commitment that future appointing authorities have difficulty avoiding. It may well be that the dominant party organization has been more quick to respond to the claims of new minorities in the judicial or other elective arenas; perhaps there have been occasions in these areas where the Democratic party has actually taken the initiative. These factors would vary with the relative concentration of a given ethnic group in each electoral district. But if power within the party hierarchy is prerequisite to representation on elective as well as appointive slates, initiative by the minority is probably far more often true than not. If the appointments pattern is to any degree representative of the political pattern in general, we can propose that reform has slowed up economic mobility while it has speeded up ethnic circulation. The ethnic component of reform is probably a mani-festation of a general tendency of minority party attraction of most elements without access in the dominant party.

ANTICIPATED CONSEQUENCES OF REFORM

In a city the size of New York one could hardly expect many spectacular and deliberate innovations. With size has come complexity, specialization, and differentiation. Each specialized center of decision-making, as we have seen, becomes an arena of power, and those who gain access to the centers of power develop a desire and a capacity to resist any changes that might imperil that position. As a consequence, "every proposal for change must run a gauntlet that is often fatal. The system is more favorable to defenders of the *status quo* than to innovators. It is inherently conservative." [39] However, to let explanation rest here would be a misrepresentation by overemphasis of dominant relations. The governmental and political system in New York has shown itself capable of an occasional important innovation, a deliberate attempt to adapt to changing conditions. But, given the tremendously strong forces of inertia, every deliberate change becomes a remarkable achievement. Thus, the significant question remaining is not "Why does an immense urban center tend toward *stasis?*"—answers to which are all too apparent—but

"How and under what conditions are changes in the system managed at all?"

At the local level, innovation has many sources. Initiative as well as leadership sometimes comes from a single unpredictable individual outside government like Henry George, or inside like Robert Moses. More often, innovation has its source outside the City itself, especially from State and Federal governments. Tenement house regulation, public educational advances, and nomination by direct primary, for example, were imposed upon the City by the State. Shifts in local welfare policies have come primarily from either State or Federal decisions, and this is likely to continue. Urban renewal received its major impetus from the Federal government; Mayor Lee's now-famous achievements in New Haven, for instance, would not have been possible without a conspiracy of Title One moneys, the interstate highway system and Hartford's agreement to help wipe out the downtown slum with an interchange. Innovation sometimes is even provided by the dominant party as is seen in the establishment of the Budget Bureau and Purchasing Department during Mayor Hylan's administration and in the direct election of AD Leaders during DeSapio's leadership of Tammany Hall.

The reform system is of particular importance, however, because it has been the most frequent, if not regular, source of innovation in the City. As its name would indicate, the reform movement is generated out of a widely felt need to change something. Here at least is one channel of innovation, one more or less institutionalized feature of the political system manifestly devoted to change. But what has the reform system changed, how much and for how long?

Each reform movement has left its mark on the City's governmental structure. The Charter of 1901 was as much a part of the reform movement as candidate Seth Low himself. Within three years of his first inaugural, La Guardia gave the City another Charter. Mitchel instituted a comprehensive zoning setup, including a new Board of Standards and Appeals, and was responsible for probably the first massive studies of City government structure and activity.[40] Before World War II, practically all new Departments and major reorganizations were carried out during reform mayoralties.[41] But these structural changes form only a small part of the reform program because so much depends on who fills the offices and how the offices and powers are to be used.

The perpetual bane of the reformer's existence is the ease with which the party leaders adapt new structures to old purposes. For probably the first quarter-century after its birth, the civil service system was more often than not a means by which patronage appointees could insulate themselves from political vicissitudes. Party leaders quickly learned how to dominate the direct primary and, for that matter, proportional representation. A charter with even the best forms and structures was no guarantee of real reform. Centralize administration toward a strong-Mayor system and you increase the possibilities of spoils system if the next Mayor is an organization man. Weaken the mayoralty by creating autonomous, tenured Departments and a long period of machine rule will render the next reform Mayor impotent. This is why the reform movements have been so strongly personnel-oriented and essentially negative. All three reform mayors spent most of their energies creating a record clear of corruption, attempting to set an example, hoping to raise the level of public expectations about local government. Every "party hack" replaced by a skilled administrator would show such an improvement that the succeeding organization Mayor would not dare reappoint the party hacks, especially if the office was as exposed as a commissionership. A combination of merit and tenure from below and creation of the proper "job image" from above has been the fundamental policy of the reform movement.

PARTY AND REFORM

Statistically and otherwise, the most significant difference between the traditional and reform cabinets is in party appointments (Figure 8.3; see also Table 8.5). The dramatic departures

Table 8.5   Changes in Degree of Party Recruitment Accompanying Reform Mayors

Mayor	Net Per Cent Change from Predecessor	Net Per Cent Change by Successor
Low	− 37	+ 12
Mitchel	− 14	+ 33
La Guardia	− 56	+ 26

of reform from traditional mayoralties in the appointment of party functionaries to cabinet posts show the basically anti-party nature of the reform program. Most of the top party functionaries

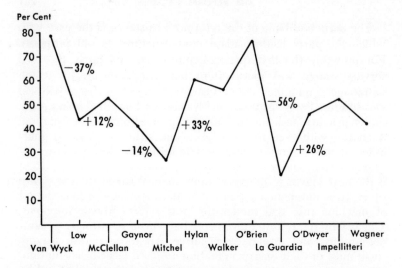

Figure 8.3 Active Party Members in the Cabinet

in reform administrations are the Democratic and Republican "regulars" holding fixed-tenure positions. When a reform Mayor does appoint a party functionary, he is typically either a minor functionary or merely a club member. Mayor Low appointed only three Republican Leaders, Mitchel appointed four, La Guardia five, three of whom had served with distinction under Mitchel.

In this regard, reform has been self-defeating. Republican Leaders have a very low expectation of reward from reform victories. They are coy partners of reform before the election and usually desert afterward, successfully opposing Mitchel's renomination, vainly opposing La Guardia's second renomination. With their leverage in Albany, New York City's Republican leaders can extract as many, if not more than as many, benefits peacefully from the City Democrats as they can by a full-scale assault; nor are the risks so great. And the stronger the Democratic position, the more likely the Republican leaders are to conspire with them. In the Bronx, for example, Republicans very frequently endorse Democratic candidacies in opposition to the Liberals.

On net, the impact of reform on party recruitment has been structural. It was only for a short period after Mayor Mitchel that the Democrats were able to recover at all from the reduction of access forced upon them by reform. After Low, and certainly after La Guardia, there was no restoration of earlier party controls on appointments. As a result of reform, interest-group access to many Departments has been strong enough to resist the full recovery of the machine. The degree to which groups and the organized departmental bureaucracies are able to commit succeeding traditional mayors to reform patterns varies, of course, according to the area of governmental activity in question (compare with Chapter 7). For example, all changes in the Inputs arena have been purely cyclical. However, if we treat that arena separately, the structural impact of reform emerges all the more clearly in the others, particularly in the Welfare and Services arena, where the "job images" created by reform appointments tend to take hold.

SKILLS AND REFORM

Machine and reform mayors alike prefer the "best man" for appointment to the top posts, but obviously their notions of "best" are derived from rather different standards. Most traditional mayors (at least before World War II) chose men with good, general capabilities and a measurable strain of loyalty to chief and party, party loyalty being the first prerequisite. In every respect, reform notions of merit were opposed to these. Already we have seen the extent to which reform carried out their anti-party policies and affected, to a certain extent, the appointment policies of succeeding organization mayors. On the positive side, however, they were less successful. Not all displaced "party hacks" were replaced by job-oriented personnel, and such changes that were made failed to accelerate the fairly well-established secular pattern of traditional Mayors (Figure 8.4).

Seth Low, the first Fusion Mayor, was *sui generis*. In many respects his administration was virtually a return to pre-Civil-War patterns. His cabinet was filled largely by "generalists" from the old and established merchant families. Such men were recruited neither by party nor career, but essentially through Social Register clubs. Almost 40 per cent of his top appointments were Gentlemen; eliminating the Board of Education, over 50 per cent were from high society. Low's concept of the mayoralty antedated both the machine system and the reform system. His reputation for honesty made him an ideal reform candidate, but he was not a reformer. Thus, on the fundamental reform issue, *skill*, he made no contribution (see Figure 8.4).

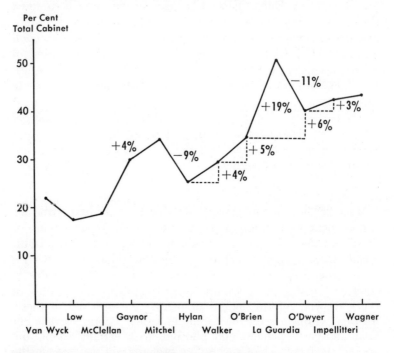

Figure 8.4   Job-Oriented Skills in the Cabinet

But merit, or job-oriented skill, was a novel doctrine in Low's day when even the mayoralty itself was treated largely as a ceremonial office.[42] The true test of reform innovation, therefore, comes later with Mitchel, perhaps the ideal chief executive,[43] and La Guardia. Following Low, the incidence of job-oriented skills starts on an upward trend that is never interrupted. Each traditional Mayor contributes slightly to cabinet specialization, and although the two reform cabinets were clearly more specialized than those of their predecessors and successors, their four- and twelve-year interventions did not alter the traditional pattern.[44] Even La Guardia's twelve-year success in the mayoralty failed to accelerate the slow but steady adoption of principles of modern administrative ideas by the dominant party. Note on

Figure 8.4 that from Hylan until the present the rate of accelera-
tion among traditional Mayors was about plus-one percentage
point.[45] Since O'Dwyer, in fact, the *rate* has actually declined.

It would, however, be too easy to discount the impact of
reform. One could argue that the gradual secular increase of
job-oriented skills is due to the increasing availability of skills
plus the growing complexity of the society. There is also some
truth in the assertion that the short durations of purity and
goodness served as examples of what *not* to do. But the stronger
argument is the other way around. A great many job-oriented
appointments in Democratic administrations were essentially
concessions, either to the press or to the group alliance supporting a particular set of attributes established during reform periods. In other cases, a specialist appointment was probably a
concession to the departmental bureaucracy, a power participant
created in greatest part by civil service reform; and in all cases
the existence of these increasingly specialized bureaucracies
presented traditional Mayors with the choice of isolation from
government business through appointment of party generalists
or isolation from the party through appointment of careerists or
professionals.

After La Guardia it is clear that the perspectives of traditional Mayors had been changed. La Guardia had demonstrated
that good government and good politics are not mutually exclusive. The three postwar Democratic Mayors did not reject the
party—as can be seen in the fact that they appointed almost twice
as many Party functionaries as La Guardia—but postwar Party
commissioners were themselves of a different sort. The number
of County and AD Leaders in the cabinet dropped to less than
one third of the pre-La Guardia number,[46] and most of these and
the other high functionaries were isolated in a single arena (see
Chapter 7, "Governmental Input"). Mayors O'Dwyer, Impellitteri,
and Wagner were, in addition, fully committed to the concept of
continuing reorganization. Each instituted massive studies along
the line of the Hoover Commission. Each was the source of
important amendments to the Charter,[47] and Wagner took the
initiative for general Charter reform.

The reform spirit, the constant threat of another reform movement, and the anti-party pluralism resulting from reform have
forced a change in the perspectives of the organization Mayor.
His constituency is far broader than ever before. Where once
the party monopoly of nominations and elections made it almost

the only exclusive constituency, now the party is only one source of effective expectation and demand, seldom the most effective. As a result, each postwar Mayor has had trouble bridging the gap between his organizational background and the demands of being chief executive. The gap probably forced them to act like reformers even if they had no stomach for the role.

Mayor O'Dwyer used his patronage and unprecedented electoral strength in an attempt to alter the party leadership, to restructure the party toward the mayoralty, and he succeeded at least in getting acceptable County Leaders in Brooklyn and Manhattan. Initiative of this sort in the mayoralty was unprecedented. Impellitteri, the aftermath of O'Dwyer's failure to bring the entire party apparatus under control, spent his three years trying vainly to secure his renomination, but still felt limited in the degree of favoritism he could afford to give to the various party factions. Wagner, in every respect a product of traditional recruitment, has been particularly subject to the varieties of non-party forces. At first he was an instrument of traditional party strategies,[48] but even then his appointment pattern showed strong group representation and specialization in key Departments. In fact, Mayor Wagner felt it necessary to declare County and AD Leaders ineligible for top posts. After the dashing of his hopes to escape the City for a larger constituency in 1956 and his stunning re-election in 1957, Wagner haltingly sought real party leadership in the City in order to bring the party into closer harmony with modern governmental needs. The unprecedented alienation of all five County organizations in 1961 is indicative of his failure to bridge the gap.

But the basis of Wagner's renomination and re-election in 1961 is even more suggestive: The departmental bureaucracies and the groups organized around them offer not only a challenge that requires professionalism and group representation at the top but also offer a source of power alternative to the party, if it can be harnessed. Both of Wagner's running mates were departmental careerists, and one, Screvane, had a following in one of the most populous (non-"Hatch Act") bureaucracies in the City, one tied rather closely to the Teamsters, the TWU, and other organized City bureaucracies and local unions.[49] Wagner's campaign manager was the Fire Commissioner on leave of absence.

Thus, largely due to the efforts of the reform movement, there is independent, non-party access to the mayoralty. Perhaps of greater importance, the reform principle of insulating the bureaucracies from the parties has become so strongly operative that it has created a separate political force in the community. The departmental bureaucracies are not neutral, they are only independent. Every Mayor must now strike the pose of reformer by appointing specialists to key posts or else deprive himself altogether of administrative control. But if he can manage it at all, he gains a source of support independent of his base of recruitment. Wagner's success in this regard more or less guarantees similar strategies in the future, until abuse of agency personnel leads to further reforms.

CONCLUSIONS

Some of the effects of reform have been cyclical, others structural. But generally speaking, the values most strongly espoused by the reform movement—anti-party and pro-skill values—have not been strongly binding upon traditional mayors. Let us say that reform values have been slowly accepted by the Democrats, but this acceptance cannot be attributed in any great degree to the changes made by the reformers *while they were in office*. The constant threat of a reform movement—the constant Democratic fear that their plurality can be wiped out by a fully united opposition—has probably contributed more, through the "rule of anticipated reaction," than actual electoral defeats toward reshaping traditional political values and practices. Groups that become the core of any reform movement are the creators and/or supporters of new "job images," and their access to the departments and directly to the Mayor helps maintain any changes made.

Between the two major parties, the channel of innovation is clearly the minority party, whose electoral weakness makes it permeable to any interests without access or which have lost access to government. Maurice Duverger identifies the phenomenon of *contagion from the Left* as the factor back of innovation in political organization and practice.[50] Parties of the Right, so goes Duverger's argument, followed suit perforce. Indeed it was the Left in Europe that first developed electoral district organization and other systematic means of mobilizing voters. But it seems clear that Professor Duverger has emphasized the wrong characteristic of these left-wing parties of the late nineteenth and early twentieth centuries. It was not their "leftness" but their minority status in the electorate that led to innovation. The machine was itself an invention of the minority against upper-class, Whig mercantile control in New York. The leaders of Tammany Hall had no love for the Irish in the 1840s, but they led the way in the systematic care and handling of greenhorns, the practice of exchanging civic training for electoral support. As a definite minority party by the late nineteenth century, on the other hand, the Republican leaders became the vehicle for a new brand of political practice, the reform system or politics by social movement.

Does contagion (or innovation) continue to be from the Left when a party of the Left becomes the dominant party? M. Duverger does not ask this question; therefore, he has not attempted to determine whether his "law" of political change is a law or simply an acute observation of a few historical facts. New York political history would strongly suggest that the key dimension in political change—where the party system is concerned—is a "dominance-minority" rather than his "left-right" continuum.

In New York City this is borne out not only in the history of party organization and the pattern of cabinet appointments but also in the most important elective office, the mayoralty itself. Since 1898, seven of the twelve Democratic mayoral nominees were Catholic, and five were Protestant. Of the sixteen Republican or Republican-Fusion nominees, ten were Protestant, three Catholic, two Jewish; and since 1928, three Catholics, two Protestants, and three Jews. Ethnically, eight of the Democrats were Irish, three native-Americans, and one Italian. Of the Republicans, seven were native-Americans, four Irish, three Jewish, and two Italian. It is also interesting, though of course not conclusive, that the Republicans, not the Democrats, set the precedent of nominating a Negro for the Manhattan Borough Presidency.

None of these patterns should be taken as proof but as grounds for further investigation. These issues go to the very core of the social or "latent" functions of political organizations, and we have ample opportunities for systematically testing such hypotheses. Even in highly competitive two-party districts, the typical pattern is probably eight–twelve year cycles of dominance by each major party. Such shifts in the power positions of the two parties are bound to have some important effects upon their internal structures and external perspectives. The minority party, most significantly, is likely to be more vulnerable to the people, groups, and ideas that are motivated by new needs and novel problems.

Samuel Lubell has observed that the issues of any particular period are fought out within the majority party, thereby emphasizing the significance of the "electoral-position" variable.[51] However, these are usually battles based upon definitions and agendas the party developed as the minority and established as the norm while in the majority. But what is the source of new definitions and new agendas? Changes in what is being fought over might indeed come from within the dominant party, for no party possesses a monopoly of new ideas. But it seems more likely that the leaders in the dominant party will be taken up with the struggle to effect adjustments among the interests responsible for the formation of the winning coalition, to consolidate a position rather than to complicate it with the demands of outsiders.

The national Democratic party has been dubbed the "party of innovation," largely because of its minority status from the late nineteenth century until the 1930s. The minority Democratic party found the way out of sectional politics into the class politics of the pre-World-War-I period. It had absorbed the personnel and ideas of the populists and progressives.[52] But before the Civil War and for a period of time afterwards, the new Republican party was innovator. And after Wilson, the Republican party answered class politics with interest-group politics. Republicans in the 1920s still held strongly to a *laissez-faire* ideology, but this did not prevent them from changing the emphasis of politics from issues that involved the total economy to issues that ran parallel to the basic sectoral lines of the economy—e.g., railroad policy, shipping policy, agricultural policy, tariff policy,[53] power policy, communications policy, and labor policy along these same lines. It was, therefore, the Republicans of the 1920s who first gave special emphasis to the now widely accepted notion that expertise follows subject-matter rather than technological lines.

The New Deal coalition was essentially a result of the group structure emerging out of class and subject-matter policies, an intensification of all earlier cleavages once government became clearly involved in economic affairs. The "Roosevelt coalition" was based upon a more specialized discrimination among organized sectors of the economy—agriculture in commodity groupings; organized phases of manufacturing and capital processes, that is, production, processing, merchandising, credit, and exchange; and reflection of the class distinctions among these in the use of the personal and corporate income tax, mandatory collective bargaining, and so on.

The settlements within the alliance of one period of party control contribute to the creation of new alliances for another period. It is not inevitable that any innovation at all will take place as a result of party changeover. The 1950s might be considered such a period.[54] But if innovations are to come, the most likely channel is through the minority party. Lubell's "sun and moon" theory[55] of political dynamics misses the mark because it overemphasizes shifts of *electoral blocs* from one party to the other, giving the impression that certain ethnic and economic groups, through attraction and repulsion, vote overwhelmingly for one party, then the other. Voting studies more systematic than Lubell's support a contrary thesis: first, the party affiliations of voting blocs are never overwhelming even when statistically significant; and second, that these voting patterns tend to be generational, not quadrennial or decennial.[56] Probably, the distribution of votes is neither direct cause nor direct effect of party politics, except that the extreme lag between party policy and electoral support sets limits on how much or how often innovation is possible. Clearly the most reasonable hypothesis would be that innovation is a function of minority electoral status, the minority being more susceptible to new leaders bearing new commitments, with only a long-run relationship to broader voting patterns. Interest groups seldom write their policies into law—although this is probably occurring with increasing frequency in direct relation to the secular decline of party organizations; the function of groups is the definition of new problems, the setting of new agendas, the creation of new kinds of leaders. The strategies of new interest-bearing leaders are not likely to be limited by their own earlier commitments or those of their constituencies. The interest constituency is simply one resource, deliver or not, through which interest-group leaders attempt to influence government or, if the group is one without access, government-in-the-making.

In New York City, the Republican party has been the channel of innovation, either by deliberate policy when in power or by threat of victory. In New Haven and Philadelphia, where the Republican party had been dominant, the Democratic party has become the sentinel of reform. The role of minor parties in America and the problem of innovation in multi-party systems are even further beyond the present scope of our study than the observations already made, but they do offer an additional opportunity for testing hypotheses about the functions of political parties and the relations between them and interest aggregates in the system.

NOTES

1. Report of the Mazet Committee, Albany, vol. I (1900), p. 442.

2. When the owner of the American Ice Company went to jail for his attempts to create through bribery and misrepresentation a monopoly of ice sales in the City, Van Wyck turned out to be one of the major shareholders. See Syrett, *op. cit.*, p. 166.

3. *Ibid.*, p. 167.

4. In spite of their dominance in the City, Democrats seldom win the citywide posts with clear majorities. Their comfort lies in the usually split opposition (Cf. Sayre and Kaufman, *op. cit.*, pp. 182-184).

5. McClellan's Commissioner of Accounts (later renamed Investigations). Mitchel's probing led to the removal of two "Tammany" Borough Presidents.

6. Gustavus Myers, *op. cit.*, pp. 388-389.

7. Under the new direct primary laws of 1911.

8. See Key, *op. cit.*, p. 588; and also Louis Bean, *How to Predict Elections*, Knopf, New York, 1948.

9. *Ibid.*, p. 405.

10. Lasswell and Kaplan, *op. cit.*, p. 247.

11. *Ibid.*, pp. 246-250.

12. Richard Hofstadter, *The Age of Reform*, Knopf, New York, 1955, pp. 8-9.

13. Cf. Ferdinand Tönnies, *Fundamental Concepts of Sociology*, American Book, New York, 1949 (trans. C. P. Loomis); and Karl Mannheim, *Freedom, Power and Democratic Planning*, Oxford, New York, 1950.

14. E. E. Schattschneider, *Party Government*, Rinehart, New York, 1942, pp. 35-36.

15. Rudolph Heberle, *Social Movements*, Appleton-Century-Crofts, New York, 1951, pp. 131-136.

16. Edward J. Flynn, *You're the Boss*, Viking, New York, 1947, p. 227.

17. Gerth and Mills, *op. cit.*, p. 110.

18. Edward J. Flynn, *op. cit.*, p. 140.

19. See Justin N. Feldman's classic article, "How Tammany Holds Power," *National Municipal Review* (July, 1950).

20. This must be emphasized because many of the Leaders in all three reform movements have been State and National Democrats.

21. Cf. Rexford G. Tugwell: "The machines . . . had been challenged and defeated before . . . , but these reform movements had never found the formula for perpetuation. They tended to crumble when enthusiasm died away and the evils they had set out to combat were no longer embodied in obvious dragons to be slain.

"La Guardia found the answer to this problem of impermanence. He kept his dragons alive and attacked them every day. *His ripost lay essentially in the paradox of a machine that was anti-machine* . . . ." (*The Art of Politics*, Doubleday, New York, 1958, p. 15).

Cf. also Warren Moscow, *Politics in the Empire State*, Knopf, New York, 1948, pp. 105-108.

22. *The New York Times* (January 13, 1918), p. 5.

23. Richard Hofstadter, *op. cit.*

24. David Riesman, *The Lonely Crowd*, Anchor edition, Doubleday, New York, 1953, pp. 200-201.

25. *Ibid.*, pp. 206-208.

26. Cf. Max Weber in Gerth and Mills, *op. cit.*, pp. 84-85.

27. Unlike earlier movements, the reformers of the late 1950s are almost entirely liberal, "Stevenson Democrats," another good reason for seeking reform within the local Party apparatus.

28. Cf. James Q. Wilson, *The Amateur Democrat: Club Politics in Three Cities*, University of Chicago Press, Chicago, 1962.

29. Cf. Hofstadter, *op. cit.*, pp. 254-269, who suggests that it generalizes into hostility toward *all* big organization.

30. Rexford Tugwell, *op. cit.*, p. 15.

31. Raymond B. Fosdick, *Chronicle of a Generation*, p. 85.

32. Syrett (ed.), *op. cit.*, p. 181.

33. Charles Adrian, *Governing Urban America*, McGraw-Hill, New York, 1955, p. 62. Emphasis in the original.

34. This may be the reason that the 1950s' reform movement has sought to take over the Democratic party, for although the job of extending the merit system is about over, much remains to be done about professionalizing the top.

35. Sayre and Kaufman, *op. cit.*, p. 692.

36. Cf. E. E. Schattschneider, *The Semisovereign People*, Holt, Rinehart and Winston, New York, 1960, p. 80.

37. The pattern of civic and professional group representation in the Mitchel cabinet is exceptional largely because Mitchel followed an exceptional Democrat, Mayor Gaynor. In many respects Gaynor followed the reform patterns, and he was led all the more strongly to group leaders as a result of his bitter feud with the Democratic party leaders. In the Gaynor cabinet, 58 per cent of all appointees were civic leaders—an all-time high. Forty-one per cent of all his appointees were professional leaders—a record that he held until La Guardia. Mitchel's cabinet was extremely high in group representation compared to all other Democratic Mayors of his time. Furthermore, since so many of Mitchel's appointees were youthful like himself, their professional prominence was not fully established at the time of their appointment. However, in the Departments fundamental to the reform spirit, Mitchel always found his commissioners among professional leaders. In particular, these were in the Departments of License, Accounts, Tenement House, Law, and Police.

38. Of the Fusion appointees 175 were natives (including English), and thirty-two were Irish.

39. Sayre and Kaufman, *op. cit.*, p. 716.

40. Commissioners of Accounts and New York Bureau of Municipal Research, *Government of the City of New York: A Survey of Its Organization and Functions*, J. J. Little and Ives Co., New York, 1915.

41. A few examples are: Citywide Board of Education (1902); Board of Standards and Appeals (1916); Department of Markets (1917); abolition of

office of Coroner (1917) ; abolition of Park Board (1933) and, as a result of the 1936 Charter, Deputy Mayor, City Planning Commission, Department of Finance (abolishing City Chamberlain), Department of Investigation; and replacement of County sheriffs and registers by one City Sheriff and one City Register under civil service.

42.   Leonard White notes that "The principal historical fact concerning chief executives as administrators is that, until 1900, most of them had little to do with administration," 3rd ed., *op. cit.*, p. 40.

43.   Cf. Sayre and Kaufman, *op. cit.*, pp. 692-694.

44.   Again Gaynor is seen as an exceptional case. The independent Judge, building on the gains made during McClellan's last years, lifted Cabinet specialization to levels not reached again until La Guardia. Both McClellan and Gaynor broke with traditions, sought personal followings—the one through insurgency, the other through sometimes eloquent appeals to civic groups—and thus brought their political careers to an end.

45.   The dotted lines and figures below the solid line indicate the net increases among Democratic Mayors.

46.   County and AD Leaders in the Cabinet:

Before La Guardia		After La Guardia	
Hylan	16	O'Dwyer	5
Walker	18	Impellitteri	4
O'Brien	15	Wagner	5

47.   For example, the following Departments were created after 1946: City Construction coordinator (1946), Traffic (1950), Air Pollution Control (1952), Labor (1954), the Division of Administration (1954), and the Commission on Intergroup Relations (as of 1958 a real governmental unit operating under the Fair Housing Practices ["Sharkey-Brown-Isaacs"] Law).

48.   Cooperating with the Bronx and Manhattan, he attempted to punish those Leaders in Queens and Brooklyn who had opposed him in the primary.

49.   Neither Beame nor Screvane had been prominent party members before their appointments to Budget Directorship and Sanitation Commissionership respectively. This was probably the first time since 1914-1918 that the organized City bureaucracies had been involved in a coordinated electoral effort. But this, too, illustrates how far New York has escaped its past. The earlier efforts were pro-"Tammany," anti-reform (Sayre and Kaufman, *op. cit.*, Chapter XI).

50.   Maurice Duverger, *Political Parties*, Wiley, New York, 1954, p. xxvii.

51.   Samuel Lubell, *The Future of American Politics*, Doubleday, New York, 1956, p. 212.

52.   Wilson's major domestic achievements ran along class lines; for example, Clayton Act, Income Tax, Federal Reserve, direct election of Senators —all antibigness, antiprivilege.

53.   The significant fact about the Fordney-McCumber Act of 1922 was *not* the reinstitution of high protective tariffs but the inauguration of the flexible provision that gave the President discretion to raise or lower duties by as much as 50 per cent of the statutory rate, *commodity by commodity*.

54.   The closeness of the two parties in the electorate since 1946—such that four of seven Congresses were controlled by the Presidential minority party and such that the 1960 Presidential election was as close as any in our history— suggests that a Party system with almost two evenly matched parties is not

innovative at all. When neither party is clearly in the minority, when the outs are always on the verge of being the ins and vice versa, the efforts of both are probably consolidative. Neither will move very far from the "center" of the existing issues or strike out along new lines if a slight marginal success along existing lines might produce the big payoff. It may well be that the viable two-Party system is one in which the minority party is a weak, not strong, opposition. The British concept of "mandate" is probably much more important for the minority party than for the Government.

55. Lubell, *op. cit.*, pp. 210 ff.

56. The pattern of Party control in *Congress* tends to reflect the inter-generational electoral shifts, the Presidential cadre reflecting the shorter term shifts of organized groups and leaders, particularly marginal groups. Cf. V. O. Key, *Politics, Parties and Pressure Groups*, pp. 608, 707-708. See also his *Public Opinion and American Democracy*, especially Parts II and V; and Berelson, *et al.*, *Voting*, especially Chapters 4 and 5.

CHAPTER 9

PARTY, PLURALISM, AND

POPULAR GOVERNMENT

Some Conclusions on Political
Meaning and Method

I HOPE THAT the preceding chapters have shed new light on two important problem areas in the study of political systems. The first is substantive and concerns the meaning of modern urban politics and the relationships among the political organizations and governmental institutions that have shaped the system; the extent and manner by which the present departs from the past; and how these changes have been accomplished, exposing to a certain extent the roles and functions of the major channels of recruitment, the impact of *types* of governmental decisions on the political structure, and the significance of dominant and minority party status. The second problem area is methodological and concerns the manner in which studies of community political systems have been and ought to be made. This final chapter is an attempt first to elaborate upon some of the normative questions raised by the findings, and second to propose some improvements in the design of future studies.

URBAN POLITICS: FUNCTIONAL FEUDALITIES

A specter is haunting the modern urban system. The specter is *pluralism*. The political system of New York City, created by and for political parties, is changing in ways that are difficult, if not impossible, for the parties to adapt to. The rise of large and effectively organized interest groups has altered in a fundamental way the relationships between parties and government, and in so doing has transformed the composition of the policy-making elite as well as the environment in which this elite is to operate.

This is not the first great transformation of the pattern of politics in the City, but, to oversimplify history, it is probably only the second. In other words, pluralism is deemed to be the third of three identifiable phases in the development of urban political history. The first was a government by an elite of status and mercantile wealth. It was a system of power that antedated universal suffrage, although it persisted for a period of time afterwards, perhaps until the Civil War. During that time there was a discernible shift from status *to* wealth in the makeup of the local elite—D. R. Fox, for instance, shows "how Federalists became Clintonians and Clintonians turned into Whigs";[1] nevertheless, it appears as though a fairly small, homogeneous upperclass elite held a virtual monopoly of power. It was not possible, however, for the old elite to maintain its position without mass support. Its social position and wealth could be matched, then overpowered, by electoral resources concentrated in the machine.

The old elite was displaced by machine control of the City's politics and government during the period between political consolidation under Tweed in the 1870s and governmental Consolidation in the 1890s. Earlier references in this book to the "traditional" system are thus references to the second period of political history. If the power holders in this period can be called an elite at all, it must be understood to be a very diffuse and heterogeneous elite that included elements of the old aristocracy as well as socially detested professional politicians. The fundamental feature of the period was the fact that political power was centered in the party. But just as it was not possible for the old elites to survive without mass support, so it turned out to be impossible for the machines, successor to the ancient regime, to maintain a monopoly of power, despite their monopoly of nomination and electoral business.

The third epoch began at some point after World War I. The decline of party-centered power in part reflected the profound social changes recorded by the City in the twentieth century. Perhaps these changes were not at first so evident as the expansion of the electorate and the mass immigration that ushered in machine control; yet there is little controversy now as to their importance. Industrial development and universal public education have created a vast middle-income skill group that has little in common with the upwardly mobile ethno-economic classes of the machine period. The second, third, and fourth generations of new and old ethnic groups share few perspectives of the immigrant mentality. The sons and grandsons perceive a host of alternative channels of success and recognition rather than simply politics, sports, or the underworld. Traditional political values— party loyalty and service and personal, in-group norms—are being displaced by skill, occupational and professional attainment, civic virtue, and, as a consequence, formal, rationalistic norms.

In the not so long run, some changes in political structure and practice would have been inevitable in face of these developments. But still other intervening developments are probably responsible for the specific political outcomes we have identified. Gideon Sjöberg has observed that " . . . once a high decree of industrial-urbanization has been achieved, it is doubtful that a small elite [of wealth *or* of party] can maintain a monopoly of power in a society." [2] The modern urban center is a highly complicated, differentiated, and specialized society. Differentiation and specialization of function in the economy are both causes and effects of the proliferation of organized interests, and a complex and differentiated governmental structure is the most favorable milieu for interest-group politics. The cult of neutrality insulates the civil service from party politics, but provides no equivalent defense against other nongovernmental political organizations; quite to the contrary, the neutral civil servant, the specialized administrator, finds his allies among his interest-group constituencies.

Party organizations, too, have become specialized as a consequence. Their monopoly now extends only to nominations and elections. Beyond that, their advantage appears great only among those sectors of government where the Weberian dilettante still prevails, where discretion is wide and choice is obscure. Party leaders are not excluded from the other arenas of government, but in such arenas they bargain with resources that are no longer telling; electoral power no longer wins hands down. The power of the masses could overwhelm the power of status and wealth, but only seldom does it appear to be a match for the authority of esoteric knowledge and the intensity of specialized, subject-matter interest.

One cannot now say that power is centered anywhere. In the earlier two periods of history there was probably a single "power structure," probably one elite for the entire City, whatever its composition or base of power might have been. In the third or modern period power is dispersed. There appear to be several, although not an unlimited number of, arenas of power, each with its own power structure and elite; or, according to Sayre and Kaufman, there are several functionally specialized decision centers with corresponding "core groups" and "satellite groups." [3] At least four such arenas have been identified in this study (see Chapters 6 and 7); more intensive analysis is likely to reveal still others and probably will expose even sharper distinctions among them. What meaning does this political context have for the governing of the City in the final decades of the twentieth century?

PLURALISM AND THE MAYOR:
THE "ORDEAL OF THE EXECUTIVE" [4]

The governmental structure of the City is highly articulated. In a sense there are as many "governments" as there are areas of public responsibility:

Functionally specialized officials constitute the core groups for decisions in particular functional areas of governmental action. . . . Each of these decision centers is surrounded by satellite groups especially concerned with its decisions. . . . Usually, the groups concerned chiefly with particular functions are uninterested in other, unrelated functional areas, so that most of the decisions (about appointments as well as programs and policies) in each decision center are worked out by an interplay among the specialized core and its satellite groups.[5]

Functional specialization of officials and governmental activities has subordinated "widely shared community values to the special interests of the separate and numerous 'islands of power' within it." [6]

These "islands of power" helped to create, and then became supported by, interests that were specialized and organized along parallel lines. Together the agencies and their supportive constituencies have become guilds, and their identifications with each other are guild identifications. In 1933, Luther Gulick ob-

served that each field of public endeavor tends to form a guild,
and that

It is a central dogma of each of these guilds, first, that what is
good for them is good for society, and second, that they know
their own business and that no nonmember of the guild is qualified
to make any comments or suggestions. . . . With such a foundation,
then, of group consciousness, it is almost inevitable that each guild
should desire to pull the government apart so that the guild may
take to itself the management and the control of its special part
of the governmental system.[7]

In such a governmental system where the separatist tendencies
are growing stronger there is an increasing need for more powerful instruments of central control and coordination at the very
time when many of these instruments are weakening. The canons
of good government provide for strengthening the Mayor through
Charter grants of greater authority over his Departments. But
however salutary these devices may be, strong-mayor principles
are not self-executing. As often as not they heap further responsibilities on the Mayor without giving him commensurate *real*
power. No formal device yet contrived has shown itself to be an
automatic centripetal factor.

In response to these separatist challenges, New York Mayors
very early began to turn to job-oriented political executives, because this type of appointment promised at least minimal satisfaction: a degree of participation in agency decisions. But, in the
long run, neither was this an entirely satisfactory adaptation
because each skill appointment tended to reduce the discretion of
the Mayor and his successors. Each appointment to a degree is
a commitment. Once the nexus between a "guild" and a top
appointment is established, a new set of expectations and demands appears on the Mayor's horizon concerning the decisions
the commissioner ought to make, who his successor ought to be,
and in general to whom the agency is supposed to be responsible
and accountable. Repetition makes these demands more legitimate; through usage they became internalized as "obligations"
and "responsibilities." "At the pleasure of the Mayor" takes on
greater irony.

That mayors often see these demands as good in themselves
does not necessarily indicate that a satisfactory adaptation has
been made. For, with each of these new commitments over the

years has come new liabilities: *viz., the weighing of power against skill.* Like Jacob's Ladder, the party in New York has been cut loose from the top as well as from the bottom of the political structure. As a consequence, the Mayor more and more often must face the alternatives of *either* a party-loyal commissioner *or* a skilled and experienced one. Thus the Mayor lacks his most dependable weapon of central control: a party.

In Great Britain civil service reform came from within the parties so that the fates of merit system and party discipline became tied together.[8] In New York City, if not all over the United States, civil service reform came from without and grew only at the expense of party control. The departmental bureaucracies grew and became highly politicized—*but not in party terms.* Thus, the parties did not develop pools of leadership groomed both in party and departmental affairs. The commissioners tend to bear only the weakest of employer-employee loyalties to the Mayor; they are formally responsible to him, but their loyalties often are focused elsewhere. As a candidate, the Mayor has a party; as a Mayor, whether he has a party or not is at least a matter of controversy.

Where there is real party government, where the Mayor is either the head of party or is effectively supported by it in all key posts and key decisions, there is a "strong mayor" regardless of charter, statutory, and administrative arrangements. Mayor Richard Lee, for example, brought about a number of spectacular innovations in New Haven despite his "weak-mayor" charter. In a democratic system without party-centered power, power will be "centered" in a variety of places, and governmental decisions will tend to become residues of the interplay of these independent centers of power. In the process, groups have the one great advantage of specialized knowledge and intense interest. At every turn the Mayor faces participants dedicated almost exclusively to a few specific governmental activities; and the intensity of their demand, not to mention the intrinsic virtue of it, is likely to make the Mayor yield. The relationship between Mayor and Department thus becomes deranged so that instead of having the upper hand, the chief executive typically negotiates at a disadvantage. Since the Mayor can fight only a few battles at a time, his role becomes very largely the passive one of moving from one crisis to another. Under such conditions, it is difficult to view each claim in terms of all other claims.

Pluralism and the Party

In the City proper and in all Counties except the Bronx, the day of the old machine is long since done. But the process of transformation continues. The Party grip on each new generation is increasingly flimsy. Social services once provided by the clubs have been taken over by governmental agencies. Citizenship training is given at free, compulsory public schools rather than over the pinochle table. Public employment, once the exclusive domain of the victorious party, is now the exception rather than the rule. Party Leaders still possess the sanctions of nomination and election for officials who disregard their merchandise; nonetheless the role of the Party organizations beyond the election continues to narrow because they have fewer and fewer attractive goods to offer. The needs of governing officials have changed faster than the Party's ability to adapt to them.

To a great and growing extent the one outstanding reform value, *skill*, is now a constant in the political processes of the City. If party government is to remain legitimate and functional, the party organization must coopt the people who possess the skills, the "middle-income skill groups." This has put the machines on the horns of a dilemma: The middle-income skill groups do not assimilate well into the traditional ways of doing party business; in large doses they promise to destroy many fundamental bases of local party cohesion. On the other horn, to resist such types is to default further to groups virtually organized around each new set of skills and subject-matter specialties, which in turn brings about a further narrowing of the party-in-government role.

The Results of Infiltration: In the 1957 Democratic primary one of the traditional Tammany clubs on the West Side was taken over by a group of insurgents made up primarily of young professional people and their wives, new to the District as well as to politics. At one of the first meetings of the new reform club in 1958, the order of business was to decide between the endorsement of Representative Adam Clayton Powell for renomination and his "Tammany-backed" opponent. A rather lively debate ensued during the course of which the new Leader of the club (and the Assembly District) tried to gain the floor. His own loyal followers tried to seat the Leader on the grounds that he was *violating strict parliamentary procedure.* Only the support

of the *old, traditional members* saved the Leader from ignomin-
ious silence.

This brief case illustrates the strong reasons why traditional
clubs are reluctant to seek appropriate talent. In the first place,
to seek is not an important term in the party lexicon. The politically ambitious always *sought* the party and allowed themselves
the privilege of party grooming. In this sense, the urban machine
was more like the Communist parties than the mass parties of
modern democracies. Like the Communist organization, the
club units of the machine worked on the principles of limited
membership, long probation, apprenticeship, and slow movement up the promotion ladder.

Secondly, the orientation of the white-collar "meritocrat" is
not like the older, upwardly mobile political activist. His presence
"changes things." He perceives many avenues of success and
recognition, and in politics is not likely to be satisfied in the short
run by older types of political incentives. But the "meritocrat"
is not simply more ambitious and self-reliant; and personal,
material reward is not his only interest. Typically, he is more
sophisticated. Inevitably he becomes interested in the organization itself—its meaning and its function, worse yet, its *proper*
meaning and function. Organization mysteries are to him subjects of inquiry, not objects of reverence, therefore subjects of
rational alteration, not mere objects of acceptance. The way of
life of the "meritocrat" is shaped by the very rational and formal
bureaucracies from which he draws his salary; and geographically
he is highly mobile. Thus he is usually new to the District, if
not to the City, and is accustomed to the formal, impersonal ways
of secondary or "contractual" association. He is educated, has a
sense of his own importance, and thus is usually in search of
"extracurricular" democracy to compensate for the hierarchical
sources of his daily bread. Without question the in-group quality
of the traditional party clubs and inner cores is altered by the
formality and impersonality of the middle-income skill groups.
With old cronies one can say "What's a constitution among
friends?" Strict parliamentary procedure is one of the minor
consequences of heterogeneity.

The fraternal, *bund* basis of party cohesion is weakened by
the entry of skill groups. Consequently the problems of discipline
grow at a time when sanctions in jobs and governmental access
are diminishing and the available patronage is less effective.
Party cohesion under such conditions demands more vigorous

theorizing and the promulgation of more distinct policies and ideologies; for these are operations ordinarily associated with the transition from *gemeinschaft* to *gesellschaft*.[9] These are the very operations for which traditional party leaders are most poorly equipped.

Resistance to Infiltration: The party's reluctance to coopt the new classes is understandable, even if not justifiable, because new values alter established patterns.[10] In the long run, party organization would survive the transition, but short-run changes of leadership and practice would appear to the old guard to be the beginning of the end. However, the alternative—full-scale resistance—is worse.

The organization of new values creates new effective demands. Eventually these demands are either reflected in governmental personnel and policy or else find satisfaction in a social movement. In either case, parties are weaker. As long as parties control nominations and elections the party system cannot be destroyed. But the parties can be further insulated from governmental processes; their role can be narrowed exclusively to the electoral arena. Already the group nature of reform in New York has, in Hofstadter's excellent terms, "weakened party government and party responsibility." [11] Party and party government are weaker *not* because reform innovations in New York have been populist, as Hofstadter argues,[12] but *pluralist.*

Eliminating parties does not "depoliticize" or "deorganize" politics; it only alters its form toward interest-group politics. Elimination of party from departmental affairs usually throws the administrator into the arms of his clientele.[13]

Toward Restoration of the Machine

The political machine, by its very entrepreneurial essence, is a neutral apparatus. There can be good machines as well as bad. The proper solution is not to reject power but to reject self-indulgence and venality in power. With enlightened leadership the urban machine could adapt itself to the real needs of city government. By absorbing pools of twentieth-century talent the machine could reduce the separation between power and skill. Party government and merit are not mutually exclusive values; in fact, if they became joined it would be possible to have organized partisanship in the public interest rather than for its own sake. This is what is required for the restoration of the machine.

But adaptation by the party is not the only requirement. The new white-collar class also has some adjustment to make. The great mistake of respectable classes as reformers is their poor understanding of the invaluable function of party as a force drawing separatist groups toward each other and bringing about a certain amount of accommodation among "pure" claims before they reach the policy agenda. Reform movements generally pursue a politics of *disintegration.*

In the past the hostility of reform leaders to organization was so strong that they could no better allow it in themselves than to the party leaders. The effect, as we have seen, was the contraction of the party domain and the expansion of group access. The reform movement of the 1950s, more clearly than any before a movement of middle-income skill groups, promises to be even more devastating in its effects, for it is taking place within the majority party. The Republicans, being the minority, have had an easier task of accommodation. In the Democratic party, especially in the all-important Manhattan organization, infiltration of the new elements is largely through insurgency. Victory through insurgency has tended to confirm the antiorganization proclivities of the reformers, setting them off in revolutionary directions.

The rhetoric of reform in the Democratic party is "democratization." In practice it takes the form of holding the District Leader continually responsible to his membership; generally, all-important decisions require a vote of the District club. While this might be a salutary practice in issues involving a single district, its impact on the County and City is strongly decentralizing. Practically all nominations involve more than one District, and, of course, party programs are the concern of all Districts. A fully "reformed" Democratic party would handle the business of nomination through a form of international relations. It would be extremely difficult for a party made up of program-oriented but leadership-hostile personnel to enunciate a program at all. In the months following Mayor Wagner's re-election in 1961 it was already clear that his position as a new kind of boss was highly questionable.

Due to the independent election of the Comptroller, the power of the Board of Estimate, the many independent commissions and authorities, and the special sway of the unionized bureaucracies, New York has, in effect, a "weak-mayor" form of government. The weakness of the decentralized government

could, however, be offset by the strength of a strong party centralized toward the Mayor.[14] Decentralization into the clubhouses
with rather severe limitations on the discretion and flexibility of
the District Leader is far from conducive to responsible, organized partisanship. The influx of new blood into local party politics
has undoubtedly raised the caliber of the average political activist and should eventually raise the level of public morality.
But extreme decentralization is the best way to prevent these
new forces from being felt at the centers of administrative
power.

In a city the size and diversity of New York the role of the
ordinary citizen is inevitably limited. If he is to be effective at
all he must act in concert with others. And if he desires to be
an activist his choice lies not between the "bosses" and the town
meeting but much more likely between party affiliation and
interest-group affiliation. Responsible party government needs
the new middle class of education and skill. On the other hand,
this group needs to learn that enlightened followership is as
important as enlightened leadership. All these things are required
to restore the machine.

Well-established civil service practices, widely accepted professional norms and hosts of legal safeguards reduce the threat
of an "old-line" machine almost to zero. Opening up many
channels of success, regardless of religion or ethnic identification, and the regularization of most of the City's contractual
relations, takes away most of the underpinnings and potential
support of the self-indulgent boss. The responsiveness of Carmine DeSapio to pressures for reform between 1953 and 1958
and his eventual replacement along with the drastic shake-up
of four of the five County organizations in 1961 prove not that
strong party organization is evil but that reformers have nothing
very much to fear from organization and from strong party
leaders at the County and City level.[15]

The City has little to fear and very much to gain from
restoration of the machine. If parties do not reclaim primacy
in policy-making and implementation, the chief executive will
continue to be faced with the ad hoc adjustment of claims.
Particularism will continue to spread, and the "ordeal of the
executive" will remain unresolved. Executive discretion—and
therefore elective responsibility—will continue in its secondary
role to a kind of functional representation. That is to say, the
parceling out of increasing responsibility to the functional areas

reduces the area of collective responsibility, the *sine qua non* of self-government. For restraint of *functional* power is not electoral but "jurisdictional," accountability being not to electorates but to professional ethics and organized clientele. Government by specialists is a world of *intra vires-ultra vires,* not good or bad.[16]

In contrast, a viable party system is integrative. Functional power in a *party*-political framework is subject both to jurisdictional and electoral restraint. The gross yes-no, winner-take-all, mechanism of election dictates a political calculus that must balance all functional areas together, each single area becoming a mere factor in the equation. Without the common ties of party in the executive command posts the governmental system is not the den of bosses but a chamber of administrative boredom: "Why blame us? After all, I appointed the best man in the New York Association of Sanitary Engineers."

No governmental system is committed to or responsible for maintaining political parties. Rather, the relationship is the other way around. Parties must adapt to the new scheme of things or their role in the political system will be further narrowed. The new skill groups must adjust to the realities of party politics or there will be no party system at all associated with City government. When party ceases to function after elective offices have been filled, popular government is the loser.

For the casual reader the book ends here. The final section is addressed primarily to the serious student of politics and "community power structure." In the past decade, great progress has been made in the study of communities as whole political systems, and in the next few years the bulk of publication, if not the rate of progress, is likely to increase markedly. The remaining pages will attempt to give future students the benefit of my trial and error.

COMMUNITY POWER STRUCTURE: THE FORGOTTEN CRAFTS OF PUBLIC ADMINISTRATION AND HISTORY

Appointments comprise only a single strand of political history, a limited segment of the political process. The pattern of appointments and the characteristics of the appointees and appointing authorities have been used as indicators of broader social and political forces. The offices and powers involved in these appointment transactions cut across practically every aspect of governmental activity and, so it has been assumed, eventually involve practically all of the organized interests in the community. Many of the generalizations in preceding chapters had to be offered tentatively, as hypotheses for further study, because they go too far beyond the data—that is, many of the generalizations are suggested but not fully confirmed by the data. However, data limited to the top political appointments are sufficient to reveal at least two fundamental weaknesses in community power analyses: weaknesses of scope and weaknesses of depth.

"Community power structure" has become virtually a new discipline in the field of social science. Since the publication of Floyd Hunter's pioneering study of Regional City,[17] increasing numbers of scholars have been occupying themselves with community studies. Hunter's contribution lies perhaps in his weaknesses, for they have provoked a renewed interest in the total context of policy making. A host of excellent empirical and critical reports have followed hard on the heels of what has come to be called the "Hunter approach." It is not my intention here to review the literature of criticism but to contribute to it by suggesting some improvements in the design of studies.[18]

GOVERNMENTAL STRUCTURE AND POLITICAL POWER: THE PROBLEM OF SCOPE

It is indeed ironic that the factors political scientists know best tend to be neglected in studies of power. The behavioral approach to politics was sought as an escape from the formalism and legalism of traditional political science, but the escape has been all too complete. *None of the studies of community leadership take governmental structure and activity sufficiently into account.* One weakness of the "Hunter approach" consistently criticized is his assumption that there is a single set of power holders, that "beneath the facade of democratic politics a social and economic elite will usually be found actually running things."[19] Since in social science one can usually find what he sets out to find, the scholar must guard against overly specific and biased expectations. Professor Dahl suggests such a defense and employs it very well in New Haven.[20] "Only by studying influence-groups *in the context of particular decisions*," says Dahl, "is it possible to isolate the scope of each group's influence. . . . "[21] In other words, one should of course be prepared to find a single elite, but he must also be prepared for some kind of leadership group in each of several "issue areas":[22] then it becomes an empirical question whether all, part, or none of the leadership groups are made up of the same people. If the overlap among leadership groups is complete, one might then conclude that the community under study is governed by a "power elite." But if the overlap is a good deal less than complete, then a different image is required.

However, Professor Dahl's issue areas still do not seem to be sufficient. In the urbanized community the most important public decisions, except those involving nominations, are governmental; the power of all political participants must be exercised *through* some formal governmental agency. Government activity is continuous; agency decisions are repetitive. The particular impact of these decisions and the manner in which each agency of government is organized are probably the most important determinants of the power structure in any modern political system, because *structures form around relatively well-established and widely shared expectations.* On any given issue one can identify *alliances* and other political arrangements for combat, but if the issue is transitory so will the alliance be.[23] Key issues like the ones analyzed in Professor Dahl's book are fought out within an established context; no full-scale study of the community has yet determined that context.

Political scientists know well that there is an intimate interrelation between governmental structure and activity and political structure and power, yet few systematic studies by political scientists have been aimed at revealing the precise nature of these relationships. The discipline has itself become so specialized that some political scientists are experts in "government" and others in "politics." To date, most of the studies combining the two areas are case studies that deal with the roles of major participants in the generation and settlement of specific policy issues. The trouble with case studies is that they are not cumulative; we have no basis for comparing all the cases in order to discover underlying conditions that would explain the peculiarities and similarities among the discrete observations. This, it seems to me, is because we have no framework within which to define the *meaning* of each discrete instance; without a general framework, each case remains a mass of interesting but essentially unassimilated fact. For facts to become *factors* some theorizing, some *a priori* generalization, is required. Professor Dahl's book is unquestionably the most exhaustive study of the politics of policy yet produced. But suppose another study of other issues were made in New Haven and a different set of participants were discovered, or, for that matter, the same set of participants? We would then be in a position to say with greater authority than before that the community is either more or less governed by a single elite; but we could not explain these phenomena in a theoretically interesting way and we could not place these findings against studies of other systems, for we have not defined beforehand what the outstanding attributes of these issues are and would thus have no *basis* for making any comparisons.

My argument is at bottom an argument in favor of starting a study with a full understanding of the basic functions of government and how they are being performed. I would propose that we take each decision-making agency and determine the *nature* of the typical decision; in other words, that we determine at the beginning precisely what are the stakes that participants can expect to gain in each segment of government. Once this is determined, we should move next to a grouping of specific governmental agencies into a small number of meaningful categories, so that no agency or issue eventually studied is unique. To some degree, we go through this procedure very often, in referring to the politics of public health, the politics of urban redevelopment, the politics of education. But we do not go far enough. These categories, like Dahl's issue areas, are too specific and too descriptive to escape the problem of uniqueness and so are lacking theoretical interest. Abstractly, what are the relevant attributes —the *stakes*, therefore—of public health policy, redevelopment policy, and education policy? Just as we work with *types* of people—attributes of class, status, occupation, group membership and so on—rather than with individual persons, so should we employ categories of policy; and, as far as possible, these ought to be congruent with the institutional-legal arrangements of government. Otherwise we deny, completely without justification, much of the traditional wisdom of political science. An attempt was made in Chapters 6 and 7 to contrive a set of categories based upon the nature of the typical decisions made by governmental agencies. It was an attempt to reach some kind of balance between Hunter's single power structure assumption and the overly specific, transitory "scopes of power" assumptions made by Dahl. The assumptions underlying my four "arenas of power" are simply: (1) that the scope of power (i.e., power *for* what, *over* what) does not extend beyond a participant's perspectives or expectations; (2) that a participant's perspectives are shaped by the institutional arrangements of government (at least in modern communities, where governmental boundaries are clearly demarcated); and (3) that the structure of the agency and the relations of participants to the agency and to each other (i.e., power structure) follow the function of the agency, and that agencies performing similar functions will develop similar power structures. Thus, some participants are involved in the "issue area" of public health, which may be *their* scope of power; but it is of great importance whether the decisions in question are regulatory (e.g., inspection, quarantine) or redistributive (e.g., outpatient clinics, polio shots). Participants may have public health policies in common, but their relations to each other and to the public health agencies—the power structure, therefore—will differ. And the utility of their resources will vary accordingly.

The four arenas I have identified may turn out to be too broad and too loosely defined. But there were some rather striking differences in the distribution of attributes among them that could hardly be explained except in terms of differences in the nature of the decisions involved and the way in which the agencies within each arena were organized.[24] Many key issues that appear from time to time involve more than one functional alteration and thus may "cut across" the more stable arrangements. This alone suggests that the telling influences in a given issue may be exceptional, a result of peculiar rather than typical alliances. It also suggests that there is a rather high probability that efforts will be made to fit issues into established alliance structures and to define issues so that they are "give-away programs" or "coercive measures" rather than a combination of both. In 1946, for example, something as novel and complex as atomic energy development was defined as "civil versus military control," even though this factor was not even strongly relevant, in order to fit it better into the "liberal-conservative" cleavages of the 1930s.[25]

Objection can be raised that the analysis in this volume is limited to only one type of political transaction—appointments— and that other patterns can be expected to prevail elsewhere. But this only serves to emphasize the point: The formal structures of government must be clarified—in good public administration fashion—and a determination of *what things are to be gotten from government* must be made *before* an elaborate and sophisticated study of informal behavior patterns is undertaken. The pattern of appointments is a valuable indicator of some real cleavages in community power. Data on appointments have the great virtue of being quantifiable while being intimately involved in relations between government and politics. They are necessary but not sufficient in the study of power.

Who Got What?

The dimension most consistently neglected in studies of power, as I have taken pains to point out in several places, is the time dimension. If techniques for identifying leaders and their scopes of power were perfected they would still fail to reveal *structures* of power, elites of power, or ruling classes. There are no standards to tell us whether a given cross-section of time is normal or a peculiar departure from the norm. If we desire to understand the *structure* of power, we need to know not only "who gets what" but who *got* what over a considerable period of time. There is no other way to determine the probability of a given type of participant making his claims effective and to discover the conditions underlying that effectiveness.

Future studies must incorporate a much larger span of time than has heretofore been the case. The "reform cycle" amply demonstrates that the relationships among all major participants often depends as much upon transitory factors as upon the arena in question. The type of Administration in office, the nature of the struggle that led to its formation, and the changing personalities and commitments of formal office holders must all be accounted for. The leadership of nongovernmental groups is almost always more stable than governmental leadership, but any significant changes in the latter are most likely to affect the access and effectiveness of the former. The intra-party struggle of 1961 and Mayor Wagner's post-election attempts to reorient both his party and his administrative leaders suggest that the politics of 1961–1965 will be materially different from that of the 1953-1961 period.[26]

Without history, or more particularly *time series,* we are deprived of one of our best means for discovering new "laws" of politics and testing old ones. We need a very clear understanding of the *sequence* of events before imputing to them any notion of relationship. In social science, the testing of hypotheses in time is always likely to prove more intuitively satisfying than the single sampling or stop-time photographic test. This is no argument against the use of various statistical tests of association. On the contrary, the same tests will probably show greater power if they are used by political historians rather than political chroniclers. Ideally, political scientists should be equipped to take successive samplings of political participants and events and in a variety of contexts; we need to establish continuing relations between ourselves, the observers, and the universe of events. Until we are so equipped, we have precious few opportunities for trending the perishable phenomena of opinions, attitudes, and perspectives. But many other kinds of data are not so transitory. In sum, until we turn to history we must severely limit, if not eliminate, our use of the concept of "structure." The development of a fairly elaborate taxonomy of government action —closely tied into traditional understanding of the nature of the public domain—and the employment of such a scheme in the history of the community promise a way out of the trap of high-class and rather expensive journalism. The proper question for political scientists is not "Who rules?" but "What are the conditions for rule?"

NOTES

1. *The Decline of Aristocracy in the Politics of New York*, p. v. See also Gabriel Almond, *op. cit.*, and Robert A. Dahl, *Who Governs?*, *op. cit.*, especially pp. 11-86.

2. "Comparative Urban Sociology," in Robert Merton, *et al.*, *Sociology Today*, p. 351.

3. *Op. cit.*, pp. 710-719.

4. This poignant phrase is taken from David B. Truman, *The Governmental Process*, Chapter XIII.

5. Sayre and Kaufman, *op. cit.*, p. 711. Emphasis added.

6. *Ibid.*, p. 719.

7. Quoted in Meyerson and Banfield, *Politics, Planning and the Public Interest*, pp. 38-39.

8. Cf. Pendleton Herring, *The Politics of Democracy*, Rinehart, New York, 1940, pp. 351 ff.

9. Karl Mannheim, *Ideology and Utopia*, Harvest edition, Harcourt, Brace, New York, 1955, p. 131.

10. Cf. Robert E. Park: "The political machine is . . . an attempt to maintain, inside the formal administrative organization of the city, the control of a primary group." *The City*, p. 35 f.

11. *Op. cit.*, p. 265.

12. I.e., "direct government." See *ibid.*, Chapter VI.

13. Cf. James W. Fesler's excellent study, *The Independence of State Regulatory Agencies*, Public Administration Service, Chicago, 1942.

14. Cf. Meyerson and Banfield, *Politics, Planning and the Public Interest*, Free Press, New York, 1955, p. 287.

15. The most important reform outstanding is the requirement for direct election of Assembly District Leaders throughout the State, so that, among others, Charles Buckley's leadership in the Bronx can be put to the popular test.

16. Cf. Karl Mannheim, *Freedom, Power and Democratic Planning*, Oxford, New York, 1950, pp. 51-59.

17. *Community Power Structure*, University of North Carolina Press, Chapel Hill, 1953.

18. A review of criticisms and some noteworthy additions are provided in Nelson Polsby, *Community Power and Political Theory*, Yale University Press, New Haven, 1963.

19. Robert A. Dahl, *Who Governs?* p. 6.

20. *Ibid.*, Chapters 8-12.

21. Some Notes and Models for Political Systems, a paper presented to the S.S.R.C. seminar on urban leadership in August, 1957, p. 30. Emphasis added.

22. *Who Governs?* pp. 102 ff. The issue areas in the Dahl study were urban redevelopment, education and nominations for electoral office. Specifically, he took eight important redevelopment decisions between 1950 and 1959, eight decisions of varying importance on public school policy and nine elections and eighteen nominations for Mayor between 1941 and 1957. (p. 333.)

23. For example, a "log-rolling" alliance is composed of two or more bloc leaders who have no interest at all in common. The basis of their alliance requires that each cares intensely (if not exclusively) about and has some influence in one issue and each is indifferent to the cause of the other. Their alliance can usually be sustained on those matters they have least in common. Still other alliances form around tangential relations and are only sustained as long as those issues last.

24. Two observations from Chicago politics might serve as illustration even though they were published twenty years apart: Harold Gosnell discovered that tax assessment had been run "by a bipartisan combination which included the leaders of the Democratic and Republican parties." (*Machine Politics: Chicago Model*, p. 7. The special position of the party in this "Inputs" arena was discussed at length in Chapters VI and VII above.) In contrast, Meyerson and Banfield describe a highly fluid, pluralistic context in urban redevelopment decisions, a "regulatory" arena. (*Politics, Planning and the Public Interest*, pp. 96 ff. Compare with my description of the regulatory arena in New York, Chapters VI and VII above.)

25. See Byron Miller, "A Law Is Passed—The Atomic Energy Act of 1946." *University of Chicago Law Review*, Vol. 15, No. 4.

26. See *New York Times* reports almost daily following the 1961 election but especially November 9 and 14 and December 2-6.

SOME PROBLEMS OF DEFINITION

AND DESIGN

THE DATA

IN THIS STUDY the top patronage has been treated as a series of strategic political decisions in which the identities as well as policies of the appointees and candidates for appointment are intimately involved. The fact of this involvement is the basis upon which the characteristics of political appointees have been used as indices for a variety of political values and practices that cannot be assessed by direct observation, especially in a political system so complex and dynamic as a large urban center.

Each appointment, except for numerous illustrative purposes, was treated as a nameless unit in the flow of men and characteristics through institutional positions. This can be thought of as a "decision flow," providing the political scientist with firm data in a manner not unlike that of the economist in his national income analyses. The first considerable advantage in the use of political personnel and their characteristics as indices is, then, that they provide both relevant and objective data. A second, no less important advantage is that the items are sufficiently numerous to allow systematic quantitative analysis. Without offering the reader a personal judgment on the value of the analysis in this volume, it seems at least fair to say that with a set of variables clearly defined and theoretically relevant, a great many

significant hypotheses can be put to truly historical and comparative tests with data of the kind I have used. Political scientists
have been very late in using the quantitative resources readily
available to them, and personnel data is one of the most sorely
underutilized types.

The data of the study were collected from conventional biographical sources,[1] including questionnaires that were sent to a
considerable number of commissioners serving in 1957–1958. In
this respect New York City was a particularly happy choice
because of the *New York Times* Annual Index. A *Times* obituary
in particular is an item to be prized. Further, the Index also
served as a key to other local dailies that were bound but not
indexed. All of the data were coded and punched on IBM cards,
and most of the analyses came directly from the counter-sorter
device.

THE POPULATION

Since there were literally thousands of strategic appointments
made in New York City during the six decades in question, some
delimiting criteria were needed. Two general considerations were
uppermost in the choice of criteria: *workability* and *comparability*. The study had to be manageable as a one-man operation,
and the positions chosen had to be clearly identifiable and stable
so that comparisons could be made within this study over time
and with studies of the future. The most important initial choice
was that of the appointments process itself. It was felt, as was
explained in Chapter 1, that the statistical population ought to
be defined in the most meaningful, institutional terms. Along
these lines the other criteria followed more or less logically:

1. *All appointments by a single appointing authority, the
Chief Executive:* Regarding these decisions, all influential forces
in the community must necessarily focus upon the Mayor, be
he weak or strong, because he must sign the commission. Therefore, there is a single dimension or focus of political activity.

2. *Only bona fide Departments of Government:* Here both
considerations of comparability and workability came into play.
First, although departmental status may vary from city to city,
the Department was found to be the most stable and identifiable
unit. Second, this criterion allowed the omission of several agencies and therefore a considerable number of appointments—for

example, the City Chamberlain (officially a bureau of the Department of Finance until abolished), the old bureau of purchases, the Mayor's executive office, and so forth.

3. *Of the Departments, only those whose powers are formally derived from the City Charter:* This excluded the authorities, the Board of Higher Education, the Board of Water Supply, and others. The Departments of Traffic and Labor Relations were not included until they were given full Charter status. Objections might be raised to this criterion, but it was strongly felt that if the project had to be cut in some fashion, this seemed the least arbitrary and the way most favorable to comparison with future studies.

4. *Only the heads of Departments:* Not even in the American sense is there a Cabinet in New York, but "cabinet" is a convenient designation for the particular *level* of government involved. Admittedly, the Mayor makes other administrative appointments of great importance, but positions below the top vary in influence and nature over time and from city to city, whereas the Department and head remain fairly stable.

5. *Finally, the unit of analysis was taken to be the* appointment, *not the individual office-holder:* This enlarged the population without substantially increasing the research. Close to 850 individuals were identified in the City Record *Civil List* as holding the positions that fell within the above criteria. However, the resulting N is 1,191, because:

a. Many of the individuals held more than one of the posts included by my criteria. Some, in fact, held more than one of these positions simultaneously.

b. Whole hosts of individuals were reappointed to the same job: (i) by a new mayor if the post did not have a fixed term, or (ii) by the same or succeeding mayor if the individual was reappointed to a fixed-term post. Here it should be emphasized that *continuation* in office as such did not constitute reappointment unless there was an explicit appointment decision, the signing of a new commission.

Each separate appointment was recorded on a separate card. Separate cards on the same individual were identical in biographical data but were different on such matters as tenure, job just before and after appointment, appointing mayor, and so forth.

The results of these criteria and choices were as follows:

OFFICES AND OFFICERS WITH CABINET STATUS

I. Under 1938 Charter as Amended to 1958

    A. Appointment and Removal at the Pleasure of the Mayor

        1. Deputy Mayor
        2. Division of Administration—City Administrator (from 1954)
        3. Tax Department—President
        4. Department of Finance—Treasurer
        5. Police Department—Commissioner
        6. Fire Department—Commissioner
        7. Parks Department—Commissioner
        8. Hospital Department—Commissioner
        9. Welfare Department—Commissioner
      10. Department of Correction—Commissioner
      11. Department of Buildings—Commissioner
      12. Department of Public Works—Commissioner
      13. Department of Marine & Aviation—Commissioner
      14. Department of Sanitation—Commissioner
      15. Department of Licenses—Commissioner
      16. Department of Purchase—Commissioner
      17. Department of Personnel—President of Civil Service Commission[a]
      18. Department of Markets—Commissioner
      19. Art Commission—three members[b]
      20. Department of Traffic—Commissioner
      21. Department of Labor—Commissioner (from 1954)
      22. Bureau of Budget—Director
      23. Board of Assessors—three members
      24. Department of Water Supply, Gas & Electricity—Commissioner

    B. Appointment Restricted, Removal at Pleasure

        1. Law Department—Corporation Counsel[c]
        2. Health Department—Commissioner[c]
        3. Department of Investigation—Commissioner[c]
        4. Department of Air Pollution Control—Commissioner[c] (from 1952)

OFFICES AND OFFICERS WITH CABINET STATUS (Cont'd)

    5. Art Commission—four members[b, c]

    6. Tax Department—six Tax Commissioners[e]

C. Appointment at Pleasure, Removal Restricted

    1. City Planning Commission—seven members (eight-year terms)

    2. Board of Health—two members[b] (eight-year terms)

    3. Board of Standards & Appeals—one member (six-year term)

D. Appointment Restricted, Removal Restricted

    1. Board of Health—two members[b, c] (eight-year terms)

    2. Board of Standards & Appeals—four* members[c] (six-year terms)

    3. Department of Personnel—Civil Service Commission—two[†] members[d] (six-year terms)

    4. Board of Education—nine[‡] members[b, a]

    5. City Record—Supervisor[c]

    6. City Sheriff[c] (1942)

    7. City Register[c] (1942)

    8. Chief Medical Examiner[c]

II. Under 1901 Charter as Amended

A. Appointment and Removal at the Pleasure of the Mayor

    1. Police Department—Commissioner

    2. Fire Department—Commissioner

    3. Health Department—Commissioner

    4. Tenement House Department—Commissioner

    5. Commissioner of Accounts

    6. Department of Street Cleaning—Commissioner (abolished 1929)

    7. Department of Bridges (Plant and Structures)—Commissioner

    8. Department of Public Charities—Commissioner

    9. Department of Correction—Commissioner

    10. Department of Docks and Ferries—Commissioner

    11. Department of Taxes and Assessments—Chairman of Board

    12. Board of Assessors—three members

    13. Art Commission—three members[b]

    14. Department of Licenses—Commissioner (from 1914)

Offices and Officers With Cabinet Status (Cont'd)

15. Board of Standards and Appeals—two members (1916)
16. Department of Markets—Commissioner (1917)
17. Department of Purchases—Commissioner (1923)
18. Budget Bureau—Director (1924)
19. Department of Hospitals—Commissioner (1929)
20. Department of Sanitation—Commissioner (1933)
21. Department of Water Supply, Gas and Electricity— Commissioner

B. Appointment Restricted, Removal at Pleasure
1. Law Department—Corporation Counsel[c]
2. Department of Parks—Board of three members (four after 1906, five after 1920, abolished 1933)[e]
3. Department of Taxes and Assessments—Board of four members[d, e] (one lawyer required)
4. Municipal Civil Service Commission—"Three or more" members[d] (three members with fixed terms after 1922)
5. Commissioner of Accounts[c]
6. Art Commission—three members[b, c]
7. Board of Standards and Appeals—two members[c]
8. Board of Health—one member (1919),[c] two members (1928)[c]

C. Appointment at Pleasure, Removal Restricted
None

D. Appointment Restricted, Removal Restricted
1. Board of Education—1902-1916: forty-six members (five-year terms)[b, e]; 1917-   : seven members (seven-year terms)[b, e]
2. Civil Service Commission—after 1922: three members (six-year terms)[d]
3. Chief Medical Examiner (1918)[c]
4. Sanitary Commission—three members[c] (Established 1929, abolished 1933)

III. Under 1897 Charter

A. Appointment at the Pleasure of the Mayor[2]
1. Fire Department—Commissioner
2. Street Cleaning Department—Commissioner
3. Department of Water Supply—Commissioner

OFFICES AND OFFICERS WITH CABINET STATUS (Cont'd)

4. Department of Sewers—Commissioner[f]
5. Department of Public Buildings, Lighting & Supply—Commissioner[f]
6. Department of Parks—Board of three members
7. Department of Bridges—Commissioner
8. Department of Highway—Commissioner[f]
9. Board of Public Improvements—President[f]
10. Department of Public Charities—Board of three members
11. Department of Correction—Commissioner
12. Department of Docks and Ferries—Dock Board of three members
13. Department of Taxes and Assessments—President and three Board members
14. Board of Assessors—Board of five members
15. Health Department—President of Board
16. Commissioners of Accounts—Two
17. Art Commission—three members

B. Appointment Restricted
1. Police Department—Board of four Commissioners[d]
2. Law Department—Corporation Counsel[c]
3. Department of Buildings—Board of three members[c, f]
4. Department of Taxes and Assessments—one Board member (lawyer)
5. Department of Health—Board of three members[c]
6. Civil Service Commission—"Three or more" [d]

Legend:
a. Created 1954
b. Non-salaried
c. Job-oriented skills restrictions

d. Partisan restrictions
e. Geographic restrictions
f. Powers transferred in 1901 to Borough President

* 2 before 1956
† 3 before 1954
‡ 7 prior to 1948

SOME OPERATIONAL DEFINITIONS

As the reader will note in the abbreviated code reproduced below, very few elaborate procedures of coding or indexing have been used. Categories developed for documentary or "dead" sources are necessarily cruder than those appropriate for survey research because the researcher cannot affect the form of the data. Therefore, all categories have been kept as close as possible to conventional usages, allowing the reader to judge the strength and weakness of each for himself. It is only necessary here to present the operational definitions of the major concepts that were adapted to the particular needs of this study.

ETHNICITY AND RELIGION

1. *"Native-American" or "Old Stock":* Individuals (white only) whose families could claim American citizenship for at least three generations and who displayed no ethnic identification whatsoever. Those of English birth were combined with this group.

2. *Irish:* Individuals either born in Ireland, or whose parents were Irish-born or who displayed some clear Irish identification.

3. *Italian:* Same.

4. *Jewish:* Birth and/or identification; "Jewish" is used as an ethnic as well as a religious designation; and although the distinction may be an issue of some importance in some contexts, it seems to matter little in political transactions whether an individual is a German Jew or a Russian Jew.

5. *Other:* All other ethnic groups are combined into this residual category.

6. *Negro.*

7. *Not ascertained:* All individuals whose ethnic origins could not be identified and who were not affiliated with ethnic organizations of any sort.

For a number of purposes, particularly in Chapters 2 and 8, each of the major ethnic groups was treated separately. On other occasions these categories were collapsed in order to employ a simple native-Ethnic (including Negro) dichotomy, in which case categories 2 through 6 were combined as against 1. For religion, no refinements beyond the three major types of affiliation were employed; and at all times the three major religions were dealt with separately.

SOCIAL MOBILITY

By income and prominence, all cabinet officials belong to a relatively high socioeconomic stratum. What I sought, then, was a means of differentiating them in terms of their class positions *prior* to appointment, more importantly their class origins. What was the relative *social distance* traveled in reaching high public office?[3] The ideal approach to this and related questions would start with original class position, that is, the class position of father and grandfather; the ideal measure of class position would include, *inter alia,* the income of the family during the childhood at least of the appointee. However, so little information could be found on fathers and grandfathers or on income that a second best solution was determined: An arbitrary index combining level of formal education and status of the *initial* occupation of the appointee himself.[4]

Four levels of class origin or degrees of mobility are employed:[5]

1. *High mobility*—i.e., low original class position—is composed of those with less than a college education and whose initial occupations were manual labor.

2. *Medium high mobility* includes a very few manual laborers who attained college degrees (less than one per cent of the total), all of whose initial occupations were clerical or *salaried* technical-managerial-professional (white-collar) with less than a college degree (again a small number), and all officialdom and salesmen with less than a college diploma.

3. *Medium low mobility* includes the initially higher white collar worker, official, and salesmen with at least a college degree; all independent professionals; and a few people whose entire carrers were in nonsalaried, civic, or philanthropic work (mainly women).

4. *Low mobility* includes all Cabinet officials who were in the New York Social Register.

Thus, class 4 is in largest part not derived from the index. The members of this class are by occupation and education indistinguishable from most of the members of class 3; the Social Register is by far the best criterion for making the distinction.[6] Class 4 also includes a few commissioners whose initial occupation was "business leader"—having joined a large, family-owned firm—but by virtue of ethnicity, religion, or newness to the City were not in the Social Register.

In analyzing degree of mobility and the "class representativeness" of the cabinet and by comparing mobility rates of politics and business, I have made use of United States Census of Occupation statistics along the lines of Warner and Abegglen.[7] Because of the arrangement of the census data it was for this particular purpose impossible to break the categories down any further than those on Table 2.3. Thus, the ratios of class origin in the cabinet to class strata in the work force were based on the following comparisons: Low original class position compares the high-mobility cabinet members (manual labor-low education) with all counted as "employees" in the Census. Lower-middle original class position in the cabinet (medium-high mobility) is compared with the total number of clerical workers, foremen, and inspectors listed in the Census. Finally, it was necessary to combine all professional, trade, and "official" occupations in the Census to compare with both medium-low and low-mobility personnel (upper-middle and upper original class) in the cabinet. One further refinement was the choice of Census figures of thirty years prior to each cabinet. The average age at the time of appointment to the cabinet was about 51.5, and the average age at the time of initial employment was about 19.5. The Census data of thirty to thirty-four years prior to appointment will therefore yield a rough idea of the economic milieu in which the adult lives of the cabinet members began.[8]

SKILLS AND OCCUPATIONS

Use of occupations in the analysis of social class and mobility depends mightily upon reliable categories of occupational status. The typology eventually employed was an adaptation of the work of Alba Edwards, a leader in the field of occupation sociology.[9] These categories or "occupational families" are scalable in terms of median income and are therefore useful for social status ranking, irrespective of the income ranking within each family.[10] One is, for instance, a "clerical worker" either as an office boy or as a confidential secretary to an executive. The young lawyer can be considered for certain purposes as much "of the profession" as his more prominent colleague.

Thus, to analyze both social mobility and occupational careers, each appointee was classified in *one* "situs" for his *initial* occupation and, by use of the identical scheme elsewhere in the Code, one "situs" for his primary occupation or career.[11] Distinctions among these categories were not only made in terms of typical occupational duties or "heads and hands";[12] in addition, the *source of income* was an important consideration. For example, on the basis of the "heads and hands" criterion one gets the usual manual, clerical, sales, professional scheme. Adding source of income requires a few subdivisions such as salaried managerial, technical, and professional as against independent professional. It was also felt necessary to make a somewhat more arbitrary distinction between the small tradesman-proprietor and the "business leader," the latter being associated with businesses that extend throughout the City and beyond. And since the City bureaucracies are central to the present study, civil service occupations were coded separately. For the same reason "officialdom" was also kept separate.

The question of specialization, particularly the concept *job-oriented skill,* was dealt with early in Chapter 3 and in the summary of that chapter. *Merit* might have been used instead of an unfortunate neologism, but *merit* is laden with too many empirical as well as normative ambiguities. Job orientation is a relatively simply concept that requires both a judgment of the training, experience, and technology requirements of careers and their relationship to the functions of the Cabinet posts. For example, a lawyer or accountant serving as Commissioner of Investigation is clearly exercising job-oriented skills. On the other hand, Mayor La Guardia's first Commissioner of Investigation, Paul Blanshard, brought to his office only his zeal for rooting out corruption; he was, thus, a nonjob-oriented commissioner. On the Tax Commission realtors and tax lawyers were adjudged job oriented; their ordinary businessman and attorney associates were equally clearly nonjob-oriented appointments. Ferdinand Q. Morton, the first Negro to serve on the Civil Service Commission, had pursued his career as a lawyer primarily in the New York County District Attorney's office, so Morton was counted a nonjob-oriented commissioner for his first appointment and "job experienced" for his several succeeding appointments.

The skills orientation of an executive is not always an easy matter to determine. While coding for the large majority of cases was relatively simple because full biographies almost always give good educational and career profiles, there were many ambiguous cases. Reliability was maximized, first, by taking care that all coding be done by one person. Second, several informal reliability checks were made by soliciting the separate judgments of a group of graduate students. Where consensus was not reached, a "Not ascertained" was coded.

Finally, among the salaried careerists, a distinction between "bureaucrats" and "new professionals" was drawn at various points in the analysis. This distinction was based on two criteria: (1) the size of the establishment and (2) the degree of horizontal mobility. The salaried person whose career appeared to have been almost entirely contained within one large establishment (e.g., Mutual of New York or the New York City Fire Department) was adjudged a "bureaucrat." The career of the "new professional" was seen as taking place either in a single, small organization (e.g., a university or the executive office of a civic association) or for a significant amount of time in more than one large establishment. See Code item 33.

In reproducing an abbreviated version of the Code, I am following the very good example of some survey research publications and several studies closer to the approach used in this volume: namely, Morris Janowitz' *The Professional Soldier* and the Hoover Institute Elite Studies. In this effort I share Professor Janowitz' expectation that the comparative study of elites and, in particular, of urban politics will be facilitated.

ABBREVIATED CODE FOR STUDY
OF POLITICAL EXECUTIVES

Column

1-4 Identification

5-6 Department and Office of Appointee
  Punch, for example:
  01. Deputy Mayor
  09. Member, Board of Education
  24. Commissioner, Department of Markets

7 Perquisites of Office
  1. Full salaried
  2. Per diem
  3. Nonsalaried

Column

8 Appointment and Removal Standards
  0. No appointment or removal restrictions
  1. No appointment restrictions—removal restricted
  2. Job-related restrictions— removal at pleasure
  3. Job-related restrictions— removal restricted
  4. Partisan restrictions— removal at pleasure

Abbreviated Code for Study
of Political Executives
(continued)

Column

5. Partisan restrictions— removal restricted
6. Geographic restrictions— removal at pleasure
7. Geographic restrictions— removal restricted
8. Other
9. Not ascertained

9-10 Year of appointment

11-12 Year of birth

13-14 Actual age at entering gainful employment

15-16 Actual age at time of appointment

17 Place of Birth—Native Born
   1. New York City
   2. New England
   3. Mid-Atlantic (outside NYC)
   4. South and Southwest
   5. Midwest
   6. Far West
   7. Foreign born (Col. 18)
   8. Not ascertained

18 Place of Birth—Foreign Born
   1. Native born or not ascertained
   2. Italy
   3. Ireland, other

19 Place of rearing
   1. New York City
   2. Other large urban

Column

   3. Small urban
   4. Suburban and rural nonfarm
   5. Rural
   6. Not ascertained

20 National origin and ethnic identification*

21 Religious affiliation*

22 Race
   1. White
   2. Negro
   3. Other nonwhite
   4. Not ascertained

23 Political accreditation (Borough of Residence)

24 Length of residence in New York City prior to appointment
   1. Lifetime
   2. More than ten years
   3. Five–ten years
   4. One–five years
   5. Less than one year
   6. Not ascertained

25 Place of primary work and "success"
   1. New York City
   2. New York City and elsewhere
   3. Not New York City
   4. Not ascertained

   * See "Ethnicity and Religion" above in this Appendix.

ABBREVIATED CODE FOR STUDY
OF POLITICAL EXECUTIVES
(continued)

Column

26   Level of formal education
      attained
      (See classification under
      "Social Mobility" above in
      this Appendix)

27-28   Initial Occupation†
         00-02. Manual labor
         03-08. Clerical, sales
                employees
         09-13. Salaried technicians
         14-18. Salaried managers
         19-30. Salaried professional
         31-55. Civil Service
                (Breakdown identical
                to 09-30)
         56-62. Officialdom
         63-66. Semiprofessional—
                nonsalaried
         67-72. Small business
                proprietors
         73-79. Major salesmen
         80-89. Independent
                professional
         90-96. Business leader

29-30   Primary occupation or career
         Scheme identical to 27-28

30   Occupation just prior to
      appointment
      1. Same cabinet post
      2. Another cabinet post

† One hundred specific occupations
were classified within these occupational
families. For example, punch 02. skilled
laborer, punch 90. large owner, manufac-
turer.

Column

      3. Officialdom
      4. Civil service
      5. Large business
      6. Proprietor-major
         salesman
      7. Independent professional
      8. Salaried
      9. Other
     10. Not ascertained

31   Additional or complementary
      occupations
      1. Consulting and advising
      2. Part-time teaching
      3. Writing
      4. Corporation boards
      5. Other business
         associations
      6. Professional practice
      7. Military
      8. Other
      9. None ascertained

32   Orientation of skills
      1. Job-oriented
      2. Non-job-oriented
      3. Job-experienced—a year
         or more experience in
         earlier appointment or as
         deputy, or civic work in
         the specific business of the
         department, etc.

33   Institutional setting of salaried
      careers: horizontal mobility
      and size of organization*

* Items 2 and 3 "bureaucrats"; items 4
and 5 "new professionals."

ABBREVIATED CODE FOR STUDY
OF POLITICAL EXECUTIVES
(continued)

Column

1. Nonsalaried and upper managerial
2. Career in one large organization
3. Career in New York City bureaucracy
4. Career in one small organization
5. Career in two or more organizations
6. Other patterns
7. Wage-earner
8. Not ascertained

34-36　Tenure—actual length of service in months

37-40　Tenure ratio—tenure of appointee/tenure of appointing mayor

41　Number of mayors served under
1. One mayor
2. Two mayors
3. More than two

42　First post-cabinet occupation
0. Death or retirement
1. Reappointment
2. Appointment to another cabinet post
3. Officialdom
4. State or federal service
5. Return to pre-cabinet career
6. New nongovernmental occupation—non-salaried

Column

7. New nongovernmental occupation—salaried
8. Other
9. Not ascertained or Wagner cabinet

43　Primary post-cabinet occupation
Same as 42

44　Professional group affiliation†
1. Leader
2. No affiliation or not ascertained

45　*General* economic group affiliation

46　*Special* economic group affiliation

47　Unions

48　Organized City bureaucracies

49　Good government and civic groups

50　Philanthropic groups

51　Fraternal and convivial groups

52　Church and associated groups

53　Political affiliation (national)
1. Democrat
2. Republican

† Simple two-fold, Leader—no affilia tion, scheme employed for all group affilia tion items (44-52).

ABBREVIATED CODE FOR STUDY
OF POLITICAL EXECUTIVES
(continued)

Column

    3. Major third parties
    4. "Definitely none"
    5. Not ascertained

54 Political affiliation (local)
    1. Democrat
    2. Republican
    3. Major third parties
    4. Fusion
    5. "Definitely none"
    6. Not ascertained

55 Political activity: the club
    1. Leader, County, or AD
    2. Functionary
    3. Identifiable membership
    4. Inactive or slight
    5. No activity
    6. Not ascertained

56 Nonorganization political
    activity: the campaign
    1. Club member or
       functionary, high in City
       campaign
    2. Non-club member, high in
       campaign
    3. Non-club member with
       some campaign role
    4. Non-club, no campaign
       role
    5. Other
    6. Not ascertained

57 Social Register
    1. Yes
    2. No

Column

58 *Who's Who* and other
    directories
    1. National
    2. NYC or other local
    3. 1 and 2
    4. Other
    5. None

59 Appointing Mayor
    O. Van Wyck
    . . . .
    Y. Wagner

60 Sex

61 Personal relationship to mayor
    1. Yes
    2. No or not ascertained

62 Government service at any
    time prior to appointment
    0. None
    1. Civil service
    2. Federal or state
    3. Elective
       etc.

63 Education or training
    0. General
    1. Law
    2. Medicine
       etc.

64 Social mobility (based on
    items 26 and 27-28. See also
    above in this Appendix)
    1. High
    2. Medium-high

ABBREVIATED CODE FOR STUDY
OF POLITICAL EXECUTIVES
(continued)

Column

    3. Medium-low
    4. Low
    5. Not ascertained

65 Area of governmental activity
    (See Table 6.4)

Column

    1. Regulation and property
       protection
    2. Service and Welfare
    3. Governmental Inputs
    4. Overhead

NOTES

1. For specific sources, see Bibliography.

2. The Mayor's power of removal was restricted for *all* officials after the first six months, when "any such public official may be removed by the Mayor for *cause* upon charges preferred." (Section 95; emphasis added.)

3. Cf. Natalie Rogoff, "Recent Trends in Urban Occupational Mobility," in Bendix and Lipset, *op. cit.*, pp. 442-454.

4. The status of occupations is discussed in the section immediately following.

5. Level of education and status of initial occupation were combined in the following manner.

| | | | | *Initial occupation* | | | | | |
Education	Man- ual	Cleri- cal	Sal- aried	Offi- cial- dom	Sales & trade	Ind. prof.	Non-sal. civic philan.	Bus. Leader	Social regis- ter
Elem. only	1	2	2	2	2	*	*	*	4
High school grad.	1	2	2	2	2	*	*	*	4
Some post high school	1	2	2	2	2	3	*	4	4
College grad. or over	2	2	3	3	3	3	3	4	4

The four levels of mobility were established according to typical breaks in the distributions for the cabinet of each of the twelve mayors. Education and initial occupation were closely related over the entire 60-year period. Cells marked with asterisk were empty for every mayor.

6. See E. Digby Baltzell, *The Philadelphia Gentleman*, Chapter I and "'Who's Who in America' and 'The Social Register': Elite and Upper Class Indexes in Metropolitan America," in Bendix and Lipset, *op. cit.*, pp. 172-185.

7. *Op. cit.*, pp. 33-45 and *passim*. See also Natalie Rogoff, *op. cit.*, pp. 443-447.

8. Cf. Warner and Abegglen, *op. cit.*, pp. 39-40.

9. Cf. "A Socio-Economic Grouping of the Gainful Workers in the United States," *Journal of the American Statistical Association* (December, 1933), pp. 377-387; and *Population: Comparative Occupation Statistics for the United States, 1870-1940* (Government Printing Office). See also: Natalie Rogoff, "Recent Trends in Urban Occupational Mobility" and Lewis Corey, "The Middle Class," in Bendix and Lipset, *op. cit.*, pp. 372, 442-454.

10. Delbert Miller and William Form, *Industrial Sociology*, pp. 670, 799. Paul Hatt refers to these "occupational families" as "situses" in his excellent defense of occupational indices for the study of social stratification. "Occupation and Social Stratification," *American Journal of Sociology*, Vol. LV, No. 6 (1950).

11. See the Code at the end of this Appendix for the specific classifications.

12. Cf. Paul Hatt, *op. cit.*

BIBLIOGRAPHY *

GENERAL REFERENCES

Books

Adrian, Charles. *Governing Urban America*. McGraw-Hill, New York, 1955.

Bailey, Steven K. *Congress Makes a Law*. Columbia University Press, New York, 1950.

Bean, Louis. *How to Predict Elections*. Knopf, New York, 1948.

Bendix, Reinhard, and S. M. Lipset (eds.). *Class, Status and Power*. Free Press, New York, 1953.

Berelson, Bernard, *et al. Voting*. University of Chicago Press, Chicago, 1954.

Dahl, Robert A. *Who Governs?* Yale University Press, New Haven, 1961.

Dahl, Robert A., and Edward Lindblom. *Politics, Economics and Welfare*. Harper, New York, 1953.

Duverger, Maurice. *Political Parties*. Wiley, New York, 1954.

Faulkner, Harold U. *Politics, Reform and Expansion*. Harper, New York, 1959.

Fesler, James W. *Area and Administration*. University of Alabama Press, Tuscaloosa, 1949.

---

* A comprehensive, annotated bibliography on all aspects of New York politics and government can be found in Sayre and Kaufman, *op. cit.*, following each chapter. This bibliography is a more specialized listing.

Fesler, James W. *The Independence of State Regulatory Agencies.* Public Administration Service, Chicago, 1942.

Fish, Carl Russell. *The Civil Service and the Patronage.* Longmans, Green, New York, 1905.

Friedrich, Carl J. *Constitutional Government and Democracy.* Ginn, Boston, 1950.

Gerth, Hans, and C. Wright Mills. *From Max Weber.* A Galaxy Book, Oxford, New York, 1958.

Gosnell, Harold F. *Machine Politics: Chicago Model.* University of Chicago Press, Chicago, 1937.

de Grazia, Alfred. *Public and Republic.* Knopf, New York, 1951.

Gulick, Luther, *et al. Papers on the Science of Administration.* Institute of Public Administration, New York, 1937.

Handlin, Oscar. *The Uprooted.* Grosset's Universal Library, Grosset & Dunlap, New York, 1951.

Heberle, Rudolph. *Social Movements.* Appleton-Century-Crofts, New York, 1951.

Henderson, A. M., and Talcott Parsons. *Max Weber: The Theory of Social and Economic Organization.* Oxford University Press, New York, 1947.

Herring, Pendleton. *Federal Commissioners: A Study of Their Careers and Qualifications.* Cambridge University Press, 1936.

Herring, Pendleton. *The Politics of Democracy.* Rinehart, New York, 1940.

Hofstadter, Richard. *The Age of Reform.* Knopf, New York, 1955.

Hunter, Floyd. *Community Power Structure.* University of North Carolina Press, Chapel Hill, 1953.

Janowitz, Morris. *The Professional Soldier.* Free Press, New York, 1960.

Key, V. O. *Politics, Parties and Pressure Groups.* Crowell, New York, 1958.

Key, V. O. *A Primer of Statistics for Political Scientists.* Crowell, New York, 1954.

Key, V. O. *Public Opinion and American Democracy.* Knopf, New York, 1961.

Knight, Maxwell E. *The German Executive.* Hoover Institute Studies #4, Stanford University Press, 1952.

Lasswell, H. D. *The Analysis of Political Behavior.* Kegan Paul, London, 1947.

Lasswell, H. D. *Comparative Study of Elites.* Hoover Institute Studies, Stanford University Press, 1952.

Lasswell, H. D. *Politics: Who Gets What, When, How.* Meridian, New York, 1958.

Lasswell, Harold D., and Abraham Kaplan. *Power and Society.* Yale University Press, New Haven, 1950.

Leiserson, Avery. *Parties and Politics.* Knopf, New York, 1958.

Lerner, Daniel. *The Nazi Elite.* Hoover Institute Studies #3, Stanford University Press, 1951.

Lipset, S. M., and Reinhard Bendix. *Social Mobility in Industrial Society.* University of California Press, Berkeley, 1959.

Lubell, Samuel. *The Future of American Politics.* Doubleday, New York, 1956.

Lynd, Robert and Helen. *Middletown in Transition.* Harcourt, Brace, New York, 1937.

Macmahon, Arthur, and John D. Millett. *Federal Administrators.* Columbia University Press, New York, 1939.

Mannheim, Karl. *Freedom, Power and Democratic Planning.* Oxford, New York, 1950.

Mannheim, Karl. *Ideology and Utopia.* Harvest Books, Harcourt, Brace, New York, 1955.

Marvick, Dwaine (ed.). *Political Decision-Makers: Recruitment and Performance.* Free Press, New York, 1961.

Matthews, Donald. *The Social Background of Political Decision-Makers.* Doubleday, New York, 1954.

Merton, Robert, *Social Theory and Social Structure,* Free Press, New York, 1957.

Merton, Robert, *et al.* (eds.). *Reader in Bureaucracy.* Fress Press, New York, 1952.

Merton, Robert, *et al.* (eds.) *Sociology Today.* Basic Books, New York, 1959.

Meyerson, Martin, and Edward Banfield. *Politics, Planning and the Public Interest.* Free Press, New York, 1955.

Miller, Delbert, and William Form. *Industrial Sociology.* Harper, New York, 1951.

Mills, C. Wright. *White Collar.* Oxford University Press, New York, 1953.

Morstein Marx, Fritz (ed.). *Elements of Public Administration.* Prentice-Hall, Englewood Cliffs, 1949.

Mosca, Gaetano. *The Ruling Class.* McGraw-Hill, New York, 1939.

Neustadt, Richard E. *Presidential Power*. Wiley, New York, 1960.

Pareto, V. I. *The Mind and Society*, Vol. 3. Harcourt, Brace, 1935.

Park, Robert E. *The City*. University of Chicago Press, Chicago, 1925.

Polsby, Nelson W. *Community Power and Political Theory*. Yale University Press, New Haven, 1963.

Riesman, David. *The Lonely Crowd*. Doubleday Anchor Book, Doubleday, New York, 1953.

Schattschneider, Elmer E. *Party Government*. Rinehart, New York, 1942.

Schattschneider, Elmer E. *The Semisovereign People*. Holt, Rinehart & Winston, New York, 1960.

Speier, Hans. *Social Order and the Risks of War*. Stewart, New York, 1952.

Taussig, F. W., and C. S. Joslyn. *American Business Leaders*. Macmillan, New York, 1932.

Tönnies, Ferdinand. *Fundamental Concepts of Sociology* (C. P. Loomis, trans.). American Book, New York, 1940.

Truman, David B. *The Governmental Process*. Knopf, New York, 1951.

Warner, W. Lloyd, and James C. Abegglen. *Occupational Mobility*. University of Minnesota Press, Minneapolis, 1955.

Wecter, Dixon. *The Saga of American Society*. Scribner's, New York, 1937.

White, L. D. *Introduction to the Study of Public Administration* 3rd ed. Macmillan, New York, 1948.

Wilson, James Q. *The Amateur Democrat: Club Politics in Three Cities*. University of Chicago Press, Chicago, 1962.

Wolfinger, Raymond W. *The Politics of Progress*. Yale University Press, New Haven, 1964.

ARTICLES

Arensberg, Conrad, "Industry and the Community," *American Journal of Sociology* (July, 1942).

Aron, Raymond, "Social Structure and the Ruling Class," *British Journal of Sociology*, Vol. I (1950), pp. 1, 126.

Baltzell, E. Digby. " 'Who's Who in America' and 'The Social Register': Elite and Upper Class Indexes in Metropolitan America," R. Bendix and S. M. Lipset (eds.), *Class, Status and Power*, p. 172.

Bendix, Reinhard. *Bureaucratization in Industry*. Reprint No. 68, Institute of Industrial Relations, University of California, Berkeley, 1955.

Bendix, R., "The Problem of Bureaucratic Power," Robert Merton, *et al.* (eds.), *Reader in Bureaucracy.*

Corey, Lewis, "The Middle Class," R. Bendix and S. M. Lipset (eds.), *Class, Status and Power*, p. 371.

Cornwell, Elmer E., "Party Absorption of Ethnic Groups: The Case of Providence, Rhode Island." *Social Forces*, 28 (March, 1950).

Dahl, Robert A., "Some Notes and Models for Political Systems," a paper presented to the SSRC seminar on urban leadership (August, 1957).

Edwards, Alba E., "A Socio-Economic Grouping of the Gainful Workers in the United States," *Journal of the American Statistical Association* (December, 1933), p. 377.

Fesler, James W., "Field Organization," in Morstein Marx (ed). *Elements of Public Administration*, Prentice-Hall, Englewood Cliffs, 1949, p. 264.

Gouldner, Alvin W., "Cosmopolitans and Locals," *Administrative Science Quarterly*, 2 (1957-1958), p. 281.

Hatt, Paul K., "Occupational and Social Stratification," *American Journal of Sociology*, Vol. LV, no. 6 (1950).

Hughes, Everett C., "The Study of Occupations," Robert Merton, *et al.* (eds.), *Sociology Today*, p. 457.

Kornhauser, Ruth, "The Warner Approach to Stratification," R. Bendix and S. M. Lipset (eds.), *Class, Status and Power*, p. 229.

Maass, Arthur, "Congress and Water Resources," *American Political Science Review*, Vol. XVIV (September, 1950).

Miller, Byron F., "A Law Is Passed—The Atomic Energy Act of 1946," *Chicago Law Review*, Vol. 15, no. 4.

Myers, Jerome K., "Assimilation in the Political Community," *Sociology and Social Research*, Vol. 35 (1950-1951), p. 175.

Rogoff, Natalie, "Recent Trends in Occupational Mobility," R. Bendix and S. M. Lipset (eds.), *Class, Status and Power*, p. 443.

Rossi, Peter H., "Power and Community Structure," *Midwest Journal of Political Science*, Vol. IV (November, 1960).

Rossi, Peter H., and Alice S. Rossi, "An Historical Perspective on the Functions of Local Politics," a revision of a paper presented at the 1956 meeting of the American Sociological Society, Detroit (mimeo.).

Schlesinger, Joseph, "Lawyers and American Politics," *Midwest Journal of Political Science* 1 (February, 1957).

Shulze, Robert O., "Economic Determinants in Community Power Structure," *American Sociological Review*, Vol. XXII (1958), p. 3.

Sjöberg, Gideon, "Comparative Urban Sociology," *Sociology Today*, p. 334.

DOCUMENTS

Commission on Organization of the Executive Branch of Government. *Report on Personnel and Civil Service*, and *Task Force Report*. Government Printing Office, Washington, 1955.

United States Bureau of the Census. *Population: The Labor Force*. The Bureau, 1943.

United States Bureau of the Census. Vol. V: *General Report on Occupations*. The Bureau, 1933.

United States Bureau of the Census. Vol. IV: *Occupations, by States*. The Bureau, 1933.

United States Bureau of the Census. Vols. I-II: *Population: 1901-1902*. The Bureau, 1902.

Edwards, Alba E. *Alphabetical Index of Occupations by Industries and Social-Economic Groups*. United States Bureau of the Census, 1937.

Edwards, Alba E. *Comparative Occupation Statistics for the United States, 1870 to 1940*. United States Bureau of the Census, 1943.

United States Bureau of the Census. Vol. I. *The Statistics of the Population of the United States*. The Bureau, 1870.

SPECIAL REFERENCES ON NEW YORK CITY

BOOKS

Almond, Gabriel. *Plutocracy and Politics in New York City*. Unpublished Doctoral dissertation, University of Chicago, 1939.

Coler, Bird S. *Municipal Government as Illustrated by the Charter, Finances, and Public Charities of New York*. Appleton, New York, 1900.

Cuneo, Ernest. *Life with Fiorello*. Macmillan, New York, 1955.

Curran, Henry H. *Pillar to Post*. Scribner's, New York, 1941.

Finegan, James E. *Tammany at Bay*. Dodd, Mead, New York, 1933.

Flynn, Edward J. *You're the Boss*. Viking, New York, 1947.

Fosdick, Raymond B. *Chronicle of a Generation*. Harper, New York, 1958.

Fowler, Gene. *Beau James: The Life and Times of Jimmy Walker*. Viking, New York, 1949.

Fox, D. R. *The Decline of Aristocracy in the Politics of New York*, Longmans, Green, New York, 1919.

Gosnell, Harold F. *Boss Platt and His New York Machine*. University of Chicago Press, Chicago, 1924.

Haig, Robert M., Carl S. Shoup, and Lyle C. Fitch. *The Financial Problem of the City of New York*. Mayor's Committee on Management Survey, New York, 1952.

Hylan, John F. *Autobiography*. Rotary, New York, 1922.

Klein, Henry H. *My Last Fifty Years*. Author, New York, 1935.

Lewis, Alfred Henry. *Richard Croker*. Life, New York, 1901.

Limpus, Lowell M. *History of the New York Fire Department*. Dutton, New York, 1940.

Low, Benjamin R. C. *Seth Low*. Putnam's, New York, 1925.

McAdoo, William. *Guarding a Great City*. Harper, New York, 1906.

Moses, Robert. *La Guardia: A Salute and a Memoir*. Simon and Schuster, New York, 1957.

Moscow, Warren. *Politics in the Empire State*. Knopf, New York, 1948.

Myers, Gustavus. *The History of Tammany Hall*. Boni and Liveright, New York, 1917.

Nevins, Allan, and John A. Krout (eds.). *The Greater City: New York, 1898-1948*. Columbia University Press, New York, 1948.

Northrop, W. B. (ed.). *Some of Mayor Gaynor's Letters and Speeches*. Graves, New York, 1913.

Peel, Roy V. *The Political Clubs of New York City*. Putnam's, New York, 1935.

Pink, Louis A. *Gaynor: The Tammany Mayor Who Swallowed the Tiger*. International Press, New York, 1931.

Riordan, William L. *Plunkitt of Tammany Hall*. Knopf, New York, 1948.

Rodgers, Cleveland. *New York Plans for the Future*. Harper, New York, 1943.

Rodgers, Cleveland, and Rebecca B. Rankin. *New York: The World's Capital City*. Harper, New York, 1948.

Sayre, Wallace S. and Herbert Kaufman. *Governing New York City*. Russell Sage, New York, 1960.

Shaw, Frederick. *History of the New York City Legislature*. Columbia University Press, New York, 1954.

Smith, Mortimer. *William Jay Gaynor: Mayor of New York*. Regnery, Chicago, 1951.

Stead, W. T. *Satan's Invisible World Displayed; or, Despairing Democracy. A Study of Greater New York*. Review of Reviews, London, 1898.

Syrett, Harold C. (ed.). *The Gentleman and the Tiger: The Autobiography of George B. McClellan, Jr*. Lippincott, Philadelphia, 1956.

Syrett, Harold C. *The City of Brooklyn, 1865-1898: A Political History*. Columbia University Press, New York, 1944.

Thomas, Norman, and Paul Blanshard. *What's the Matter with New York?* Macmillan, New York, 1932.

Tugwell, Rexford G. *The Art of Politics as Practiced by Three Great Americans: Franklin Delano Roosevelt, Luis Munoz Marin, and Fiorello H. La Guardia*. Doubleday, New York, 1958.

Valentine, Lewis J. *Police Night Stick*. Dial, New York, 1947.

Werner, M. R. *Tammany Hall*. Doubleday, Doran, New York, 1928.

ARTICLES

Carmer, Carl. "From Van Wyck to O'Dwyer," Allan Nevins and John A. Krout (eds.), in *The Greater City: New York 1898-1948*.

Feldman, Justin N. "How Tammany Holds Power," *National Municipal Review* (July, 1950).

Hamburger, Philip. "The Mayor: Profile of Robert F. Wagner," *The New Yorker*, Vol. 32 (January 26, 1957), pp. 39-67; (February 2, 1957), pp. 54-55, 59-60.

Heilbroner, Robert L. "Carmine G. De Sapio: The Smile on the Face of the Tiger," *Harper's Magazine*, Vol. 209 (July, 1954), pp. 23-33.

La Guardia, Fiorello H. "Bosses Are Bunk: A Reply to Ed Flynn," *Atlantic Monthly*, Vol. 180 (July, 1947), pp. 21-24.

McBain, Howard Lee. "John Purroy Mitchel," *National Municipal Review*, Vol. 7 (September, 1918).

Moscow, Warren. "Exit the Boss, Enter the Leader," *The New York Times Magazine* (June 22, 1947).

Rovere, Richard. "The Big Hello," *The New Yorker*, Vol. 21 (January 12, 1946), pp. 29-34; (January 19, 1946), pp. 22-30.

DOCUMENTS AND GUIDES

Ash, Mark (ed.). *The Greater New York Charter as Enacted in 1897.* Weed-Parsons, Albany, 1897.

Bureau of Municipal Research. *Municipal Year Book of the City of New York, 1913.* Pratt, New York, 1913. For 1915, *Brooklyn Eagle* Press, Brooklyn, New York, 1915. For 1916 and 1917, Municipal Reference Library, New York.

Commerce and Industry Association of New York. *Annual Reports.* From 1942.

Daily News. New York City Guide and Almanac, 1957-58. New York University Press, New York, 1957.

Democratic Party. *Rules.* (County and State.)

Haig, Robert M., Carl S. Shoup, and Lyle C. Fitch. *The Revenue Problem of the City of New York and a Proposed Program.* Mayor's Committee on Management Survey, New York, 1952.

Institute of Public Administration. *Governmental Organization Within the City of New York.* The Institute, New York. Five editions through 1949.

Lee, Henry J. (ed.). *The Charter of the City of New York, with Amendments to May 1, 1930. Brooklyn Eagle* Library, New York, 1930.

McKinney's Consolidated Laws of New York, Annotated. Edward Thompson Co., Brooklyn, 1944. Annual Supplements.

New York City, Board of Elections. *Annual Reports.* Annually from 1909.

New York City, The City Record. *Civil List* (a roster of all City employees). Published annually.

New York City, The City Record. *Official Directory* ("The Green Book"). The City Record, New York. Published annually from 1916.

New York City, Civil Service Commission. *Annual Reports.* 1900 to date.

New York City. *Charter and Administrative Code, Annotated.* William Press, Albany, six volumes.

New York City, Commissioners of Accounts and New York Bureau of Municipal Research. *Government of the City of New York: A Survey of Its Organization and Functions.* Little and Ives, New York, 1915.

New York City, *Mayor's Annual Reports.*

New York City, Mayor's Committee on Management Survey. *Modern Management for the City of New York.* The Committee, New York, 1953. Two volumes.

New York City Charter Adopted at the General Election Held November 3, 1936 (as amended to May 31, 1954). The City Record, New York, 1954.

New York Social Register. Published annually.

New York State. Assembly, Investigation of the Offices and Departments of the City of New York by a Special Committee. *Report of Counsel* [Mazet Committee]: December 22, 1899. Lyon, Albany, 1899.

New York State, Constitutional Convention Committee. *New York City Government: Functions and Problems.* Vol. 5 of *Reports and Studies,* Burland Printing Co., New York, 1938.

New York State. Senate Committee to Investigate the Police Department of the City of New York. *Report and Proceedings.* Lyon, Albany, 1895. Five volumes.

New York State. Special Committee to the Assembly Appointed to Investigate the Public Officers and Departments of the City of New York and of the Counties Therein Included. *Final Report* [Mazet Committee]. Lyon, Albany, 1900. Five volumes.

Rankin, Rebecca B. (ed.) :
New York Advancing: World's Fair Edition. Municipal Reference Library, New York, 1939.

New York Advancing: Victory Edition. Municipal Reference Library, New York, 1945.

Guide to the Municipal Government of the City of New York. Record Press, New York, 1952.

Regional Plan Association. *Regional Survey*, Vol. II. The Association, New York, 1928.
Republican Party. *Rules.* (County and State.)

BIOGRAPHICAL SOURCES*

The American Catholic Who's Who. Walter Romig, Grosse Point, Michigan. Issued biennially, 1934-1960.
The American Catholic Who's Who, 1911. Herder, St. Louis, 1911.
American Women; the Official Who's Who among the Women of the Nation. American Publications, Los Angeles, 1935-1936.
America's Young Men; the Official Who's Who among the Young Men of the Nation. American Publications, Los Angeles, 1934.

Biographical Directory of the State of New York. New York, 1900.
Biographical History of Westchester County, New York. Lewis, Chicago, 1899.
The Brown Book: A Biographical Record of Public Officials of the City of New York for 1898-99. Brown, New York, 1899.

Citizens Union Collection. A collection of pamphlets, scrapbooks, and office files. Columbia University, Special Collections, Butler Library.
The City Club of New York. *Yearbook.* The City Club, 1886-1900. Published annually.

Hazelton, Henry I. *The Boroughs of Brooklyn and Queens, Counties of Nassau and Suffolk, Long Island, New York, 1609-1924.* Lewis Historical, New York, 1925. Three volumes.

Italian American Who's Who. Vigo Press, New York. Issued annually, 1920-1959.

Journalism Library, 303 Journalism Building, Columbia University, New York 27, New York. Clippings File, 1890 to date.

McGuire, James K. (ed.). *The Democratic Party of the State of New York.* United States History Company, New York, 1905. Three volumes.
Mayoralty papers. Official papers of all Mayors and Acting Mayors of Greater New York arranged chronologically by administration. Municipal Archives, New York City.

* All standard biographical references from *Who's Who in America* to White's *Conspectus* were covered systematically. Listed here are only the somewhat more specialized sources.

Morris, Charles. *Men of Affairs in New York: An Historical Work.* Hamersley New York, 1906.

New York *Daily Tribune* Index. New York *Tribune* Assoc., 1876-1907. Issued annually.

New York State. *The New York Red Book.* J. B. Lyon Co., Albany, New York. Published annually from 1892.

New York Times Index. *New York Times,* 1913-   ; also issued annually from 1863-1905.

Nowinson, Richard (ed.). *Who's Who in United States Politics and American Political Almanac.* Capitol House, Chicago, 1950.

Queens County, New York. *Portrait and Biographical Record of Queens County.* Chapman, New York and Chicago, 1896.

Silberman, Murray. "Biographies of the Mayors of New York," Working Papers for the Russell Sage Foundation Project on New York City Government, Columbia University, New York, 1957.

Wells, James L., Louis F. Haffen, and Josia A. Briggs (eds.). *The Bronx and Its People, A History: 1609-1927.* Lewis Historical, New York, 1927.

Who's Who in American Jewry. National News Association, New York. Three volumes, 1926, 1927, and 1938.

Who's Who in Colored America. Who's Who in Colored America, New York. Two volumes, 1927 and 1938/40.

Who's Who in Commerce and Industry. A. N. Marquis, New York. Issued serially, 1936-

Who's Who in the East. Larkin, Roosevelt & Larkin, Boston, 1942-1943; Marquis, Chicago, 1953.

Who's Who in Engineering. Lewis Historical, New York. Issued serially from 1922.

Who's Who in Government. Biographical Research Bureau, New York, 1930.

Who's Who in Labor. New York, 1946.

Who's Who in New York (City and State). Who's Who Publications, Inc. Issued biennially, 1904-1914; periodically 1918-1960.

Who's Who in Queens, 1936.

Who's Who in World Jewry; a Biographical Dictionary of Outstanding Jews. Who's Who in World Jewry, Inc., 1955.

INDEX